Urban Space for Pedestrians

Urban Space
for Pedestrians

A Report of the Regional Plan
Association

by Boris Pushkarev,
with Jeffrey M. Zupan

The MIT Press
Cambridge, Massachusetts
and London, England

This book was designed by The MIT
Press Design Department.
It was set in IBM Composer Baskerville
by Technical Composition,
and printed and bound
by Halliday Lithograph Corp.
in the United States of America.

Library of Congress Cataloging in
Publication Data

Pushkarev, Boris
    Urban space for pedestrians.

    Includes bibliographical references.
    1. Pedestrian facilities design.
2. Cities and towns—Planning. 3. Space
(Architecture) I. Zupan, Jeffrey M.,
joint author. II. Regional Plan
Association, New York. III. Title.
TE279.5.P87   711'.4'3   75-29242
ISBN 0-262-16063-3

Pedestrians should be loved.

Pedestrians comprise the greater part of humanity. Moreover—its better part. Pedestrians created the world. It is they who built cities, erected multi-story buildings, laid sewerage and water mains, paved streets, and illuminated them with electric lights. It is they who spread civilization throughout the world, invented book printing, gunpower, deciphered Egyptian hieroglyphics, introduced safety razors, abolished slave trade and discovered that 114 nourishing meals can be cooked from soybeans.

When everything was finished, when our beloved planet assumed a fairly habitable look, motorists appeared on the scene.

One should note that the automobile itself was invented by pedestrians but somehow the motorists forgot that very quickly. Gentle and intelligent pedestrians began to get squashed. Streets, created by pedestrians, were usurped by motorists. Roadways were widened to double their former size, sidewalks narrowed to tape width and pedestrians began to cower in fear against the walls of buildings.

In a large city, pedestrians lead a life of martyrdom. A kind of transportation ghetto was set up for them. They are allowed to cross streets only at intersections, that is precisely in those places where traffic is heaviest and where the hair by which a pedestrian's life usually hangs is most easily broken.

In our large country, the automobile, intended by pedestrians for peaceful transportation of people and goods, assumed the proportions of a lethal weapon. It puts out of commission row upon row of trade union members and their families and if, on occasion, a pedestrian succeeds in escaping from under the silver nose of an automobile, he is promptly fined for violating the traffic law.

In general, the authority of pedestrians has been shaken considerably. They, who gave the world such outstanding figures as Horatio, Boyle, Lobachevsky, and Anatole France, are now forced to clown in the tritest manner just to remind the world of their existence. God, oh God, Thou who in reality art dead, where did Thou, who dost not exist, leave the pedestrian!

Ilf and Petrov,
The Golden Calf,
Moscow, 1931.

Foreword

To build a better urban America will require more compact, well-designed development, yet high urban densities are not popular these days. In the spread cities of North America, however, higher densities do promise the realization of objectives that are increasingly in the public mind: preservation of nature, richer opportunities for cultural interaction, a resource-conserving environment with workable public transit and more occasions for walking and strolling.

The physical shape of the central city as it evolved over the past century or more is in many ways ugly and inhospitable. Its negative features must be overcome, if we are to reap the benefits of urban concentration. We must learn how to design for higher densities without congestion. This, in essence is the message of the Second Regional Plan, which has guided the policies of Regional Plan Association over the past decade. Some qualitative design principles for a high density urban center were dealt with in our earlier book *Urban Design Manhattan* (Viking Press, 1969). In it, we promised that "some of the quantitative aspects . . . will be covered more fully in subsequent reports." This book fulfills that promise.

The tools of modern travel analysis are enlisted to answer some of the questions that have vexed planners for decades: What is the proper relationship between building bulk and circulation space? How much crowding is too much and how does one avoid congestion in public places? While the book touches on space requirements for various kinds of movement in cities, it focuses on pedestrian circulation and amenities as being most pertinent to the city center.

This work shows that the degree to which urban spaces are filled with people can, to a large extent, be calculated and predicted. It suggests that such spaces should not be dimensioned abstractly, for the sake of architectural proportions or administrative convenience, but rather in relation to the number of people that can be expected to use them.

The first purpose of the book is to provide urban policy makers with quantitative methods of proportioning pedestrian space in downtowns in relation to the adjoining buildings. As a text on theory and application, the book is directed to urban designers, planners, traffic engineers and civil engineers, architects and landscape architects, real estate developers, and lawyers specializing in zoning matters. It will also be of interest to behavioral scientists concerned with human responses to the man-made environment, to environmentalists and citizens working toward pedestrian improvements.

The second purpose is to apply the methods which are relevant to urban centers in general to the specific situation of Manhattan, and to propose steps for eliminating pedestrian congestion and so improving the journey "from the train door to the elevator door."

In the six years since the study on which this book is based was commenced with the then Chairman of the City Planning Commission and the then Chairman of the Metropolitan Transportation Authority serving on its Advisory Committee, some progress was made in New York toward achieving its objectives. Zoning regulations governing the provision of open space around buildings in high density areas were revised in several ways to make such space more useful to people. Street closing experiments were conducted and several modest pedestrian mall projects got underway. An effort was launched to raise the design standards of subway stations on lines under construction, and the rebuilding of several old subway entrances was accomplished. Most of these projects benefited directly from the output of this study; the details are treated in the text.

Nevertheless, much still remains to be done. Our recommendations are basically threefold.

1. In any future comprehensive zoning revision, the amount of pedestrian circulation space provided by a building must be linked to its bulk and use as a matter of right, not as an elective option. The principle must be applied comprehensively, and not be limited to the highest density districts. Furthermore, protection from inclement weather must receive much greater attention.

2. The principle of automobile-free streets must receive much wider application in dense downtown areas, where movement on foot and by public transit is by far the dominant form of locomotion, and where truck deliveries, occasional limousines, and municipal services can be satis-

fied by a fraction of the existing vehicular pavement.

3. Most urgently, a large-scale reconstruction of the below ground public environment—primarily of subway stations—must be launched. The cost will be high, nine-digit dollar figures, but so will be the payoff of a livable city. Then there will be sunlight in transit stations and the below-ground environment will invite people instead of repelling them. To expedite the realization of this goal, and to provide a meaningful integration of the building spaces above ground and the walkway spaces below ground, the task cannot be left to public agencies alone; a public-private partnership must be established.

The policies and standards advanced by this book grew out of a fortunate combination of theory and practical experience in implementing them. Neither would have been possible without the interaction with agencies and individuals listed in the acknowledgments. Especially do we recognize the helpfulness of Martha R. Wallace of the Henry Luce Foundation for providing the initial grant for this project and for advice during its course.

John P. Keith, President
Regional Plan Association

Acknowledgments

This book reflects a broad spectrum of work on transportation and space in urban centers carried out at Regional Plan Association over the past decade. Its core is based on the results of a study of pedestrian movement in Midtown Manhattan, funded by a grant of $150,000 from the Henry Luce Foundation in 1969. A key input—helicopter aerial photography of Midtown Manhattan—was provided by the Port Authority of New York and New Jersey. Other essential data were furnished by the New York City Transit Authority. The book also incorporates some findings from an unpublished study of urban density by Rai Y. Okamoto and Robert Beck, consultants to Regional Plan Association, funded by the National Institutes of Mental Health.

Early results of the Midtown study were reviewed by an advisory committee including Max Abramovitz, Donald H. Elliot, James Landauer, Roswell B. Perkins, and William J. Ronan. An abstract was published in Regional Plan Association's press release no. 1125 in May 1971 and reprinted in the *Proceedings of the Pedestrian/Bicycle Planning and Design Seminar* in San Francisco, 1972. Excerpts from Chapter 2 appeared in *Highway Research Board Record* no. 355 in 1971, and excerpts from Chapter 3 were presented at the Transportation Research Board meeting in January, 1975. Further excerpts were used in testimony at public hearings, in the joint Municipal Art Society —Department of City Planning brochure *Humanizing Subway Entrances: Opportunity on Second Avenue* (September 1974), and in the Mayor's Office of Midtown Planning and Development brochure *Madison Mall*, October 1971.

Results were also discussed in a number of meetings with New York City agencies—the Department of City Planning, the Office of Midtown Planning and Development, the Office of Lower Manhattan Planning and Development, the Office of Downtown Brooklyn Development, the Transportation Administration, the Traffic Department, and the Steering Committee of the Second Avenue Study, jointly sponsored by the City Planning Commission and the Municipal Art Society. All of these provided valuable direction.

The book incorporates extensive revisions and a broader framework, based particularly on the suggestions of Jacquelin Robertson, Jeffrey Ewing, John J. Fruin, Paul M. Friedberg, and William H. Whyte. Further valuable advice was received from Martin Growald, Eugene J. Lessieu, Herbert Levinson, Norman Marcus, Michael Parley, Peter Pattison, Raquel Ramati, Frank Rogers, Richard Rosan, Richard Roth, Jack C. Smith, Edward F. Sullivan. Permission to use unpublished Tri-State Regional Planning Commission data was granted by J. Douglas Carroll, Executive Director.

In addition to the coauthors, the following persons on the staff of Regional Plan Association participated in the preparation of this study: C. McKim Norton, Counsel; Sheldon Pollack, Information Director; Dick Netzer, Economic Consultant; F. Carlisle Towery, Urban Design Consultant; Ira S. Kuperstein, Survey Manager; Felix Martorano, J. Douglas Peix, Katrin Wenzel, and Danny N. T. Yung, Architectural Designers; Jerome Pilchman, Cartographer; Richard M. Zinner, Legal Assistant; Craig L. Atkinson, Adrian Boland, Anthony Callender, Paul Cardell, Robert Connolly, Kenneth Feldman, Jessica Fromm, Noelle A. Melhado, Robert G. Tannenhaus, Kay Sunday Xanthakos, and Lawrence Zupan, Research Assistants; Rosalyn Ader and Linda Streeseman, Secretaries; Edward Ciok, Steven Kuperstein, Judith Mills, Joshua Tankel, Martha Valazco, Harriet J. Zagor, Interviewers. Marina Sultan provided research and administrative assistance and typed the final manuscript. The photographs are by the authors, unless otherwise indicated.

List of Figures

Chapter 1

Urban Space: A Framework For Analysis

It is curious that most of the concern with functionalism has been focused upon form rather than function . . . design professionals—city planners, landscape designers, architects . . . —would gain by adopting a functionalism based on user behavior.

Robert Sommer,
Personal Space

The Setting: Density and Human Space Needs

The premise that overcrowding is bad for people and other living beings is probably beyond dispute. After all, the rats in Dr. John B. Calhoun's experiments did develop severe psychological disorders due to stress from overcrowding.[1] However, in an atmosphere of antiurban bias, such findings have led some people to equate high urban population density with overcrowding. The retort that people are not rats is quite beside the point. Much more to the point is the question, Exactly how much crowding is overcrowding among humans? To have meaning, the question must be asked in great detail and cover a variety of human situations. The large contemporary city is an assemblage of spaces, or channels, for human interaction, infinitely more complex than the simple pens in which Dr. Calhoun's rats lived and died. A seemingly low average density can conceal acute points of congestion, while a comparatively much higher one can accommodate a smooth flow of human interaction when spaces are appropriately proportioned and arranged.

The question of how much space man needs to live without overcrowding is further complicated by the fact that man does not live by space alone. If spaciousness and privacy were the only objective, there would be no need for cities. Every person would live on his or her separate share of the habitable portion of the earth—presently about 2.5 acres (1 ha) each—with twice as much earth surface left in mountains, deserts, tundra, and ice. This is somewhat the way people lived in the simple society of prehistoric times, though they had about a thousand times more space. Today, people in a complex society depend on constant direct and indirect contact with countless other people and, to maintain that contact, have to arrange themselves in fairly compact settlements, which in the United States occupy less than 2 percent of the land. Such clustering enables people to have access to each other, which allows society to function. In fact, society values access very highly: because of its accessibility, land in Midtown Manhattan sold for around $20 million an acre ($50 million per hectare) in 1970, about 20,000 times more than land away from the highway some 80 miles (130 km) to the north.

Manhattan may be unique, and yet the centers of other large cities are becoming more like it. Responding to the growth of communications-oriented white-collar activity, between 1960 and 1970 Manhattan added 65 million sq ft (6 million m^2) of office space to its skyline. Yet downtown Washington added 18 million (1.7 million m^2), the core of Los Angeles, 17 million (1.6 million m^2); downtown Chicago, 13 million (1.2 million m^2); and figures in the millions can be recited for dozens of cities all over the world. Before 1960 New York was one of 25 world cities with rapid transit. In the next 15 years 35 more cities in the world opened new rail transit systems or substantially progressed in their construction, greatly enhancing the potential for concentration.

Given the number of people on earth and their interdependence in a complex society, urban concentrations are here to stay. If they are to become more oriented toward communication rather than production, if they are to house a population with fewer children and more education and income, their downtowns and subcenters will have to be reinforced. The real issue of human space arrangements thus is how to allow the needed concentration without causing congestion. The issue gains in importance if we look toward a future in which the "good life" will not require the massive expenditures of energy and materials to which North Americans became accustomed in the past half-century.

In this book the broader question of what determines the magnitude of needed concentration will be put aside. Rather, the amounts of space available to people at various levels of concentration will be examined in an attempt to pinpoint symptoms of congestion. After an overview of the general components of urban space use, one component in particular will be focused on: space for pedestrian circulation in dense urban centers. We will analyze pedestrian behavior and on that basis propose standards for design.

Components of Urban Space

To provide a sense of the dimensions of urban use of space, Table 1.1 compares the densities of seven major urban areas: Los Angeles, New York, Philadelphia, Chicago, London, Paris, and Mos-

cow. The measure of density is the inverse of the customary "people per unit of land area," namely, "area per person," which will be used throughout this book for arithmetical and psychological convenience.

It can be seen that the shares of land devoted to the different uses are remarkably stable; but the total rises from 644 sq ft (60 m²) per person in Moscow—essentially a preautomobile city at the time the data refer to—to 5,516 sq ft (512 m²) in Los Angeles, with 2.2 people per auto at that time.

The amount of space per person in an urban area is powerfully influenced by the population's command over material resources —especially the means of transportation. The means of transportation, of course, not only provide space but also consume space, as illustrated by the street area per person. Added to the price for space paid in space must be the price paid in energy and other resources.

However, the figures in Table 1.1 also suggest that areawide averages of population density are limited in their meaning, even when carefully defined. The regions of Los Angeles and New York are shown to have about the same per capita area in residential land. This happens to be the case because New York City and its suburban counties, taken together, average out roughly to the residential density of Los Angeles. The fact that such extremes exist within an urban region can in no way be inferred from Table 1.1. Moreover, density measures related to land area

take no account of space in buildings, where people spend most of their lives, and of the arrangement of the buildings that define the urban environment.

Therefore, in exploring the livability of urban space, one cannot start with areawide geographic averages. The argument that Holland has the highest population density of any country in the world, and yet its social pathology is very low, may mean only that the average density figure for Holland says nothing about the delicate distribution of urban space within that country. An individual's daily environment is very small indeed, and, in exploring human behavior in relation to space, one must start from the smallest possible scale, from the daily "path of the feet and the eye," to borrow a phrase from the late architect George Howe. Only when a step-by-step analysis of human needs for space is done can one ask the incidental question: What average density does this add up to?

A simplified diagram of an urban resident's daily space needs is shown in Figure 1.1. Located in the center at the top is indoor residential space, that is, space in dwellings. Connected to it is outdoor residential space, that portion of the residential plot which is not covered by the building. Public open space located separately from the dwelling may or not be within walking distance. Bodies of water near built-up areas are obviously another form of open space important for amenity but are not included in the diagram or in the statistics. From the indoor dwelling space one proceeds via some *walkway*

Table 1.1
Allocation of Urban Space in Seven Major Metropolitan Areas

	Los Angeles area	New York Region	Philadelphia area	Chicago area	Greater London	Paris agglom.	Moscow city
Base year	1960	1970	1960	1956	1971	1962	1956
Population (× 1,000)	7,579	18,682	4,023	5,170	7,418	6,457	4,839
Land area per person (sq ft)							
Residential	2,121	2,180	1,823	974	785	363	286
Public open space	1,301	1,219	327	619	330e	202	105
Streets	1,201	758	577	788	261	269	78
Nonresidential	893	612	758	654	425	203	175
Total in urban use	5,516	4,769	3,485	3,035	1,801	1,037	644
(in m²)	(512)	(443)	(324)	(282)	(167)	(96)	(60)

Sources: Los Angeles Regional Transportation Study, *Base Year Report,* 1963. Tri-State Regional Planning Commission, *1970 Land Use Estimate,* Interim Technical Report 4335-3209, 1972. Penn-Jersey Transportation Study, vol. 1, *The State of the Region,* 1964. Chicago Area Transportation Study, vol. 1, *Survey Findings,* 1959. Greater London Council, *Annual Abstract of Greater London Statistics,* 1972. Institut d'Aménagement et d'Urbanisme de la Région Parisienne, "Paris et huit métropoles mondiales," *Cahiers de l'Institut...,* vol. 2, 1965. Akademiia Stroitel'stva i Arkhitektury SSSR, *Moskva: planirovka i zastroika goroda 1945-1957,* 1958.
Note: Street use in Philadelphia, London, and Moscow may be underestimated due to peculiarities of definition; institutional use, elsewhere listed under "nonresidential," appears under "open space" in Los Angeles.

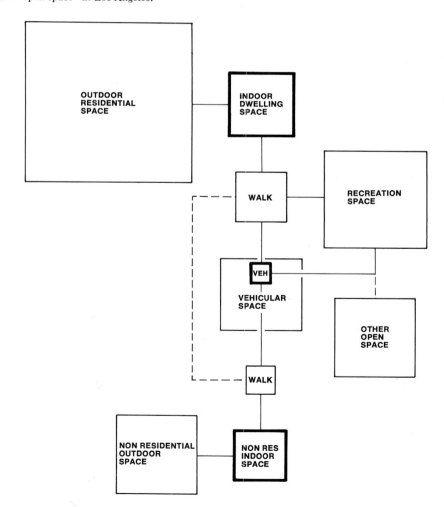

Figure 1.1
Components of urban space

space to a vehicle (private or public), which moves within vehicular space. Disembarking from a vehicle one uses walkway space again, usually to enter some nonresidential building, which has its own nonresidential outdoor space. In higher density areas the vehicular trip itself may be short-circuited by a walk, indicated by the dashed line.

The magnitudes of the major urban space components shown in Figure 1.1 are listed in Table 1.2 for three parts of the New York urban region: (1) the island of Manhattan, (2) the other four boroughs of New York City, and (3) eighteen suburban counties in the states of New York, New Jersey, and Connecticut. The variation in outdoor density among these parts of one region is far greater than that among the urban areas listed in Table 1.1. In fact, the New York region encompasses the full spectrum of outdoor densities encountered in the other metropolitan areas. It can serve as a convenient laboratory for studying the urban use of space. A trip through parts of it, with Figure 1.1 as a guide, will enable us to look in more detail at space allocations that seem relevant to human well-being and will place our analysis of pedestrian movement into a broader framework.

Residential Space
The place where crowding is perceived most acutely is at home, and in this respect Manhattan, in some ways the world's highest density urban place, does not stack up badly at all. Subtracting about 15 percent from the "gross residential floor space" in Table 1.2 (to account for hall-

ways, stairways, elevator shafts, and exterior walls), we find that on the average in 1970 a resident of Manhattan had 327 sq ft (30 m^2) of net dwelling space, about the same as a suburban resident of the New York Region, perhaps even slightly more. Of course, Table 1.2 does not show that this allocation varies substantially by income: in low-income public housing it is closer to 215 sq ft (20 m^2), while in upper-income apartment houses it often exceeds 450 sq ft (42 m^2). Nevertheless, the average is close to the target set by the American Public Health Association[2] and is twice as high as it was in 1900, when net residential space in Manhattan was on the order of 166 sq ft (15 m^2) per person and overcrowding was a major problem.

We do not know how New Yorkers' indoor space compares with that in other parts of the country; after four decades of government concern with housing, a national inventory of floor space still does not exist. We do have some idea how it compares with other countries. For example, in post World War II construction in Western Europe, allocations of around 270 sq ft (25 m^2) per person were common. In Moscow total dwelling space per resident dropped from about 108 sq ft (10 m^2) in 1913 to 73 sq ft (6.8 m^2) in 1940 and reached only 145 sq ft (13.5 m^2) by 1970.[3] In a different setting even lower limits seemed tolerable: low-income housing in Hong Kong in the mid-sixties was built to a norm of 35 sq ft (3.2 m^2) of living and sleeping space per person,[4] which translates into about 45 sq ft (4.2 m^2) of

net dwelling space, lower than the Moscow average of 1940 but an improvement over previous conditions.

In contrast to indoor space, Manhattan does not have much residential outdoor space: only about 36 sq ft (3.3 m^2) per person, compared with seven times as much in the other boroughs of New York City and nearly one hundred times as much in the suburban counties, as Table 1.2 shows. Outdoor residential space is the dominant element in low-density settlement.

The race for private outdoor yards began in the streetcar suburbs around the turn of the century, when improved transportation made an escape from the evils of the tenement house possible. The tenement house, with dark and narrow shafts instead of yards, left about 0.05 units of outdoor space for each unit of indoor space, roughly half of what Manhattan has on the average today.

In the then new environment of the three-family house on a 25-ft (9 m) wide lot, there was more than ten times more outdoor space for each unit of indoor space. As detached structures, these houses could be cheaply built of wood without posing a fire hazard; the alley between them provided additional windows. The trouble was that the outdoor space was broken up between front yard, side yard, and back yard, the latter eventually further reduced by a garage, so usable yard space was small, and looking into one's neighbor's windows was not conducive to privacy. So urban re-

Table 1.2
Allocation of Urban Space in the New York Region, 1970

	Manhattan	Rest of N. Y. C.	Rest of Region*	Region av.
Floor space in buildings				
(sq ft)				
Gross residential per resident†	385	310	334	330
Gross nonresidential per employee‡	267	400	630	472
Land Area in Urban Use				
(sq ft)				
Residential land per resident				
Land covered by buildings	60	109	167e	138
Outdoor residential space	36	266	3,373	2,042
Open space per resident				
Public parks	57	149	1,178	736
Other open space§	1	44	810	483
Street area per resident				
In vehicular pavement	66	182	735	492
Other (including sidewalks)	40	102	395	266
Nonresidential land per employee				
Land covered by buildings	41	218	574e	338
Nonresidential outdoor space	22	644	1,858	1,051
Total area in urban use per resident	382	1,075	7,572	4,769
(m²)	(35.5)	(100)	(703)	(443)
Total land area per resident	403	1,234	18,944	11,391

Source: Tri-State Regional Planning Commission, *1970 Land Use Estimate*.
Also related data files.
*Includes 18 suburban counties within Region as defined by Tri-State Regional Planning Commission.
†Population in thousands: Manhattan, 1,539; rest of New York City, 6,356; rest of Region, 10,787.
‡Employment in thousands: Manhattan, 2,556; rest of New York City, 1,637; rest of Region, 4,050.
§Watershed reservations, military properties, cemeteries, and quarries.
e = estimate

Indoor residential space—a Midtown Manhattan example. The half-floor in a building designed by I.M. Pei contains 13,600 sq ft (1,251.2 m^2), of which about 84 percent —the un-shaded portion—is net residential floorspace. With an average of 1.75 residents in each of the 14 apartments shown, net residential floorspace per person is about 470 sq ft (43.2 m^2). Because of the income level of the residents, this is about 40 percent above the average for Manhattan.

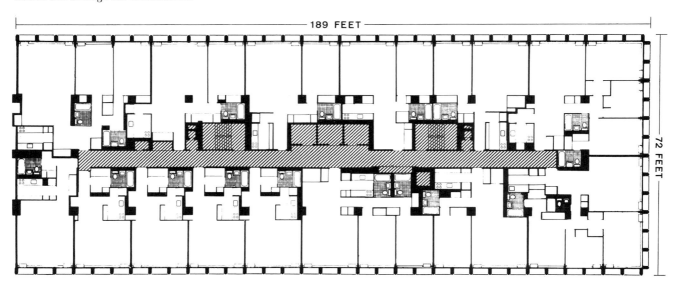

Outdoor residential space for the building illustrated is about four times the Manhattan average, or 147 sq ft (13.5 m^2) per resident. This is achieved by low coverage (16 percent of the site is covered by buildings) at a moderately high density (FAR 3.5 or 140 apartments per acre) in 20-story towers. During times of peak use, about 8 percent of the residents can be found in the outdoor space, meaning that each user has 1,800 sq ft (165.6 m^2) available. The 25 people seen in the photograph have about 1,200 sq ft (110.4 m^2) per person.

formers concentrated on insuring wider lot sizes through zoning ordinances and subdivision regulations. In response to such standards and to rising affluence, lot sizes in new detached-house developments in the New York Region grew steadily throughout the nineteen twenties, thirties, and forties—from the 1/17 acre (0.02 ha) that a 25-ft lot represented to 1/4 acre (0.1 ha) in 1950 and 1/2 acre (0.2 ha) in 1960. A one-story house on a half-acre lot has 20 times more outdoor space than the turn-of-the-century frame house.

This would seem to be plenty, but in fact lot sizes in suburban subdivisions continued to expand. Part of the trend was due to exclusionary zoning, which had nothing to do with standards of spaciousness, but part of it reflected genuine market demand by an affluent minority. From the viewpoint of the person who can afford it, a half-acre lot still has neighbors running and shouting within a 50-ft (15 m) range. Unfortunately, the size of the lot increases as the square of the distance from one's neighbors, so that if the goal is to provide privacy through spatial, rather than structural separation, perhaps as many as 10 acres (4 ha) on a wooded site are needed. As a general principle of urban settlement, this is clearly absurd.

Exploring the lower limits of private outdoor space, Kevin Lynch writes: "A space of about 40 feet by 40 feet is likely to be the minimum if it is to be usable for sitting, playing and raising a few flowers."[5] With a two-story house and a little front yard, this translates into a density of 16

dwellings per acre (40 per hectare)—perhaps the maximum density of single-family houses with direct access to land in their exclusive use. Of course, the condition is firm structural separation between the lots, meaning an investment in labor and masonry instead of the vehicles and energy to propel them which a large-lot pattern requires.

Even as the suburbs strove for larger and larger lot sizes, in Manhattan the pursuit of spaciousness took the vertical route. The reasoning was that if the floor space contained in a tenement block is differently arranged and covers, say, 15 percent instead of 75 percent of the site, in a building that is not 6 but 30 stories high, then 3.4 times more outdoor ground space per dwelling can be provided, keeping the same floor space density. The floor space density, or floor-to-lot-area ratio (FAR), is the number of times the floor space in a building exceeds the size of its lot. An important added amenity would be the long view from the higher floors and escape from street-level noise: the real estate market had demonstrated that people are willing to pay a premium for higher floors and good views.

The low-coverage, high-rise principle was implemented in Manhattan for low- and middle-income housing primarily through publicly aided urban renewal and for private luxury housing through the revised zoning law of 1961. Contrary to popular impressions, densities in urban renewal projects were generally below the prevailing average; the FAR for Manhattan as a whole

was 4 in 1970; in urban renewal projects it ranged from about that level down to 2, the floor space density of a four-story town house. In addition, the coverage of the land was reduced dramatically from Manhattan's 63 percent average down to about 15 percent. The gain in open space was purchased at the price of greater height—generally 6 to 25 floors, compared with Manhattan's average of 6.4 floors. Admittedly, in private luxury apartment zones, where the permissible floor-area ratio was lowered only to 12, reducing the site coverage to 30 or 40 percent of the lot resulted in residential skyscrapers 30 to 45 stories high, with densities of over 400 dwelling units per acre (1,000 per hectare).

The increasing provision of outdoor space at the ground level by means of greater building height, however, came under attack from two different directions. In a study sponsored by the U.S. Department of Justice, Oscar Newman[6] found crime rates in low-income buildings over 15 stories to be twice as high as those in buildings of less than 6 stories. He attributed this to the isolation and lack of identity in high-rise towers, which place the environment beyond the control of its residents. The anonymity of large open spaces between buildings and their sparse use made them, too, the locus of above-average crime rates.

He found no objection to separate high-rise towers for the elderly, provided their design incorporates "defensible space" features, and stated that "high-income families . . . who can afford to pay for doormen . . . can afford to live at almost any densities they choose".[7]

But high-rise, high-income towers came under attack from local neighborhoods, where the intrusion of tall buildings was felt to be disruptive in its own right. Ironically, the feeling that tall buildings were intrusive was made worse by the setback and plaza provisions of the 1961 zoning law; the new open space at the ground level sometimes broke up the continuity of the street in a haphazard manner and set the building apart from the community. In a study of zoning reform in 1973, the New York City Urban Design Council[8] went so far as to recommend that maintaining the existing building line is more important than providing added space at the ground level and that maximum permissible coverage limits should be abolished. It did, however, suggest requirements for the provision of strictly recreational space (located indoors, to a large extent) and some incentives for landscaping whatever was left of outdoor space. One might add that neither new apartments in Moscow nor public housing in Hong Kong cover more than 25 percent of their sites.

In summary, most people would probably agree that the average ground-level outdoor space provided in residential lots in Manhattan is not enough. Yet incredibly, there is evidence that some efforts to supply more resulted in providing too much for an urban setting. Meanwhile, under suburban conditions, even one hundred times as much is

not considered adequate. Clearly, a much better understanding of actual use is necessary before we will know how to allocate space in residential environments so that they are responsive to human needs and ecologically responsible.

Recreation Space
The provision of public open space is one case in which some early empirical work was done on user behavior, notably in the *Regional Survey of New York and Its Environs,*[9] which investigated the needs for neighborhood play areas based on the children's access distance, nature of the activity, average duration, and frequency of use. It also investigated the then notorious crowding on beaches. Aerial photography found less than 50 sq ft (less than 5 m^2) of sand per bather on some sections of Coney Island and Rockaway beaches in August 1926; three times that amount was recommended as a comfortable standard.

The aerial count was repeated on a broader scale in August 1971 by Regional Plan Association, as part of its planning for the Gateway National Urban Recreation Area.[10] On 100 mi (160 km) of ocean-front beach around noontime on a Saturday it found close to 1 percent of the Region's population. Space standards, however, were much improved. Minimum area per person was 110 sq ft (10.2 m^2) at Coney Island, 120 sq ft (11.1 m^2) at Rockaway, and reached 400 sq ft (37 m^2) on Fire Island, reflecting wider transportation access to the beach front. These space allocations increased very sharply

as one moved away from the access points, about tenfold within one-third of a mile (0.5 km), and long stretches of beach were still practically empty.

The increase in people's preference for space around themselves on the beach is indicative of the broader demand for —and provision of— more urban park land in the course of this century. Even in Manhattan public park land per resident increased 84 percent between 1900 and 1970, with only one-third of the increase due to a decline in population and two-thirds due to physical additions, mostly during the thirties in the reign of Robert Moses. Similar trends occurred in other large cities, although in Moscow there was a net decline— from 142 sq ft (13.2 m^2) of park land per capita in 1912 to 104 sq ft (9.7 m^2) in 1956.[11]

In the New York Region as a whole, land in public parks (excluding the large reservations in the Catskills, along the Delaware River, and in the Pine Barrens of New Jersey) increased from 253 sq ft (23 m^2) per person in 1921 to 757 sq ft (70 m^2) in 1974, reaching nearly 60 percent of the ambitious goal set by Regional Plan Association in its *Race for Open Space* report.[12] Roughly half of the land is in large, regional tracts, mostly on the fringes of the settled area. The acquisition of local park land has been lagging. We should stress that the existence of regional open space, important as it is on ecological grounds or for weekend outings, is rarely perceived by the urban or suburban resident in his daily path, unless he happens to live right next to it.

Outdoor recreation space—examples from a beach occupancy study prepared for Regional Plan Association by Skycomp Data Corporation of Princeton, N.J. Top view, Kismet on Fire Island, about 500 sq ft (46 m^2) per person. Middle view, Sandy Hook Beach of the Gateway National Urban Recreation Area, about 150 sq ft (13.8 m^2) per person. Lower view, Brighton Beach on Coney Island, about 125 sq ft (11.5 m^2) per person. The figures cited pertain to the sand area only, and exclude people on the boardwalk or in the water.

Thus, it in no way obviates the need for intimate-scale public greenery.

Aside from public parks, reserved for open space use in perpetuity, there is a category relatively immune from development but only marginally accessible to the public, shown as "other open space" in Figure 1.1 and Table 1.2. It consists mostly of buffer zones around potable water reservoirs, military reservations, and cemeteries, where most of us eventually receive our last 50 sq ft (4.6 m²) of space.

Space for Vehicles
It is the potential for access by people and the facility to bring in (or take out) goods which make most urban space useful. These requirements are realized by space that is reserved for circulation, nowadays mostly vehicular circulation. As can be calculated from Table 1.2, vehicular pavement, even in the New York Region, exceeds the area covered by buildings. In the United States as a whole, roadways cover several times more area than buildings. So it should come as no surprise that human behavior in travel by mechanical modes has received much research attention.

Human needs for space in travel depend, most importantly, on the type of vehicle chosen and on the speed at which it moves. Group vehicles require less ground space per person than individual vehicles. Movement at slow speed requires less space than movement at high speed.

Table 1.3 illustrates the ground space requirements of some typical urban modes of travel. The space in each case should be viewed as a kind of portable territory, which moves along with the traveler and is located mostly outside the vehicle. The size of the traveling group in each case is shown in the column "assumed occupancy per vehicle." These occupancies are daily averages that represent behavior in the New York Region around 1970 and reflect the impossibility of matching equipment to travel demand at all times and on all segments of a route. Except for the auto, which has typically about one-third of its seats occupied, the occupancy figures represent roughly one-half of seated capacity. Of course, packed with standees, the bus and the subway carry about six times more passengers than indicated in Table 1.3, with the space per person shrinking proportionately; but for the moment we are concerned with fairly relaxed, non-rush-hour conditions, not with extremes of crowding.

The speed figures, likewise, do not show extremes—the maximum possible speed with no one else on the road or the minimum observable speed under congested conditions. They illustrate the borderline of free flow, with only marginal interference from the traffic stream. They exclude access time and waiting time and, in the case of the airplane, represent speed on approach.

Apart from the space requirement of airplanes, which explains why airports are big, the salient figure in Table 1.3 is the space needed by the auto on local streets. Of course, space allocations for traffic on local streets are extremely volatile and depend on the traffic, the area, and, most importantly, on stop signs and traffic lights. Nevertheless, the figure of 5,500 sq ft (510 m²) per person in a car carrying 1.5 people is a reasonable illustration of what it takes to attain a speed of 21 mph (34 km/h) on a grid of local streets.

Now, if everybody tried to claim that amount of space on the streets at once, movement would be virtually impossible. Fortunately, most people stay put most of the time. Travel during the peak hour generally amounts to about one-tenth of the daily travel demand. Those who travel by auto, however, do spend an average of about an hour a day in it. So we might say that the average auto user "rents" some 5,500 sq ft (510 m²) of street space for an hour each day; but because only 10 to 11 percent of that demand is realized during the peak hour, the land requirement per auto user becomes one-tenth of the space needed in travel, about 550 sq ft (51 m²). *It is important to distinguish between the space needed while in movement and the fixed supply of pavement required to provide it.* This basic distinction will be employed again when pedestrian space is analyzed.

As can be seen from Table 1.2, suburban areas in the New York Region provide an average of 735 sq ft (68 m²) of vehicular pavement per resident, allowing average speeds higher than 21 mph (34 km/h). At the other extreme, in Manhattan, pavement per resident shrinks to 66 sq ft (6 m²), severely curtailing auto ownership and average speeds. Tokyo and Moscow have a similar amoung of street pavement per resident.

Even with an average of 550 sq ft per person, though, peak-hour speeds on major streets usually do drop below 21 mph because traffic is not uniformly distributed. Typically, over two-thirds of the pavement is in streets that serve primarily their own neighborhoods and do not lead to where most people want to go. With travel concentrated on the remaining third,[13] available space per traveler in a car with 1.5 occupants is no longer 5,500 sq ft. If it is cut in half, a peak-hour condition typical of suburban arterials, average speed drops to 17 mph (27 km/h); cut in half again, as it is often on major urban streets, speed drops to about 13 mph (21 km/h); cut in half once more, speed is down to 9 mph (14 km/h)—quite typical of downtown business districts. At that speed the maximum possible traffic flow on a grid of local streets, with a space of about 750 sq ft (70 m²) per auto traveler, is achieved. This progressive compression of space, perceived through the progressive reduction in speed, is experienced as worsening congestion.

The inefficiency of urban streets for moving auto traffic was understood by engineers long ago. The answer was the freeway. Because of the advantage of uninterrupted flow and the much higher speed that results, a freeway can "rent" the same piece of pavement to more users in a unit of time and achieve a greater flow of vehicles in the same space. Thus, freeways in the New York Region in 1970 carried 32 percent of all automobile travel,[14] while freeway pavement, even including shoulders, accounted for only 6 percent of the total paved

space. However, designed to relieve congestion, freeways did create some of their own. They not only relieved local streets of the longer trips but also induced new travel, which would not have occurred had it not become possible to traverse much longer distances in the same time. Hence, the question: Can the spiraling demand for travel space, created by better facilities, ever be satisfied without congestion?

To answer by way of an example: in exurban areas with about 10 acres (4 ha) of land per family and no clusters of activity, a very high per capita travel demand is being satisfied at very high average speeds by roadway pavement on the order of 2,000 sq ft (186 m²) per resident, which includes some rather empty freeway mileage. With that ratio of pavement to people, which begins to approach the nationwide average in the United States, there certainly is no congestion. But even in suburban areas, which have ten times the population density of their exurbs, provision of pavement on that scale would defeat the very purpose of a green environment. In cities with one hundred times the population density, achieving 2,000 sq ft of roadway per resident would mean devoting all land to pavement.

Public transportation is usually proposed as a cure for congestion created by too many autos in a limited space. The tiny space needs of bus and rail transit are evident in Table 1.3. But, there is a catch. These high-density modes developed in a symbiotic relationship with a high-density environment. A mode that uses

roughly ten times less space than the auto also requires roughly a ten times greater population density in the surrounding area to be competitive. Otherwise there simply are not enough potential riders within walking distance of a stop to fill a bus or a train on a frequent schedule. If the schedule thins out, waiting time increases, further diminishing ridership. As it is, public transportation tends to be inherently slower than the auto because it has to make stops to pick up passengers. This is reflected in the operating speeds shown in Table 1.3. But added to that must be access time to and from a transit stop and waiting time, which on the average just about equal the time in transit. Thus, effective door-to-door speed of public transit is about half what is shown in Table 1.3.

With improved technology, transit speeds can be raised above the the New York averages shown in Table 1.3. But much of the improvement, whether on exclusive bus lanes or on new transit systems, is purchased at the cost of reducing the number of stops, which creates only single-purpose routes to one major destination. To provide any more diversified service independent of the auto, high population density is needed at both ends of the trip.

Thus we come to the irony that lack of congestion, if it is to be achieved by public transit, requires less, rather than more, urban space per person. This, of course, is even more true should one expect walking to become a significant substitute for mechanical travel. According to the census, 25 percent of the Man-

Table 1.3
Ground Space per Traveler in Comfortable Movement

Travel mode	Assumed operating speed		Assumed occupancy per vehicle	Ground space per person at assumed speed and occupancy		Flow per hr per unit of paved width	
	mph	(km/h)		sq ft	(m²)	ft	(m)
Pedestrian	3	(5)	0	130	(12)	120	(400)
Bicyclist	10	(16)	1	200	(42)	260	(860)
Local bus	12	(19)	15	225	(21)	280	(925)
Auto on street	21	(34)	1.5	5,500	(510)	20	(66)
Express subway	23	(37)	25	235	(22)	520	(1,695)
Auto on freeway	55	(88)	1.5	2,500	(232)	115	(380)
Airplane landing	150	(240)	60	1,400,000	(130,000)	0.5	(2)

Sources: Pedestrian, from Table 3.7. Bicyclist, Carlo De Rege, "An Analysis of the Traffic Stream of Bicycles in Central Park" (paper for New York University Graduate School of Public Administration, 1971; estimated curve in Figure 4.3; compare also Institute of Transportation and Traffic Engineering, University of California, *Bikeway Planning Criteria and Guidelines,* 1972, pp. 21, 27, 37. Local Bus, average space per vehicle at 12 mph calculated from Table 4.6 times bus equivalency of 1.6, divided by bus occupancy. Auto on Street, based on 4.5 percent of regionwide arterial daily flow per lane, representing midday hourly flow and midday average speed, both from Tri-State Regional Planning Commission, *Streets and Highways,* 1968, pp. 41, 43; an alternative method, based on extrapolation from Table 4.5, would yield 7,000 sq ft for Manhattan conditions only. Subway, based on 14.5 ft roadway width per track and 10-car trains on a 2-min headway. Auto on Freeway, from Table 4.6 with 4 ft per 12-ft lane added to allow for pavement on shoulders (landscaped buffers and medians are not included); Airplane Landing, based on 1-mi minimum spacing between parallel independent runways and 3-mi radar separation.

Table 1.4
Space for Travelers in Vehicles

	Net seating space per seated pass.		Minimum aisle width	
	sq ft	(m²)	in.	(cm)
School bus	3.3	(0.31)	20.5	(52)
City bus	3.6	(0.33)	21.0	(53)
Subway car (PATH and MTA R-46)	3.9	(0.36)	27.5	(70)
Commuter bus	4.1	(0.38)	15.0	(38)
Airplane coach (narrow body)	4.6	(0.43)	17.0	(43)
Rail commuter car (MTA)	4.8	(0.45)	21.5	(55)
Subway car (BART)	5.3	(0.49)	29.5	(75)
Airplane coach (wide body)	5.6	(0.52)	20.0	(51)
Small auto, 1,300 lbs (580 kg), front seat	5.7	(0.53)	–	–
Rail coach (Metroliner)	6.3	(0.59)	26.5	(67)
Airplane first class (wide body)	7.5	(0.70)	30.0	(76)
Large auto, 4,000 lbs (1,800 kg), front seat	9.7	(0.90)	–	–

Source: Regional Plan Association. Based on field measurements at seated elbow level, including leg room in autos and cushion thickness, where applicable.

hattan Central Business District residents walk to work. The proportion can be around 15 percent in some smaller old cities. It is less than 5 percent in low-density suburbs.

Space in Vehicles

While the auto (as distinguished from the auto traveler) requires some 1,100 sq ft (100 m²) of space to move even under congested conditions and multiples of that at higher speeds, the car itself covers only a small fraction of that space—between 65 and 130 sq ft (6 and 12 m²), depending on its size. Subway trains and buses likewise occupy about one-tenth of the space they need for movement. So vehicle size has little effect on the space needed for movement. However, it has a great effect on storage requirements when the vehicle is not in use. While rail vehicles spend the night in their own yards, the parking of autos becomes a well-known problem if street pavement is less than about 250 sq ft (23 m²) per capita, as is the case in most older cities with densities of 10,000 people per sq mi (3,860 per km²) or more.

Of greater interest from the viewpoint of human space needs is the room for people inside the vehicle. Table 1.4 illustrates the net seating space per seated passenger provided in different vehicles. Quite obviously this space, exclusive of aisles and service areas, is not in itself a sufficient measure of comfort. The shape of the seat related to body position (the low seat in an auto does need more leg room); vehicle operating characteristics, such as acceleration, deceleration, and lateral thrust; noise; the condi-

tion of the air; and the average length of the ride all influence the perception of comfort. Nevertheless, the reader will have no difficulty rating the seating in the vehicles listed in Table 1.4 from "crammed" to "comfortable," a progression that is likely to relate closely to the amount of space. Two of the modes in Table 1.4, subways and buses, are designed to handle large numbers of standees during the rush hour and are usually judged by standee space, rather than seating space. Just as the behind of most adults will fit into the 16.5 in. (42 cm) of seat width provided on a school bus, so can standees fit into a remarkably small space if they are sufficiently compressed. The New York City Transit Authority calculates the maximum "practical capacity" of subway cars on the basis of about 1.8 sq ft (0.17 m²) of clear floor area per standee.[15] A similar maximum standard on the Moscow metro is 1.3 sq ft (0.12 m²) of clear floor area per standee.[16] In fact, space per standing passenger on sections of some of the most overcrowded subway runs in New York City has been observed to fall as low as 1.15 sq ft (0.1 m²) in cars located in the middle of the train. Many preferred this utmost level of congestion to a price they could have paid for somewhat more space—namely, a 300-ft (90 m) walk to the front or rear car of the train, where they could have had 1.6 or 2.0 sq ft (0.15 or 0.19 m²) of standing room, respectively.[17] On the whole, however, it seems clear that people who are accustomed to nearly 10 sq ft (0.9 m²) of space per seat in an auto will not abandon it

willingly for public transit, unless transit provides, on its own terms, a reasonably comparable level of comfort:[18] more room in vehicles that require less room on the outside.

Nonresidential Space

While most trips either begin or end at home, their destination is usually some nonresidential building. Overall, there is less floor space in nonresidential buildings than in residences (the former account for somewhat more than one-third, the latter for somewhat less than two-thirds, of total floor space in the New York Region). Measured from the viewpoint of the worker, however, which is appropriate in the case of nonresidential buildings, there is on the average more floor space per employee on the job than there is floor space per resident in the home, as Table 1.2 shows.

Nonresidential buildings serve a wide variety of functions (some 270 different building types have been identified), and their indoor space allocations vary accordingly. Even in the New York Region, less oriented toward goods handling than many others, the largest single chunk of nonresidential floor space is still that in manufacturing plants and warehouses—it accounts for roughly 33 percent of the total and averages about 500 sq ft (46 m²) per production worker, a figure that varies considerably with location:[19] the more labor-intensive plants gravitate toward urban centers.

Institutional and public buildings amount to some 26 percent of nonresidential floor space and average around 1,000 sq ft (93 m²) per employee. This huge allocation is explained by the fact that employees are likely to be in the minority of all persons who are in schools, hospitals, libraries, community centers, and similar institutions. Again, those with smaller indoor space needs tend to locate in more central areas.

Commercial space represents roughly 23 percent of the total and averages somewhat less than 300 sq ft (28 m²) per employee, a space allocation that also will shrink dramatically when customers of the retail stores, retail services, restaurants, motels, and hotels that are included in this category are counted. In the next chapter we will give some examples of the interior densities encountered in such buildings, which are among the highest of any building type.

Omitting a small amount of miscellaneous use, such as power and telephone equipment buildings, the fourth major category consists of private and public office buildings. Regionwide, these account for some 13 percent of all nonresidential floor space and average about 250 sq ft (23 m²) per office employee, an allocation that varies only mildly with density of development.

The four ratios of floor space per employee shown are only rough indicators of the fixed supply of building space; they do not show the space that is in fact available to a worker while on the job. This is so because employment as listed in economic statistics refers to the number of jobs; the

number of people holding these jobs is smaller (some people hold more than one job), and the number of workers at work at any one time is smaller still, because of the sequence of shifts, vacations, and other reasons for absence.[20] Thus, in Chapter 2, when we actually measure the floor space per person in selected buildings, the space allocations will be larger than shown here when only workers are involved. They will, of course, be smaller when visitors using a building are included.

As evident from Table 1.2, nonresidential buildings in most cases cover a much larger share of their lot than residences and have higher floor-area ratios. Thus, they have less *outdoor space*. Some of this outdoor space is used for yards providing light and air, some for material storage and other needs appurtenant to production, and some for ornamental landscaping, but at lower densities a very large share of outdoor space is devoted to auto parking.

One of the paradoxes of automobile access is that the greater the number of people that a cluster of buildings attracts, the more isolated that cluster has to be from other buildings because of the needs for parking around it. Thus, retail space, as we indicated, attracts the greatest number of people per square foot of floor space and in suburban areas must typically provide over twice the area in parking than it has in indoor floor space. An office building may need only 250 sq ft (23 m²) per worker, but if each worker comes by car and if it takes at least 250 sq ft to park a

100-sq ft (9 m²) car on a self-parking basis, then the building needs as much outdoor (or garage) space for parking as indoor space for its indoor activities. By that same reckoning, manufacturing, not a very people-oriented use of space, needs on the average only half the space for parking as it needs in the building itself. It is clear that mobility by auto not only allows, but positively demands, deconcentration of precisely those uses that can profit most from concentration.

If, on the other hand, access by high-density modes of travel is provided, then the building types attracting large number of trips can be grouped together in a small area, fostering mutually supportive linkages among each other. This effect of a total greater than the sum of its parts is the prime reason for downtown concentrations.

With virtually half of the New York Region's office floor space located in Manhattan, these 245 million sq ft (22.76 million m²) of floor space cover only half a square mile (1.3 km²) of lot area—about 6 percent of the land in the Central Business District south of 60th Street—leaving the rest of the land for other supporting activities, built to much lower densities, and streets.

The office floor-area ratios in the smaller downtowns are much lower than the 18 average of Manhattan, generally less than 4, but still pose very small land requirements. By contrast, in suburban, fully auto-oriented locations, floor-area ratios range from a high of 1 near shopping centers and highway interchanges to less than 0.1 on some lavishly landscaped campus sites. In other words, these campus-type office buildings use about two hundred times the land of a Manhattan office tower.

The range of floor space densities for other types of nonresidential buildings is narrower, but there still remains a steep step from the compact land requirements in or near an urban center to the expansive requirements of an outlying location. Thus, floor-area ratios of department stores, ranging from 12 to 6 in Manhattan, are typically about 2 in smaller downtowns (this includes some garage parking) and about 0.2 or 0.15 in suburban shopping centers. Land per student in universities that have a full complement of facilities is on the order of 200 sq ft (19 m^2) or less on an urban campus but 2,000 sq ft (190 m^2) or more in a spread development. Greater building height and a greater than tenfold reduction in non-residential outdoor space per worker achieve the greater compactness of an urban center.

With this kind of a range of space allocations, one would expect that a systematic measurement and evaluation of their performance, the differences in behavior they cause, and their costs to the environment would have been undertaken. Such is not the case.

One thing is clear, though. While greater compactness expedites contacts on foot, it can also reduce the space available for walking to a minimum. From Table 1.2 one can estimate that in sub-urban nonresidential areas there are over 800 sq ft (over 74 m^2) of nonvehicular street space per worker. Much of it has sidewalks, though very few walk. In non-residential areas of Manhattan, where walking is very important, there are for every worker on the order of 10 sq ft (say 1 m^2) of nonvehicular street space, all of which is, fortunately, sidewalk space.

With the overview of the general scale of urban space use as a background, we can now turn our attention to this sidewalk space. For along with the related issue of space in public transit, it emerges as a bottleneck in an urban system, which is, in many ways, quite generously endowed with space.

The Issue: Pedestrian Space in Urban Centers

No matter by what means people arrive in a downtown area, they end up as pedestrians on its sidewalks. Autos can be diverted from the surface, transit capacity can be expanded, but the ultimate limit on the smooth functioning of a downtown is its provision for pedestrian circulation. The image of a downtown is not the skyline seen from the airplane—it is the image of the spaces where people walk.

Yet, planning for pedestrians in urban centers has been badly neglected. Nineteenth century street layouts frequently did allocate as much as half the urban right-of-way to walkways, which was ample when very few buildings were more than three stories high. But when buildings in downtown areas started to get taller—and to attract more pedestrian trips—no effort was made to set them back farther from the building line. On the contrary, real estate pressures forced closer encroachment. When the motor vehicle arrived on the scene, roadways began to be widened, likewise at the expense of walkway space. Thus, in downtown areas, the pedestrian was squeezed into leftover space between the traffic and the building walls. Also, traffic signals were timed primarily to minimize vehicular delay, not to minimize total delay in all the conflicting streams they regulate. Virtually the only attention paid to pedestrians was with respect to their physical safety, not to their comfort or amenity. On the other hand, when large-scale downtown redevelopment began

Below, a view of the pedestrian's predicament from the 1920s. From *New York Tribune*, 5 April 1925.

Annihilation of pedestrian space. Top view, Park Avenue in Manhattan prior to 1928, with two-thirds of its width devoted to walkways and landscaping. Bottom view, Park Avenue today, with two-thirds of its width devoted to autos and taxis. Top view courtesy of New York Historical Society; bottom view courtesy of Paul Cardell.

to occur in recent decades, architects were frequently bent upon providing monumental urban spaces totally out of scale with potential pedestrian flow. There was no body of empirical data which would help proportion pedestrian circulation space in relation to building bulk and use and to the behavioral needs of pedestrians.

When intolerable congestion resulted, efforts to correct it were, more often than not, curiously misguided. Urban planners equated congestion with a high concentration of activity, that is, high building density, and attempted to limit the latter, often denying the very essence of the urban center in the process. Only lately has it occured to urban planners that rearranging circulation space at or near the surface can be a more direct cure to congestion than limiting building bulk; that given the same building bulk, greater building height provides more, rather than less, room for circulation on the ground.

The Legacy of the Past
The reluctance to admit the benefits of high density and to make the necessary commitment with regard to arranging space seems to have been the fate of many large cities. It is well illustrated by the case history of New York, which is worth recounting. The first tall secular building (though perhaps technically not yet a "skyscraper") was completed in Manhattan in 1875 and was, not counting an ornamental tower, 10 stories high. By 1910 the height of the tallest building shot up to 50 stories, and the legendary skyline was

born. In the same period a rapid transit system, initially above, and then below ground was hastily expanded to serve the burgeoning concentration. In February 1913 the New York City Board of Estimate authorized the establishment of a commission that was to consider whether it was desirable "to regulate the height, size and arrangement of buildings" in order, among other things, "to prevent unwholesome and dangerous congestion . . . in street and transit traffic." The commission, established under the chairmanship of Edward M. Basset, known as the father of zoning in America, called itself the "Heights of Buildings Commission." Not much reference to the "arrangement" of buildings remained in its title or in its well-known report,[21] which became the basis for New York City's first zoning law, passed in 1916. The commission report did refer to sidewalk congestion and pointed out that existing sidewalk space could not accommodate the occupants of tall buildings, should they all exit at once. But it treated walkway space as a given and made no proposals for enlarging it by rearranging buildings. Nor were such provisions included in the first zoning law, which molded the shape of Manhattan's skyscrapers for forty-five years.

In 1931, Thomas Adams, writing on "The Character, Bulk and Surroundings of Buildings" in the sixth volume of the *Regional Survey of New York and Its Environs*,[22] made some attempts to estimate pedestrian trips produced by buildings. His estimates, compared with those of today,

were exaggerated, and in general the subject appeared intellectually elusive to both him and his contemporaries. However, he did make the correct observation that "the department store throws a vastly greater burden upon the streets than the office building" and suggested that "department stores require such wide sidewalks that they would gain considerable advantage from having their front walls set back 10 to 15 feet from the street line." Generalizing, he noted that "New York City, with all its skyscrapers, suffers less from height of building than from excessive coverage of land with buildings." Unfortunately, he did not develop this point and reverted to the conventional argument that "overbuilding" causes congestion; he termed building floor areas more than 8 times greater than their lot areas "excessive."

Even as Adams was finishing his report, the Chrysler and Empire State buildings were being completed, with floor areas 30 and 32 times greater than their lot areas, respectively. Both skyscrapers—one 78, the other 102, stories high—had setbacks above the lower floors that were larger than required by the zoning law, but neither provided even a foot of extra sidewalk space at the ground level.

"Overbuilding" came to a halt for two decades because of the depression and World War II, and it was not until 1950 that the issue was raised again in the Harrison, Ballard and Allen report *Plan for Rezoning the City of New York*.[23] Starting from the premise that the 1916 zoning envelope or permitted building bulk was absurdly exaggerated compared with the development potential of the City, the report sought to lower permissible densities in order "to limit the concentration of people and their activities," to limit the loads on traffic, transit, and service facilities, and "to prevent excessive congestion." It called building floor areas 15 times greater than their lot areas "maximum." However, it did not touch on the actual relationship of building bulk to pedestrian and vehicular circulation space, except by way of proposals for off-street automobile parking, fashionable at the time but capable of attracting even more surface traffic to high-density areas. Nevertheless, the report did make a contribution by suggesting improved methods of regulating building use, bulk, and shape.

These positive features became the point of departure for a new study, *Zoning New York City,* prepared under the direction of Jack C. Smith and published in 1958.[24] The report still contained the rhetoric of "the price" being "too high in terms of overbuilding and congestion," but the main thrust was against "stereotyped designs enforced by regulations rigidly restricting the outer form [of buildings] but ineffectively dealing with the bulk and density they are intended to control." To encourage "design in the public interest," a system of incentives was proposed, among them: "In order to bring more light and air into streets surrounded by tall buildings, as well as to create more usable open space, a bonus device has been established to encourage the setting back of buildings from the street line." Thus, for the first time, there was serious concern with building "arrangement," with the liberation of the pedestrian from the tyranny of walls following the property line.

With minor amendments, *Zoning New York City* became the zoning law of 1961. It did lower overall permissible densities close to the level of existing development but pioneered, along with a Chicago ordinance of a few years earlier, the device of permitting higher density as an incentive for providing pedestrian plazas and arcades. For example, in the highest density districts, a developer who provided 1 unit of open area at or near the sidewalk level could build, in return for this sacrifice in ground floor space, 10 extra units of floor area at the top. In these districts the maximum floor area was raised from 15 to 18 times the lot area, if the extra ground level space was provided.

Manhattan's first pedestrian plazas beyond the property line must be credited to architects Gordon Bunshaft (Lever House, 1951, and Chase Manhattan Bank, 1961) and Mies van der Rohe (Seagram Building, 1957) and their clients, who sacrificed legally permissible building space under the old zoning law. As soon as the law was changed, virtually every large office building began to avail itself of the plaza bonus. By 1970 there were, in the central square mile of Midtown Manhattan, over 11 acres (4.5 ha) of public pedestrian plazas on private land and over 2 acres (0.8 ha) of ornamental space, consisting of landscaping and fountains. Most of this open space was built since 1961 under provisions of the new zoning law, which thus added to Midtown, at no cost to the public, space equivalent to two Bryant Parks.

The principle of providing open space in ground-level plazas and concentrating the building bulk in straight towers without setbacks was carried furthest in the World Trade Center in Lower Manhattan, designed by Minoru Yamasaki in 1962-64 and largely completed by 1975. The two 110-story towers have evoked some public emotion against high density, but in fact the floor-area density of the entire development is about 14, substantially below average for Manhattan office buildings. However, the World Trade Center also shows that it is not simply the amount of space, but its arrangement, that counts: the 5-acre (2 ha) plaza remains largely unused, while pedestrian circulation space in concourse corridors and on approaches to rapid transit is crowded, separated visually and structurally from the empty grandeur of the ornamental plaza. Suggestions made during the design of the project for improved pedestrian circulation and for opening to light and air the spaces where most people walk were resisted by the Port Authority, which owns the buildings. The City of New York, in its negotiations with the Port Authority at the time, was primarily concerned with vehicular, rather than pedestrian, space and successfully insisted on widening roadways around the project to 80 and 100 ft (24 and 30 m). Such vehicular pavement width turned out to be unnecessary. It isolates the project from the surrounding urban fabric and is a barrier to the dominant traffic flow in the area, which is on foot.

Of course, new construction after 1961 could not easily alleviate the shortage of walkway space created in Manhattan over the previous decades. The pattern is dramatically illustrated by Table 1.5, which is based on measurements made by Regional Plan Association in 1969 in the central 1.2 sq mi. (3.1 km²) of Midtown Manhattan as a first step in the studies on which this book is based.

Table 1.5 shows how walkway space shrinks with increasing building density in Midtown Manhattan. Buildings in the lowest density category, with floor-area ratios below 5, have 80 units of walkway space per 1,000 units of indoor space. Buildings in the highest density category, with floor-area ratios above 25, have only 10.8 units of walkway space per 1,000 units of indoor space. In other words, the greater the density of a building and the more pedestrian travel it generates, the less walkway space there is available to it. Such misallocation of walkway space constitutes the major source of pedestrian congestion in high-density areas.

The reason for the reverse relationship between building bulk and walkway space lies in the traditional rules for determining sidewalk widths. Historically, as we have indicated, sidewalk space has been treated as a constant, related perhaps to street width but in no way to building

bulk. When the Manhattan street plan was laid out in 1811, it anticipated predominantly residential development at a floor-area ratio of 2 and amply endowed the future buildings with some 100 units of sidewalk area for every 1,000 units of building area. Since then sidewalk dimensions have been either held constant or cut back in favor of vehicular pavement, even in areas where floor-space density increased tenfold; it is only logical that the sidewalk allocation in such places would shrink to about one-tenth of its former size. The notion that walkways should be dimensioned proportionately to building bulk did not occur for 150 years.

The effect of the 1961 zoning ordinance, which gave high-bulk buildings an incentive to increase their walkway space by means of pedestrian plazas, is, to some extent, reflected in Table 1.5: the walkway surface per 1,000 units of floor space does not decline proportionately from the 10-15 floor-area ratio to the 15-20 category. This is because of a heavy concentration of post-1961 buildings with plazas in the latter density range.

Steps Toward the Future
The opening of plazas in the canyons of Midtown and Downtown Manhattan brought home one very important point: high density does not necessarily equal congestion. To the pedestrian in the street, a 50-story building amply set back on a plaza can offer much more physical room for walking and is also visually less prominent (because of the laws of perspective and man's limited angle of vision)

than a 10-story building rising straight from the property line. To be sure, the rapid transit delivery capacity may have to be more than twice as high for the former, but that occurs underground, where considerable room can be made at a price. The matter boils down to balancing relative costs of different forms of transportation investment: suburban freeways for dispersed development versus urban rapid transit for development concentrated in centers.

Discarding the inhibition of several generations of urban planners, the *Critical Issues* volume of the *Plan for New York City: a Proposal,* published by the New York City Planning Commission in November 1969, said: "Concentration is the genius of the City, its reason for being, the source of its vitality and excitement. We believe the center should be strengthened, not weakened, and we are not afraid of the bogey of high density."[25] Implementation of this policy had two aspects: on the one hand, increasing pedestrian amenity and space to reduce congestion; on the other hand, increasing building density to pay for the gains in space at the ground level or to maintain other urban features, such as theaters or retail stores.

Perhaps the best-publicized step in the first direction was temporary street-closing experiments, which gave some vehicular space to pedestrians and demonstrated, in a limited way, that surface use by motor vehicles, which creates much of the perceived congestion, can be reduced even before fully satisfactory alternatives are developed.

Partial re-creation of pedestrian space. Two of the early plazas which began opening the canyons of Manhattan before zoning law provided incentives for the expansion of ground-level space. Top view, Time-Life Building (1959, Harrison and Abramovitz, architects). Bottom view, Chase Manhattan Bank (1961, Skidmore, Owings and Merrill, architects). Photographs by Jerry Spearman, reprinted by permission of Department of City Planning, City of New York.

Table 1.5
Walkway Space Related to Building Floor Space in Midtown Manhattan (38th to 61st streets, Second to Eighth avenues)

Floor-area ratio	% of total bldg. space	% of total walkway space	Sq ft (or m²) of walkways per 1,000 sq ft (or m²) of bldg. fl. space
0-5	8.6	27.0	80.3
5-10	19.9	23.0	29.2
10-15	24.5	18.9	19.5
15-20	29.5	21.4	18.4
20-25	14.1	8.2	14.7
25-30	3.4	1.5	10.8
Total	100.0	100.0	25.7
Total sq ft	196,154,000	5,036,800*	
Total m²	18,222,706	467,900*	

Source: Regional Plan Association.
*Exclusive of walkways in parks.

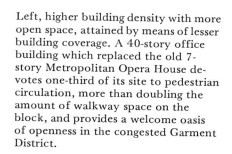

Left, higher building density with more open space, attained by means of lesser building coverage. A 40-story office building which replaced the old 7-story Metropolitan Opera House devotes one-third of its site to pedestrian circulation, more than doubling the amount of walkway space on the block, and provides a welcome oasis of openness in the congested Garment District.

Right, more space for pedestrians at the expense of motor vehicles. Experimental closing of Fifth Avenue to traffic on July 11, 1970 offers the glimpse of a new freedom of movement, of clean air and a quiet city. Space available for walking in both this and the preceding view is in the comfortable range of 150 to 200 sq ft (13.8 to 18.4 m^2) per person. Right photograph courtesy of *The New York Times.*

Pedestrian space is gaining in three-dimensional richness. Right, sculptured forms by Pamela Waters create sitting space in a widened sidewalk. Above, sunken plaza by Max Abramovtiz provides daylight and access to an underground corridor. Top photograph by Paul Cardell.

Early results of this study were made available to New York City agencies beginning in December 1969 and were used for planning the temporary street and avenue closings in 1970 and 1971, as well as for designating Broadway, Madison, and Lexington avenues as potential permanent malls in the *Movement in Midtown* study of the Mayor's Office Midtown Planning and Development.[26] The city administration's detailed plans for a Madison Avenue mall, likewise utilizing the findings of this study,[27] however, came to naught after two years of intense political maneuvering. As will be shown later, a strong technical case can be made for the exclusion of most vehicular traffic from major avenues in Manhattan; politically, however, the strategy met with more success in areas where the competition between pedestrians and vehicles, especially taxicabs, is less intense. The 125 European and 20 United States cities that had permanent vehicle-free streets in 1972[28] were joined in 1975 by only 2 smaller downtowns in the New York Region—Paterson, New Jersey, and Poughkeepsie, New York. By 1975 a number of similarly modest pedestrianization schemes in New York City were also well along toward implementation.

Less publicized but more successful in Manhattan were zoning changes to promote pedestrian amenities: the Lincoln Square Special Zoning District, calling for a continuous pedestrian arcade along a stretch of Broadway; the Special Greenwich Street Development District in Lower Manhattan, calling for a number of grade-separated pedestrian amenities; the Special Fifth Avenue District, providing for mid-block pedestrian walkways and striving to preserve the visual and functional qualities of a section of Fifth Avenue. Following specific recommendations of this study, a zoning amendment providing for off-sidewalk waiting areas in front of motion picture theaters was adopted late in 1971, together with new provisions for covered pedestrian spaces.[29]

Last but not least, a beginning was made in breaking a tyranny even more oppressive than that of the property line—that of the ground level. With the opening of the first subway in 1904 and of the two major underground rail terminals about a decade later, Manhattan became a multilevel city. Yet, Victorian esthetics and laissez-faire economics conspired in the pretense that only the ground level exists; whatever is underneath is carefully hidden and its exposure to daylight minimized. Though an overwhelming majority of people who arrive in the Manhattan Central Business District do so from underground, the connections between the underground world and the world of sunlight and air are steep, torturous, and narrow, in no way encouraging the use of underground transportation. Opportunities for breaking open the "street membrane," for merging the underground and the sidewalk into one continuous pedestrian space, present themselves whenever a new building is built near an existing subway station. Since the formulation of the "access tree" concept by Regional Plan Association in 1968 (later published in *Urban Design Manhattan*), which emphasized this issue, four new Midtown developments made some attempt to open subways to light and air, hinting at what a truly expressive, multilevel city could be like. Also, improvements to subway stations short of breaking them open to light and air were negotiated by the City Planning Commission at several other locations.

In June 1973 a zoning amendment was passed allowing depressed plazas connecting to subway stations,[30] and in December 1973 temporary legislation (made permanent in 1974) was enacted for the Second Avenue Special Transit Land Use District, which, for the first time, extended the concept of a mandatory zoning setback to below the ground level to permit off-sidewalk entrances to new subway stations, as urged by the Regional Plan Association. A comprehensive revision of plaza regulations in the highest density districts in 1974 provided detailed specifications for below ground "open air concourses" on private property, leading to subway stations.

As for the other direction of the "new zoning,"[31] that of increasing diversity of use, perhaps the best-publicized step was the establishment of the Special Theater District, where zoning provisions increased the maximum floor area to 21.6 times the lot area, if theaters, restaurants, and related features were included in an office building. A similar increase in density was granted in the Special Fifth

Avenue District for multipurpose buildings and pedestrian arcades. Inclusion of retail space in office buildings was made a mandatory feature in the Special Greenwich Street Development district in Lower Manhattan, where permissible densities were virtually doubled as an incentive to provide diversity of use and a series of elaborate pedestrian improvements.[32]

This leads naturally to the question, How high can density be allowed to go before increased pedestrian traffic catches up with the expanded space? What is a balanced relationship between building bulk and pedestrian circulation space? The answer was nowhere to be found in the "new zoning."

Moreover, the flexible, case-by-case approach in the early special zoning districts, where bonuses were granted on a "special permit" basis at the discretion of the City Planning Commission, subject to a public hearing and Board of Estimate legislative approval, contained no safeguards for maintaining a mandatory minimum of pedestrian space. The need for such safeguards is illustrated by the case of a large office building in the theater district, where the City's eagerness to have new theaters went so far that the need for added pedestrian space was disregarded. At the same time, there are plenty of cases in which ample plazas, stimulated by bonuses, remain unused because of their arrangement, while adjacent sidewalks continue to be congested.

It is quite clear that precise and generally applicable standards

of pedestrian space, allowing a proportionate volume of building floor space as a matter of right, are long overdue. To be sure, there will always be complex situations requiring individual attention and some discretionary latitude on the part of the planning body. However, these situations can be reduced in number and should not be exempt from elementary requirements for a necessary minimum of pedestrian space.

The need for a firm factual basis to guide the allocation of pedestrian space is apparent on more general grounds as well. The new zoning, having started from incentive bonuses granting the developer the right to increase building density on condition that certain parts of the site are left open, developed a trend toward permitting higher densities in return for payments toward public improvements that may even be away from the building site. This amounts to an outright *sale* to the developer of the right to increase density. In principle, an evolution in this direction would not necessarily be wrong. It could harness market forces in the private sector to become the regulator of density instead of letting the public sector determine by decree what absolute levels of activity concentration are good or bad for society. Instead of limiting density as such, the role of the public sector would become strictly one of preventing congestion and other "diseconomies" at any given level of density by carefully sealing both financial levies and design requirements to the circulation and amenity improvements necessary. The financial levies could

include those designed to recapture the "unearned increment" that accrues to private landowners as a result of public investment and might, if uniformly applied, work to curtail excessively *low* densities. However, to become practical, such an approach presupposes a knowledge of the true "external costs" that a building imposes on its neighbors and on the public at various levels of density. Such knowledge is virtually nonexistent. Determining pedestrian requirements is an essential step in closing this gap.

In summary, pedestrian congestion in high-density urban districts is a result not of high density as such but rather of inadequate allocation of space at and near the surface level for pedestrian use. Pedestrian space can be expanded—
1.
At the expense of nonessential vehicular traffic in public streets;
2.
At the expense of increased building height, but reduced site coverage, on private land;
3.
At the expense of building multilevel walkways below, and occasionally above, ground and improving their attractiveness to match that of surface walkways.

High standards of pedestrian amenity can be maintained with increasing density and future congestion prevented if the amount of walkway space required for new buildings is firmly linked to the amount and use of floor space in these buildings. Developing such quantitative relationships between building floor space and pedestrian circulation space is the purpose of this book.

The Method: Relating Walkway Space to Buildings

The conceptual tools for estimating the amount of walkway space required by a building are available from the field of travel analysis, a field that so far has mostly limited itself to the study of travel by mechanical modes. Before we plunge into the details, an overview of the methodological steps and of the pertinent vocabulary is in order.

At least one end of any trip is generally anchored to a building. Thus, one can picture all travel as emanating from buildings and these buildings as having *trip generation rates,* that is, figures that indicate how many trips in a unit of time a unit of floor space attracts, or generates. Quite obviously, the trip generation rates vary, depending on the type of use a building serves: for example, a retail store attracts many more trips than a warehouse. The use to which floor space is put as well as the amount of floor space are important variables to be considered.

Next, it is also quite clear that travel is not uniform over time. Very few trips occur at four o'clock in the morning; a great many occur at five o'clock in the afternoon. While particular individuals may have fairly erratic schedules, society as a whole develops rather stable responses to the time of the day, the week, and the season, which are reflected in *cyclical variation* in travel. If we are interested in avoiding congestion, we must be concerned with certain peak periods when travel is most intensive, and know how these relate to

total travel during a longer span of time.

Trips follow a path on which a traveler stays for a certain distance. This distance, or trip length, is important not only from the viewpoint of the traveler, who has to spend time and effort to traverse distance, but also from the viewpoint of society; for if a trip along a particular path is short, then others can use other sections of the path. If it is long, then more of the path is preempted by the same individual. The same burden is put on a path when ten people travel along it for one mile each as when one person travels along it for ten miles. Therefore, travel demand is measured not in trips but rather in person-miles or person-kilometers of travel: the number of trips multiplied by their average length. Knowing the average trip length is essential for calculating the person-miles or person-kilometers of travel, and yet very few trips have an "average" length: most are either shorter or longer. A table or a curve that shows what proportion of all trips are of what length is called a *trip-length frequency distribution.* It is governed by two factors: the geographic distribution of opportunities for making trips—mostly building floor space—and people's travel propensity, that is, their willingness or ability to overcome distance in order to reach the opportunities.

If a path is intercepted by a counting device, which records the number of trips passing a point on the path in a unit of time, then the resulting measure is known as *traffic flow,* or *traffic volume.* If, after determining it, we stop being interested merely in the number of people passing the point but rather begin to observe their behavior in movement, then we leave the field of travel demand analysis and enter the field of traffic flow analysis.

Our interest will lead us first to observe the speed at which people are moving. We will note that there is a certain relationship between the rate of flow and the speed of movement—a relationship that differs from the simple flow of water through a pipe. It is one we alluded to earlier in this chapter, in which people, or vehicles, tend to move at a faster speed if the flow rate is low.

Knowing the rate of flow and the speed, the amount of space available to each participant in a traffic stream can be easily calculated. For example, if the flow rate is 60 persons per hour, or one person passing a point every minute, and the people are walking at a speed of 260 ft (79 m) per minute, then the average distance between them is 260 ft. Multiplying that by the width of the path will give us the space allocation per person at that flow rate and that speed.

To ascertain the minimum desirable space allocation, a closer analysis of the traffic stream is necessary, one which will introduce some objective criteria of comfort or congestion. A reduction in the freely chosen speed, sharp avoidance maneuvers, actual collisions between people, and the onset of queuing, all of which occur as space per pedestrian declines, are among such

criteria. In applying them, one must realize that travel streams in most cases are not uniform but are subject to short-term fluctuation, which results in *platooning,* or bunching. Conditions in the platoons, not average conditions in a traffic stream, determine its perceived quality.

In summary, by knowing the size of buildings and their use, the amount of pedestrian travel in their vicinity can be estimated. Further, by knowing how much space a pedestrian needs to be comfortable, walkways can be dimensioned in relation to the traffic that anticipated buildings will produce.

Conventional Travel Demand Analysis

With these fairly simple conceptual tools in hand, we can now sketch out one set of steps necessary to determine the amount of walkway space a building requires. These are shown diagrammatically on the left side of Figure 1.2. The nine steps are as follows:

1.
Measure the building floor space.
2.
Count the number of trips produced by it during the day, thus obtaining a trip generation rate per unit of that particular type of floor space.
3.
Determine the cyclical pattern of these trips.
4.
On that basis, assume a peak period flow rate for which to design.
5.
On the basis of flow analysis, postulate a comfortable rate of flow.

6.
Convert the comfortable flow rate into needed walkway width per person.
7.
Multiply the needed width per person by the peak period flow. This yields the total walkway width needed to take care of the pedestrians attracted by a unit of floor space in a unit of time during the peak period.
8.
On the basis of a separate survey, determine the average length of walk.
9.
Multiply the needed width by the average trip length to obtain the needed walkway area per unit of floor space. The last step, multiplying the needed walkway width by the average trip length, takes account of the person-miles or person-kilometers of travel, which is the true measure of the pedestrian load on the walkways.

Unfortunately, having gone through these calculations, we do not really know where to put the walkway space needed. Putting it all on the same site as the building attracting the trips would not seem right, for most of the walking will undoubtedly take place off the site. On the other hand, walkers to adjacent buildings will be using the sidewalk of the building in question. Conventional travel analysis solves this problem by going through a round of fairly complex calculations known as *trip distribution,* by which each trip between each pair of origin and destination zones is assigned to a specific path. The detail required to make this approach work for pedestrian travel in a downtown area, where a great number of trips are very short, makes it extremely cumbersome.

Direct Estimation of Pedestrian Density

In this book we will go through the nine steps outlined, because the pertinent statistics are intrinsically of interest, but our primary reliance will be on a simplified approach, which might be termed *direct estimation of pedestrian density*. The approach bears some resemblance to the direct traffic estimation model of Morton Schneider, at least with regard to the underlying theory. Oversimplifying greatly, the theory is that the amount of travel to be found in a small area at an instant in time will be proportional to the area's accessibility and attractiveness.[33]

Accessibility is a rather complex phenomenon that can be considered to have at least three dimensions. The first is the amount and type of transportation facilities traversing the place in question. The second is people's propensity to travel along these facilities—the rate at which their trips are attenuated with distance. The third is a description of the geographic distribution of opportunities for making trips around the destination, that is, how much and what type of building floor space is located how far away.

The first dimension, transportation, is easily quantified; in the case of motor vehicles, it can be measured by the area of pavement provided. Thus, if two places have an equal amount of building floor space, the one that has more vehicular pavement will also attract more vehicular

trips.[34] In the case of pedestrians, it can be measured by the walkway area provided.

Concerning the second dimension of accessibility, people's propensity to travel along the available facilities, we know that pedestrian trips are attenuated with distance at a very fast rate. In Manhattan, as will be shown later, half of all trips on foot are less than about 1,000 ft (305 m). Therefore, we do not have to be concerned with the trip-generating influence of floor space located a considerable distance away from any site under investigation.

Fortunately, however, even the floor space on the immediately adjacent sites does not have to be taken explicitly into consideration. This is so because attractiveness and accessibility tend toward an equilibrium; big buildings will be erected in a place if there are enough people nearby to fill them. The third dimension of accessibility, which deals with the proximity of other floor space to the floor space on the site in question, is thus largely inherent in the measure of the floor space on the site in question. It can be disregarded if abrupt changes in land use do not occur within an area and if great precision is not required. Thus, walkway space alone remains our measure of accessibility. Attractiveness in an urban situation is more easily defined by the amount and type of floor space on a site. The other component of attractivensss, namely the natural features of a site, can be usually disregarded.

With these simplified assumptions, direct estimation of pedes-

trian density will require seven steps, shown diagrammatically on the right side of Figure 1.2. They are as follows:

1.
Measure the building floor space on a block, or a block face.
2.
Measure the walkway space in the same area.
3.
Count the pedestrians to be found in that area at an instant during a selected peak period by means of aerial photography.
4.
Develop a statistical relationship that shows what number of pedestrians at an instant are associated with a unit of floor space and a unit of walkway space.
5.
On the basis of flow analysis, postulate a comfortable rate of flow (same as before).
6.
Convert the comfortable flow rate into a space allocation per moving pedestrian.
7.
Multiply the number of pedestrians expected to be found in front of a building during the peak period by the desirable space allocation per pedestrian to obtain the needed walkway space.

We might stress that in the second approach we are dealing not with flow rates that buildings generate but rather with the density of pedestrians associated on the average with a given building density. The pedestrians caught in the act of walking near a building at an instant include some going to or from that building, as well as all the passersby who spill over from adjacent buildings. Thus, we avoid the

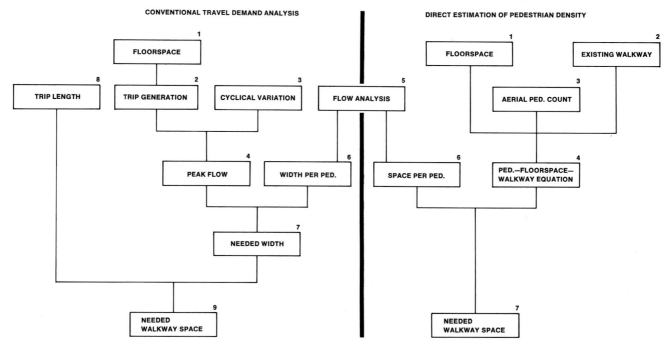

Figure 1.2
Two ways of determining walkway
space needed by a building

issue of trip distribution and trip assignment to specific paths. If we want to convert the instantaneous density into walkway flow and person-miles or person-kilometers we can, if we take a ground measurement of average speed. Moreover, the approach has the advantage of not considering the number of trips generated by a building as a rigid given: it responds dynamically to the space available for walking. More available walkway space will pull people out of buildings, an effect that is incorporated in the statistical relationship in step 4. This feedback effect will complicate the derivation of standards a little, but the added realism is well worthwhile.

In conclusion, we might warn the reader that while both approaches outlined above are rigorously based on observed behavior, value judgements do enter them at two important points. One is the decision on what kind of peak flow to design for. The

peak of the peak? Or an average sort of peak? The other one is the decision on the amount of space for walking judged to be "comfortable." While we do stick to objective criteria of congestion, symptoms of congestion begin to show up gradually as space per walker declines. At what point to draw the line between one standard of comfort and another is, to some extent, a question of judgment. These two points of judgment are common to all transportation planning. The judgments made in this book are scaled to be realistic under Manhattan conditions. In areas of less intense activity, more liberal standards might well be in order.

Notes for Chapter 1

1. John B. Calhoun, "Population Density and Social Pathology," *Scientific American,* February 1962, pp. 139-148. For a general overview of the subject, see Gwendolyn Bell, Edwina Randall, and Judith Roeder, *Urban Environments and Human Behavior; an Annotated Bibliography* (Stroudsburg, Pa.: Dowden, Hutchinson and Ross, 1973). See also Harold M. Proshansky, William H. Ittelson, Leanne G. Rivlin, eds., *Environmental Psychology: Man and His Physical Setting* (New York: Holt, Rinehart & Winston, 1970).

2. American Public Health Association, *Planning the Home for Occupancy* (Chicago: Public Administration Service, 1950).

3. The figures pertain to "overall dwelling space," a definition comparable to the rentable, or "net," dwelling space in New York. The Soviet definition of "living space," often used in the past, excludes kitchens, bathrooms, closets, and corridors within dwellings and currently equals about 67 percent of the "overall dwelling space." See Tsentral'noe statisticheskoe upravlenie, *Narodnoe khoziaistvo SSSR v 1970 godu.* (Moscow: Statistika, 1971), p. 549.

4. Robert Sommer, *Personal Space; The Behavioral Basis of Design.* (Englewood Cliffs, N.J.: Prentice-Hall, 1969), p. 27.

5. Kevin Lynch, *Site Planning,* 2nd ed. (Cambridge, Mass.: MIT Press, 1971). p. 303.

6. Oscar Newman, *Defensible Space; Crime Prevention through Urban Design* (New York: Macmillan Company, 1972).

7. Ibid., p. 194.

8. Urban Design Council of the City of New York, *Housing Quality: A Program of Zoning Reform* (1973).

9. *Regional Survey of New York and Its Environs,* vol. 5, *Public Recreation* (New York: Regional Plan of New York and Its Environs, 1928), pp. 115-133, 153-156.

10. Skycomp Data Corporation, "Gateway Beach Census," Prepared for the Regional Plan Association (Princeton, N.J., 1971).

11. *Moskva; planirovka i zastroika goroda* (Moscow: Gosstroiizdat, 1958), p. 201.

12. Regional Plan Association, *The Race for Open Space: Final Report of the Park, Recreation and Open Space Project* (New York, 1960), pp. 8-9.

13. Tri-State Regional Planning Commission, *Streets and Highways: A Regional Report* (New York, 1968). See also *Highway System Characteristics,* Interim Technical Report 4377-2104 (December 1972); *Vehicle-Miles of Travel on Major Roadways: 1970,* Interim Technical Report 4407-1205 (November 1973).

14. Tri-State Regional Planning Commission, *Cost and Performance Evaluation of Alternate Regional Highway Strategies,* Interim Technical Report 4432-2101 (New York, April 1974).

15. New York City Transit Authority, *Rapid Transit Passenger Car Data* (New York, 1965), p. 4.

16. Jaroslav Apanasevich, "Metro Systems of the Soviet Union," New York City Transit Authority, (New York, 1973), p. 16.

17. Wahab O. Dosanmu, "Effect of Subway Car Relative Position on Rush-Hour Congestion" (Paper for New York University Graduate School of Public Administration, 1969).

18. For an effort to define comfort levels on public transport, see Hermann Botzow, "A Level of Service Concept for Evaluating Public Transport," Transportation Research Board (January 1974).

19. Regina Belz Armstrong, *The Office Industry: Patterns of Growth and Location* (Cambridge, Mass.: MIT Press, 1972), p. 106.

20. Ibid., pp. 133, 141.

21. *Report of the Heights of Buildings Commission to the Committee on the Height, Size and Arrangement of Buildings of the Board of Estimate and Apportionment of the City of New York* (December, 1913).

22. *Regional Survey of New York and Its Environs,* vol. 6, *Buildings: Their Uses and the Spaces about Them* (New York: Regional Plan of New York and Its Environs, 1931).

23. Harrison, Ballard and Allen, *Plan for Rezoning the City of New York,* A report submitted to the City Planning Commission (October 1950).

24. Vorhees, Walker, Smith & Smith, *Zoning New York City,* A proposal for a zoning resolution for the City of New York submitted to the City Planning Commission (August 1958).

25. New York City Planning Commission, *Plan for New York City; A Proposal, Critical Issues* (New York, 1969):

26. Van Ginkel Associates, *Movement in Midtown,* A summary of a study prepared in cooperation with the Office of Midtown Planning and Development, Office of the Mayor, City of New York (June 1970).

27. Office of Midtown Planning and Development, *Madison Mall* (New York, October 1971).

28. U. S. Department of Housing and Urban Development, "Vehicle-free Zones in City Centers," in *HUD International Brief,* no. 16 (June 1972).

29. The City of New York, *Calendar of the City Planning Commission* (December 8, 1971), pp. 16, 17.

30. The City of New York, *Calendar of the City Planning Commission* (June 13, 1973), p. 9. The City of New York, *Calendar of the City Planning Commission* (October 16, 1974), p. 86 (Special Transit Land Use District) and p. 46 (Urban Open Space); for final wording, see post-1975 editions of the New York City *Zoning Resolution;* for a general discussion of principles, see [Raquel Ramati] *Humanizing Subway Entrances; Opportunity on Second Avenue.* New York, Department of City Planning and Municipal Art Society, September 1974; [Michael Parley] *New Life for Plazas.* New York City Planning Commission, April 1975.

31. Norman Marcus, and Marilyn W. Groves, eds., *The New Zoning: Legal, Administrative and Economic Concepts and Techniques* (New York: Praeger, 1970).

32. The City of New York, "Special Greenwich Street Development District," *Calendar of the City Planning Commission* (January 6, 1971), pp. 24-57.

33. For a mathematical formulation of this proposition and some of its consequences, see Morton Schneider (formerly Director of Research, Tri-State Transportation Commission, New York), "Access and Land Development," in *Urban Development Models,* Highway Research Board Special Report 97 (Washington, D.C., 1968), pp. 164-177.

34. Barbara A. Huvane, Frank S. Koppelman, and Edward F. Sullivan, "Express Roadways and Traffic," *Technical Review* 5, no. 3, Tri-State Regional Planning Commission (New York, 1969), pp. 9-12.

Chapter 2

Pedestrian Travel Demand
The land use planning profession was in general not well equipped by training and past practice to take full advantage . . . of the methods of mathematical models.

Britton Harris,
Urban Development Models

Conventional Travel Demand Analysis

The large-scale area transportation studies conducted in the United States in the nineteen fifties and sixties have advanced the understanding of travel by mechanical modes but have neglected pedestrian movement. Responding as they did to steeply rising auto use, they were primarily concerned with planning freeways. Most did not ask whether reducing, rather than satisfying, an ever-expanding demand for travel by mechanical means might be an appropriate goal or whether, at the very least, the significance of travel on foot might be greater than its modest share of the total person-miles or person-kilometers traveled. Therefore, even the walk segments of trips by mechanical modes have received only cursory attention.[1] And only the Chicago Area Transportation Study undertook a separate regionwide survey of purely pedestrian trips.[2] That survey made a lasting contribution to travel theory but has never been followed up. Studies of pedestrian travel in downtown areas by land use planners and business groups have been quite limited in scope. Efforts to improve such studies have been made,[3] but the data rarely lend themselves to comprehensive mathematical analysis. Only recently have transportation consultants entered this field.[4]

Still, the best-understood aspect of downtown walking probably is trips to and from parking facilities.[5] The decennial censuses now enumerate walk trips from home to work, but such trips constitute a very small proportion of all walking. In sum, information on pedestrian travel demand is deficient. Such information is essential if pedestrian needs are to be scaled. Following the outline sketched in the previous chapter, we will start with conventional measures of trip generation.

Trip Generation

The area transportation studies, despite their broad scope and rigorous methodology, fall somewhat short when it comes to determining the number of trips that different building types generate. This holds true not just for trips on foot but for mechanical trips as well. The home-interview questionnaire, their main data base, tends to undercount trips because it relies on the interviewee's recollection and knowledge of all travel for the household. For the longer trips the undercount can be corrected on the basis of screen-line checks across major arteries and need not be a problem for planning regional facilities, such as freeways. It remains, however, a problem with respect to short trips, which are more likely to be forgotten and the omission of which is more difficult to correct. One method of correcting for it is the facility-cordon count, which, instead of asking people about trips, counts people or vehicles entering and leaving a building or some other facility. A short interview with a sample of the people being counted can be a part of the method, to determine trip length and other travel characteristics.

As a part of this study, counts of this type were taken at several buildings in Midtown Manhattan. In addition, similar counts of particular establishments in a wider area were available from work done by students at New York University Graduate School of Public Administration. With respect to office buildings, comparable counts were also available for downtown Seattle. To see how these counts of people entering and leaving a particular building on foot relate to previously established trip generation rates by mechanical modes of travel, a summary of the latter, prepared by the Tri-State Regional Planning Commission, was used. These sets of data are presented in tables 2.1 through 2.4.

Before interpreting the tables, several words of caution are in order. All trip generation rates shown are expressed in terms of in and out trips and, to be comparable to one-way trip definitions, must be divided by two. The trip rates by mechanical modes, which are based on observations by the facility-cordon method in various parts of the country, pertain to vehicles, mostly automobiles. To make them comparable to our own data, which show trips by persons, somewhat arbitrary assumptions about average vehicle occupancy had to be made.[6] Lastly, no claim is made that the measurements of trips that start out on foot are in any way representative. The measurements show only what happens at the establishments listed, which were not selected with any sampling design in mind. Thus, the purpose of the comparisons in tables 2.1 through 2.4 is to illustrate the magnitudes involved, not to

provide conclusive proof. Nevertheless, the comparisons do suggest several messages.

Suburban dwellings produce on a per capita basis about as many trips by auto alone as urban dwellings do by all modes of travel, including walking. We might emphasize that all trips shown in lines 7 and 8 of Table 2.1 start out on foot at the building door, but more than one-third of them eventually become trips by taxi, auto, bus, or subway. By contrast, walk-only trips at the suburban locations and a minor number of trips by public transportation are not included. Judging by the results of the Chicago walking trip survey, the addition of walk-only trips to the suburban rates would raise the last column on the right part of Table 2.1 by more than 20 percent.

There is, undoubtedly, some substitution of auto trips for walk trips as urban density declines. However, the increase in auto trips with declining density is greater than the decline in walking and occurs in response to greater opportunities for auto travel in low-density areas, primarily higher auto ownership. Conversely, high urban density does not merely shift some travel from auto to walking and public transportation but also reduces the total demand for travel.[7]

Office buildings produce roughly twice the number of trips per unit of floor space as residences. Suburban offices seem to produce somewhat more trips by auto alone than downtown offices do by all modes, including walking. The proportion of walk-

only trips at two of the Manhattan office buildings investigated was found to be about 26 percent, a figure similar to the share of walk trips to and from the Museum of Modern Art in Midtown Manhattan established by a previous survey. On that basis, the trip generation by mechanical modes of the Manhattan office buildings appears to be roughly *half* that of the suburban office buildings.

Of course, some of the difference may be attributable to different types of occupancy. Among the urban office buildings, those that serve purely administrative functions generate the least trips. Also, large building size tends to internalize some trips, because company cafeterias and other services are located on premises. By contrast, smaller buildings and those that have tenants serving primarily the public—such as doctors, dentists, brokers, and government agencies—generate more trips. The building listed in line 5 of Table 2.2 is an outstanding example of this.

Floor space in restaurants attracts more than ten times the number of trips as office floor space. However, restaurant trip generation rates also vary, depending on the type of service and on the hours of operation, as suggested by Table 2.3.

The number of trips generated by high-intensity retailing establishments, such as supermarkets and junior department stores, is similar to that generated by intensive food-service establishments. However, all the establishments listed in lines 4 through 11 in Table 2.4 are of the high-

Table 2.1
Comparison of Vehicular and Pedestrian
Trip Generation by Residences

Location	No. of dwellings observed	Trips entering and leaving during 24 hrs.		
		Vehicles, observed		Persons in vehicles, assumed
		per dwelling	per resident	per resident
Single family dwellings				
				(assume 1.6 persons per auto trip)
1. Maryland	8,778	8.64	2.34	3.7
2. California	5,719	9.49	2.56	4.1
3. Long Island	208	11.40	2.41	3.9
Suburban apartments				
				(assume 1.4 persons per auto trip)
4. Virginia	2,508	7.58	3.45	4.8
5. Maryland	3,029	7.30	3.17	4.4
6. California	2,821	5.90	3.28	4.6
Urban apartments				

		Trips entering and leaving during 24 hrs on foot, observed		
		per dwelling	per resident	per 1,000 gross sq ft (93 m²)
7. Manhattan, 30th St.	288*	7.6	4.5	8.3
8. Manhattan, 12th St.	136†	8.0	5.0	9.1

Sources: Lines 1-6, Tri-State Regional Planning Commission, *Trip Generation Rates,* Interim Technical Report 4365-4410, 1973. Line 7, Regional Plan Association. Line 8, Elaine Spevak, unpublished paper for New York University Graduate School of Public Administration.
*914.3 sq ft (85 m²) gross floor space per dwelling.
†882.4 sq ft (82 m²) gross floor space per dwelling.

Table 2.2
Comparison of Vehicular and Pedestrian Trip Generation by Offices and a Museum

	Location	Gross fl. space, sq ft	Trips entering and leaving during 24 Hrs per 1,000 sq ft (93 m²) of fl. space	
Suburban office buildings				
			Observed vehicle trips	Assumed person trips at 1.2 persons per auto
1.	New Jersey	186,000	17.9	21.5
2.	Maryland	170,000	17.5	21.0
3.	Long Island	1,180,000	15.0	18.0
4.	Virginia	836,000	8.9	10.7
Urban office buildings				
Type			% Walk-only trips	Observed person trips in and out on foot
5. Local use	Bronx	59,000	n.a.	58.0
6. Mixed use	Manhattan	314,000	n.a.	17.3
7. Headquarters	Manhattan	1,634,000	26	14.2
8. Headquarters	Manhattan	1,048,000	26	13.2
9. 24 bldgs.	Seattle	5,241,000	n.a.	15.4
10. Museum of Modern Art	Manhattan	227,000	26.8	21.0

Sources: Lines 1-4, Tri-State Regional Planning Commission, *Trip Generation Rates*. Line 5, William M. Murphy, unpublished paper for New York University Graduate School of Public Administration. Lines 6-8, Regional Plan Association. Line 9, Herbert S. Levinson, "Modeling Pedestrian Travel," mimeographed, Wilbur Smith and Associates, 1971. 10:00 A.M. to 6:00 P.M. outbound count converted to 24-hr in and out flow based on New York cyclical pattern. Line 10, David Johnson, "Museum Attendance in the New York Metropolitan Region," mimeographed, Regional Plan Association, 1967, and updated employment and attendance figures from the Museum of Modern Art.

Table 2.3.
Comparison of Vehicular and Pedestrian Trip Generation by Restaurants

Type	Location		Trips entering and leaving during 24 Hrs per 1,000 sq ft (93 m²) of fl. space	
			Observed vehicle trips	Assumed person trips at 2.5 persons per vehicle
Suburban establishments				
1. 2 restaurants	New Jersey		72.2	180
Manhattan establishments				
		Gross fl. space sq ft	Period of count	Observed person trips in and out on foot
2. Cafeteria	57th St.	7,200	wk. day 10 A.M.- 8 P.M.*	492
3. Sandwich shop	Garment Dist.	1,000	wk. day 6 A.M.- 3 P.M.	430
4. Restaurant	Times Sq.	12,000	wk. day 9 A.M.- 9 P.M.*	173

Sources: Line 1, Tri-State Regional Planning Commission, *Trip Generation Rates*. Line 2, Harold Zombek and Line 3, Albert Herter: unpublished papers for New York University Graduate School of Public Administration. Line 4, Regional Plan Association.
*Open beyond period of count shown.

Table 2.4.
Comparison of Vehicular and Pedestrian Trip Generation by Retail Stores

	Trips entering and leaving during 24 Hrs per 1,000 sq ft (93 m²) of fl. space	
Suburban shopping centers	Observed vehicle trips	Assumed person trips at 2.0 persons per vehicle
1. Average of 21 neighborhood centers (under 100,000 gross sq ft)	79	158
2. Average of 44 Community centers (100,000 - 499,999 gross sq ft)	56	112
3. Average of 23 regional centers (over 500,000 gross sq ft)	30	60

Urban establishments

Type	Location	Gross fl. space sq ft	Period of count	Observed person trips in and out on foot	% walk-only trips
4. Delicatessen	Manhattan	2,500	Sa. 10 A.M.-10 P.M.*	2,460	70
5. Supermarket	Queens	7,500	wk. day 9 A.M.-9 P.M.	428	n.a.
			Sa. 9 A.M.-9 P.M.	536	n.a.
6. Supermarket	Manhattan	5,100	Sa. 9 A.M.-6 P.M.	509	n.a.
7. Jun. dept. store	Manhattan	69,600	wk. day 9 A.M.-9 P.M.	385	n.a.
8. Supermarket	Manhattan	14,500	wk. day 9 A.M.-9 P.M.	372	n.a.
9. Supermarket	Richmond	7,500	wk. day 9 A.M.-9 P.M.	285	n.a.
10. Dept. store	Manhattan	176,700	wk. day 9 A.M.-9 P.M.	252	n.a.
11. Boutique	Manhattan	3,400	wk. day 11 A.M.-7 P.M.*	205	61
			Sa. 10 A.M.-6 P.M.	488	81

Sources: Lines 1-3, Tri-State Regional Planning Commission, *Trip Generation Rates.* Line 4, Leonard Lowell and Elizabeth Kline; Line 5, Leonard Huber; Line 6, Richard Goldfine; Line 8, John S. Mills; Line 9, Robert M. Greene; Line 11, Mary Ortiz and Karen Countryman: unpublished papers for New York University Graduate School of Public Administration. Lines 7 and 10, Regional Plan Association.
*Open beyond period of count shown.

intensity type; most retail floor space is less intensively used. *About two-thirds of the trips to the urban stores shown appear to be walk-only trips.* Without the walk-only trips, the urban and suburban retail trip generation rates become similar in magnitude.

Clearly, the data on the choice of mode in the examples presented here are sketchy, but that need not concern us for the moment. Whether or not they use a mechanical mode of travel for part of the journey, all trips contribute to pedestrian travel demand, particularly in a downtown area.

The large differences in travel demand among different building types lead us to seek some more understanding of the mechanism by which they arise. One would suppose that buildings that attract more trips also have higher densities of indoor occupancy. Table 2.5 shows this to be, on the whole, the case. The table indicates how much floor space per occupant there is in a building during the period of peak occupancy, or *peak accumulation.* We might note that the time of peak accumulation is not the same as the peak traffic period; in nonresidential buildings peak accumulation generally occurs around midday, sometime between 11 A.M. and 3 P.M. In residential buildings it occurs, of course, at night. If at any time the number of occupants in a building is known (that is, if one knows that an office building is empty at 6 A.M.), then peak occupancy can be calculated by counting inbound trips and outbound

trips for consecutive small periods of time from then on, subtracting the latter from the former for each period, and cumulating the differences. Such counts were made for the establishments listed in Table 2.5. The areas available at peak accumulation refer to gross floor space; subtracting storage and shelf areas in stores, or kitchen areas in restaurants, the clear floor space available to workers and patrons is much smaller.

It is evident, however, that the differences in trip generation rates per unit of floor space, both within and between particular categories of building use, are greater than the differences in space available per peak occupant. Borrowing a term used in parking design, we might term the number of daily one-way trips per peak period occupant the *turnover rate,* which is also shown in Table 2.5. The turnover rate is a function of how a building is used: whether it attracts primarily employees working in it or also outside patrons, whether the patrons' transactions are short or take a long time, to what extent the employees eat in or go out for lunch, and so on. If a building or some other facility (such as a park) is being designed for a particular density at peak accumulation and if the turnover rate is known, the number of trips it will generate is automatically established.

The Daily Cycle: Building Entrances
The daily trip generation rate gives us an overall impression of how busy a place is and, in some instances, how many customers it serves, but it does not tell us

how the trips are distributed over the course of the day and what load they impose on travel facilities during the critical peak periods. To find out, we have to know the peaking pattern, or *daily cyclical variation.*

An easy way to chart the daily cycle is to express the trips occurring during each hour of the day as a percent of the daily total. This is done in Table 2.6 for trips entering and leaving a residential subdivision on Long Island by auto and a Manhattan apartment building on foot. It can be seen that the daily cycles of travel in both cases are fairly similar. Home-oriented travel is heaviest between 4 P.M. and 8 P.M.; about 33 percent of all daily trips occur during those four hours. It is lightest between 1 A.M. and 5 A.M.: less than 3 percent of the trips occur during those four hours. Roughly 10 percent of all daily travel in both residential areas occurs during one hour between 5 P.M. and 6 P.M.

Compared to these similarities, the differences are minor. The afternoon peak and especially the morning peak are sharper at the Manhattan building, while midday activity is lower. This is due mostly to the difference in household size: the average household in the subdivision has 4.7 members, while in the Manhattan building it has only 1.7 members. Thus, a much greater share of the Manhattan building residents go to work, and fewer are left to engage in midday travel near the place of residence. It also appears that the Manhattanites go to bed later and get up later than the suburbanites. Of

Table 2.5
Peak Accumulation and Turnover Rates at
Selected Buildings

Table and line of previous reference	Bldg. type	Trip rate per 1,000 sq ft (93 m²) in and out	Gross fl. space in bldg. per person during peak accumulation sq ft (m²)	Turnover rate (daily one-way trips per peak accumulation occupant)
2.4, 5	Super-market	536	73 (6.8)	19.7
2.4, 10	Dept. store	252	76 (7.1)	9.6
2.3, 4	Restaurant	173	36 (3.3)	3.2
2.2, 5	Office	58	162 (15.0)	4.7
2.2, 6	Office	17	320 (29.7)	2.7
2.2, 7	Office	14	340 (31.5)	2.4
2.2, 8	Office	13	330 (30.7)	2.3
2.1, 7	Residence	8.3	544 (50.5)	2.3

Sources: Same as tables 2.1 through 2.4.

Table 2.6
Daily Peaking Patterns in 2 Residential Areas

Time	Percentage of weekday 24-hr in and out trips during each hr.	
	Auto trips entering and leaving suburban subdivision (Table 2.1, line 3)	All trips entering and leaving Manhattan apartment on foot (Table 2.1, line 7)
0-1 A.M.	0.8	1.7
1-2	0.7	0.7
2-3	0.4	0.4
3-4	0.2	0.2
4-5	0.4	0.2
5-6	1.5	0.3
6-7	2.8	0.6
7-8	4.5	3.9
8-9	4.6	9.1
9-10	4.4	6.6
10-11	4.1	5.0
11-12	4.8	4.4
12-1 P.M.	5.1	4.7
1-2	5.2	4.6
2-3	5.2	4.2
3-4	7.5	5.4
4-5	7.6	7.2
5-6	8.8	10.7
6-7	8.5	9.4
7-8	8.3	8.3
8-9	6.1	3.8
9-10	4.0	2.9
10-11	2.3	3.3
11-12	2.2	2.4
Total, 24 hrs	100.0	100.0

Sources: Column 1, Tri-State Regional Planning Commission, *Residential Trip Generation,* Interim Technical Report 4234-4424, 1971, based on a one-week count in August 1968 and a two-week count in June 1969; Column 2, Regional Plan Association, based on counts during parts of different days in midweek during April, 1970 and 1974.

course, there is considerable random variation from hour to hour in counts of this type, so differences between particular hours taken in isolation may not be too significant.

What is significant for our purposes is the degree to which daily travel is concentrated in the peak periods, and for that purpose a breakdown finer than by hourly intervals is desirable. So as not to make such an analysis too unwieldy, we will limit it to twelve daytime hours. The buildings we will look at in more detail are familiar from previous discussion: a general-purpose office building, an administrative headquarters, a department store, a restaurant, and the apartment building just examined, all located in Midtown Manhattan. Their identification in earlier tables is shown at the head of Table 2.7. The numbers in that table show the percent of total 12-hr trips that occurs during each 15 min interval, with inbound and outbound trips shown separately in two cases. The totals on which these percentages are based are given for reference in the bottom line. The counts for the office buildings and the apartment house cover the period 7:30 A.M. to 7:30 P.M.; those for the department store and the restaurant, 9:00 A.M. to 9:00 P.M. These periods taken together account for 100 percent of the 24-hr daily traffic at the department store, almost 99 percent at the office buildings, probably close to 80 percent at the restaurant, and 78 percent at the residential building.

The data in Table 2.7 are presented graphically in figures 2.1

and 2.2 and portray familiar patterns of the ebb and flow of humanity in a downtown business district. Activity at the office buildings begins to stir about 7:30 A.M., reaches a peak toward 9:00, drops to a low level in the late morning, rises during lunchtime, falls in the afternoon, reaches its highest peak at 5:00 P.M., and then gradually peters out. Activity at the department store picks up slowly after opening, reaches a prolonged peak during the noon hours, recedes, and rises to less than half its noontime level between 5:00 and 6:30 P.M. By referring to Table 2.7, we can infer that this particular department store does almost 50 percent of its business during two and a half hours at lunchtime and only 6 percent during its late open hours. The pattern at the restaurant is similar. About 47 percent of the activity shown occurs in the three hours after 11:45; arrivals of the "a drink after work" crowd and of the dinner patrons are clearly visible. The pattern at the apartment house, which we discussed before, is quite different from the others—some activity in the morning, a long lull with a low point around noon, and a bulge around 6:00 P.M. The irregularity of the residential graph reflects its small sample size.

A convenient way to measure the sharpness of a peak is to compare it to an average period. In our case, if pedestrian flow were even, each 15-min period would account for about 2.1 percent of the 12-hr flow. Comparing the patterns in Figure 2.1 on that basis, we can see that, at the second office building, two-way pedestrian flow during the fifteen

minutes after 5:00 P.M. is 3.5 times the average. No other building in the chart exceeds three times the average flow during any fifteen minutes. However, two times the average flow is exceeded quite frequently: for 45 min by each of the office buildings, for 105 min by the department store, and for 75 min by the restaurant. Only the apartment house manages to stay below that peaking level all day. The prolonged lunch peak at both office buildings approaches the level of two times the average. If the retail, restaurant, and residential uses shown illustrate characteristic patterns (the exact percentages will inevitably vary), the question remains why the two office buildings differ so much from each other.

To answer the question, inbound and outbound pedestrian flow at these buildings is shown separately in Figure 2.2, based on Table 2.7. With respect to one-way flow, peaking is even more pronounced: at the second office building, 12 percent of the entries occur between 9:00 and 9:15 A.M., and almost 15 percent of the exits occur between 5:00 and 5:15 P.M., a factor six to seven times the average—the building is predominantly a "9 to 5" operation. By contrast, the first building has a large part of its clerical work force on an 8:15 to 4:15 shift and another part on an 8:45 to 4:45 shift, leaving less than half its employees on a "9 to 5" schedule. The result of the staggered work hours is roughly a 30 percent reduction of the peak 15-min load, as seen in the graphs of Figure 2.2.

Generally, cyclical patterns are not immutable laws of nature but, to a large extent, responses to devices of social control and to ingrained conventions. Note, for example, the surges of people returning home "just before 6" or "just before 7" for dinner, seen in the residential graph in Figure 2.1.

The effect of cyclical patterns is to magnify the difference in trip generation rates between different types when the rates refer to the peak 15-min period rather than to the entire day. This is illustrated in Table 2.8, which takes selected trip generation rates from earlier tables and applies to them their appropriate peaking proportions, such as those found in Table 2.7. We can see that on a peak-period basis the gap between residential buildings becomes much wider.

Whereas earlier we noted that office buildings produce roughly twice the number of trips per unit of floor space as residences, we can now say that *during the peak fifteen minutes office buildings produce nearly four times as many trips as residences* per unit of floor space.

Restaurants and intensive retailing establishments maintain their relative position, with trip generation rates on a peak-period basis more than ten times those of offices. We may repeat that our retail examples include only high-intensity establishments. Later on in this chapter, when we have occasion to deal with a representative cross section of retail space, we will see that on the average retail stores are a less intensive generator of trips during the noontime period than restaurants.

The Daily Cycle: Outdoor Walkways

The peak 15-min travel rates at building entrances which we have been discussing are significant for building design, the proper proportioning of elevators, building lobbies, and entrance doors. Fortunately, the peaking patterns on outdoor walkways are not as sharp. Different trip lengths and destinations, as well as different peak times at individual buildings, work together to flatten out the peak flow of pedestrians in the extensive "mixing bowl" of sidewalks, plazas, and other walkways.

Let us then proceed to look at cyclical variation in pedestrian flow on outdoor walkways. A set of such peaking patterns is shown in Table 2.9 and Figure 2.3. It is apparent that the shape of the daily cycle at any walkway depends very much on the predominate building uses in the area. This can be seen by comparing the cyclical profiles in Figure 2.3 with those in Figure 2.1. The first profile, representing the escalators leading from Grand Central Terminal to the Pan American Building, resembles the profiles at office buildings but is more attenuated. For a total of one hour, the 15-min flow slightly exceeds twice the average 15-min rate.

About a thousand feet away from Grand Central Terminal, at four sidewalk locations, represented in the second profile, the work-trip peaks in the morning and evening become still more attenuated, and the midday lunch and shopping peak begins to compete with them; no 15-min period exceeds twice the average 15-min flow rate.

The third profile represents the average of twelve counts on 48th Street between Second and Seventh avenues. It is distinguished by deep troughs in midmorning and midafternoon, indicating that the street serves primarily as a corridor for work trips and lunchtime trips and does not attract walkers in its own right. Because of the heavy concentration of offices in the areas it traverses, 48th Street displays cyclical characteristics that most resemble those of an office building in Figure 2.1. Among the five areas shown, it has the highest peak, but one that lasts only fifteen minutes and could easily be relieved by staggered exit times in adjacent office buildings.

The fourth profile is quite different and represents an average of four counts on Fifth Avenue between 44th and 47th streets. This is an area dominated by retail shopping, and the shape of its daily cycle resembles very much that of the department store in Figure 2.1, with a heavy midday concentration. For one and a quarter hours at midday, the 15-min flow is at about twice the level of the average 15-min rate. However, the morning and evening work-trip peaks are still clearly visible.

The work-trip peaks are even less prominent in the fifth profile, representing two counts on 42nd Street just east of Times Square. Heavy midday flow for shopping and lunch, as well as an unusual volume of travel in midafternoon and early evening—representing casual strollers—combine to make this profile the flattest of all. The peak fifteen minutes never even

Table 2.7
Daily Peaking Patterns of 5 Selected Buildings. Percentage of 12-Hour Flow During Each 15 Minutes

Time	Office, flat peak (Table 2.2, line 6)			Office, sharp peak (Table 2.2, line 8)			Dept. store (Table 2.4, line 10)	Restaur. (Table 2.3, line 4)	Res. (Table 2.6, col. 2)
	in	out	two-way	in	out	two-way	two-way	two-way	two-way
7:30- 7:45	1.0	0.2	0.6	0.7	0.1	0.4			1.4
7:45- 8:00	3.0	0.4	1.7	1.2	0.1	0.7			1.6
8:00- 8:15	4.3	0.8	2.6	2.2	0.1	1.1			1.5
8:15- 8:30	6.6	0.5	3.5	3.6	0.3	2.0			3.5
8:30- 8:45	6.8	0.5	3.7	6.6	0.3	3.4			3.2
8:45- 9:00	8.3	0.6	4.4	10.3	0.2	5.3			3.4
9:00- 9:15	4.6	0.9	2.8	11.8	0.3	6.0	0.0	0.0	2.9
9:15- 9:30	2.6	0.8	1.7	4.6	0.8	2.7	0.0	0.0	1.8
9:30- 9:45	2.1	0.7	1.4	3.0	0.7	1.9	0.2	0.0	2.3
9:45-10:00	1.8	1.2	1.5	1.3	0.5	0.9	0.8	0.0	1.4
10:00-10:15	1.6	1.0	1.3	1.3	0.9	1.1	0.8	0.5	1.6
10:15-10:30	1.5	1.0	1.2	1.0	0.8	0.9	0.9	0.6	1.7
10:30-10:45	1.4	1.0	1.2	1.1	0.8	0.9	1.1	0.7	1.9
10:45-11:00	1.4	1.1	1.3	1.0	0.8	0.9	1.3	0.8	1.2
11:00-11:15	1.4	1.2	1.3	0.8	1.1	0.9	1.5	0.9	1.3
11:15-11:30	1.3	1.5	1.4	0.7	1.1	0.9	1.5	0.9	1.2
11:30-11:45	1.3	2.0	1.6	0.9	1.9	1.4	1.6	1.0	1.2
11:45-12:00	1.4	3.4	2.4	1.1	5.5	3.3	2.6	2.6	2.0
12:00-12:15	1.9	5.2	3.6	1.0	5.9	3.5	4.0	3.5	1.1
12:15-12:30	2.9	5.0	3.9	1.1	6.7	3.9	5.2	5.5	2.4
12:30-12:45	4.0	4.1	4.1	2.0	4.7	3.4	6.2	4.3	0.9
12:45- 1:00	4.0	2.8	3.4	4.0	3.4	3.7	6.2	3.9	1.6
1:00- 1:15	3.5	3.0	3.2	4.6	2.8	3.7	5.4	4.9	1.3
1:15- 1:30	2.8	1.9	2.4	4.6	2.1	3.3	6.0	5.9	2.4
1:30- 1:45	2.4	1.7	2.0	5.6	1.9	3.8	5.1	4.3	1.3
1:45- 2:00	2.1	1.4	1.8	6.2	1.7	3.9	4.9	3.5	0.9
2:00- 2:15	2.7	1.3	2.0	3.8	1.1	2.5	3.5	2.9	1.5
2:15- 2:30	2.2	1.3	1.7	2.1	1.1	1.6	2.6	3.2	1.0
2:30- 2:45	2.0	1.4	1.7	2.3	1.3	1.8	2.6	2.1	1.6
2:45- 3:00	1.6	1.5	1.6	1.4	1.2	1.3	2.0	1.2	1.3
3:00- 3:15	1.2	1.7	1.4	1.1	0.6	0.8	2.2	1.0	2.0
3:15- 3:30	1.2	2.0	1.6	0.8	0.7	0.8	1.5	1.0	1.5
3:30- 3:45	0.9	1.5	1.2	0.8	1.2	1.0	1.7	0.8	1.6
3:45- 4:00	1.0	1.3	1.2	0.7	1.2	0.9	1.4	0.8	1.9
4:00- 4:15	1.0	2.5	1.7	0.7	1.7	1.2	1.5	0.8	2.7
4:15- 4:30	1.1	8.2	4.7	0.5	1.8	1.2	1.7	0.9	1.9
4:30- 4:45	1.4	5.9	3.6	0.6	2.5	1.5	1.7	0.9	2.1
4:45- 5:00	1.9	9.1	5.5	0.5	8.6	4.6	1.8	2.4	2.6
5:00- 5:15	1.2	6.3	3.8	0.2	14.6	7.4	2.5	2.4	2.9
5:15- 5:30	0.9	3.0	1.9	0.3	5.0	2.6	2.5	2.0	3.4
5:30- 5:45	0.9	2.5	1.7	0.5	4.8	2.7	2.2	1.7	3.5
5:45- 6:00	0.7	1.8	1.3	0.3	1.8	1.0	2.4	1.6	3.9
6:00- 6:15	0.7	1.6	1.1	0.3	1.6	1.0	3.0	1.6	3.1
6:15- 6:30	0.5	1.1	0.8	0.3	1.2	0.7	2.0	3.2	3.0
6:30- 6:45	0.5	0.8	0.7	0.2	1.0	0.6	1.0	3.3	2.3
6:45- 7:00	0.3	0.5	0.4	0.1	0.7	0.4	0.9	3.2	3.6
7:00- 7:15	0.1	0.5	0.3	0.1	0.5	0.3	0.9	3.0	2.9
7:15- 7:30	0.0	0.3	0.1	0.1	0.3	0.2	0.9	2.8	2.7
7:30- 7:45							0.6	2.4	
7:45- 8:00							0.6	2.8	
8:00- 8:15							0.5	2.8	
8:15- 8:30							0.4	2.5	
8:30- 8:45							0.2	1.8	
8:45- 9:00							0.0	1.1	
12 hrs	100.0	100.0	100.0	100.0	100.0	100.0	100.0	100.0	100.0
12 hr trips			5,360*			13,690	44,540	2,075	1,700
24 hr trips			5,425			—	44,540	—	2,180
12 hrs as % of 24 hrs			98.8			—	100	—	78.0

Source: Regional Plan Association. *Average of five daily counts in July, seasonally adjusted by 1.053 to represent April-November levels.

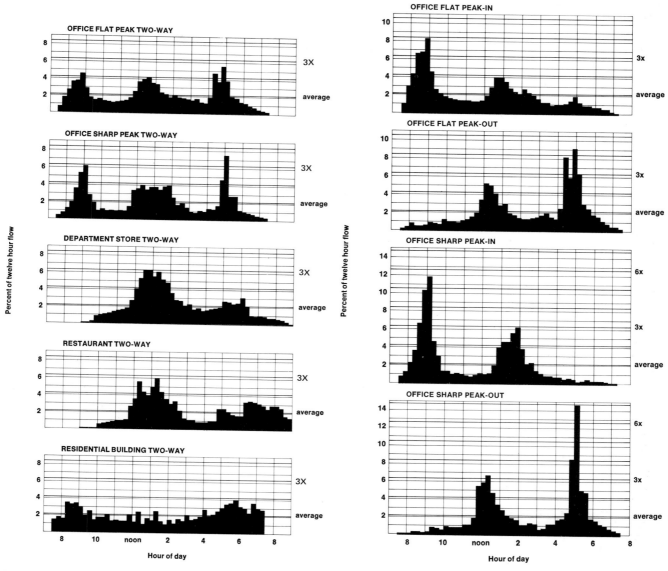

Figure 2.1
Two-way daily peaking patterns at five building types

Figure 2.2
One-way daily peaking patterns at two office buildings

Table 2.8
Comparison of Daily and Peak-Period Trip
Generation

Sources: Tables listed in column 1, and
Table 2.7.
*10-hr rate only.

Table and line of previous reference	Bldg. use	In and out trips per 1,000 sq ft (93 m²) of fl. space		
		Daily	Peak 15 min	Time of peak period
2.3, 2	Cafeteria	492*	22.36	12:00 noon
2.4, 10	Dept. store	252	15.64	12:45 P.M.
2.4, 9	Supermarket	285	11.97	5:00 P.M.
2.3, 4	Restaurant	173	10.20	1:15 P.M.
2.2, 7	Office, hdqrs.	14.2	0.98	8:45 A.M.
2.2, 8	Office, hdqrs.	13.2	0.97	5:00 P.M.
2.2, 6	Office, mixed use	17.3	0.89	4:45 P.M.
2.1, 8	Residence	8.3	0.25	5:45 P.M.

Table 2.9
Daily Peaking Patterns of Walkways in 5 Selected Areas. Percentage of 12-Hour Two-Way Flow During Each 15 Minutes

Time	Grand Central escalators (1 location)	Grand Central area (4 sidewalk locations)	48th St. 2nd to 7th aves. (12 side-walk locations)	Fifth Ave. 44th to 47th sts. (4 sidewalk locations)	42nd St. near Times Sq. (2 sidewalk locations)
7:30- 7:45	0.6	0.6	0.8	0.3	0.5
7:45- 8:00	1.4	0.9	0.8	0.3	0.7
8:00- 8:15	2.3	1.3	1.1	0.5	1.0
8:15- 8:30	3.3	1.8	1.8	0.8	1.3
8:30- 8:45	4.3	2.5	2.9	1.3	1.6
8:45- 9:00	4.3	3.2	3.0	1.8	1.8
9:00- 9:15	3.9	2.7	2.9	1.5	1.9
9:15- 9:30	3.4	1.7	1.8	1.1	1.4
9:30- 9:45	1.4	1.4	1.4	1.2	1.3
9:45-10:00	1.3	1.4	1.4	1.0	1.4
10:00-10:15	1.0	1.2	0.8	1.2	1.4
10:15-10:30	1.2	1.4	1.0	1.4	1.5
10:30-10:45	1.1	1.3	0.8	1.7	1.6
10:45-11:00	1.0	1.5	1.0	1.7	1.5
11:00-11:15	0.9	1.5	0.8	1.6	1.7
11:15-11:30	1.1	1.7	1.0	2.0	1.3
11:30-11:45	1.3	2.0	1.5	2.2	1.9
11:45-12:00	1.6	2.2	2.0	2.6	2.0
12:00-12:15	2.4	3.3	2.4	3.4	2.5
12:15-12:30	2.2	3.5	3.4	3.7	2.9
12:30-12:45	2.1	4.0	4.0	4.6	2.8
12:45- 1:00	2.5	4.0	3.7	4.2	3.1
1:00- 1:15	2.6	4.0	3.5	4.2	3.4
1:15- 1:30	2.7	3.8	3.2	4.4	3.1
1:30- 1:45	3.0	3.1	2.9	4.2	2.8
1:45- 2:00	2.4	2.7	2.7	4.1	2.7
2:00- 2:15	1.8	2.3	2.6	3.6	2.6
2:15- 2:30	1.7	2.3	2.4	2.9	2.4
2:30- 2:45	1.7	2.3	2.3	2.6	2.0
2:45- 3:00	1.4	2.2	2.1	2.6	2.3
3:00- 3:15	1.6	2.0	1.9	2.0	2.3
3:15- 3:30	1.4	1.7	1.8	1.7	2.2
3:30- 3:45	1.6	1.7	1.8	1.8	2.3
3:45- 4:00	1.2	1.7	1.7	1.8	2.1
4:00- 4:15	1.8	1.6	1.6	1.8	2.2
4:15- 4:30	1.6	1.8	1.9	2.0	2.3
4:30- 4:45	2.4	2.0	2.2	2.1	2.2
4:45- 5:00	4.3	2.9	2.9	2.4	2.3
5:00- 5:15	4.3	3.9	5.0	3.4	2.8
5:15- 5:30	4.0	3.1	3.5	2.9	3.3

Table 2.9 Continued

Time	Grand Central escalators (1 location)	Grand Central area (4 sidewalk locations)	48th St. 2nd to 7th aves. (12 side-walk locations)	Fifth Ave. 44th to 47th sts. (4 sidewalk locations)	42nd St. near Times Sq. (2 sidewalk locations)
5:30- 5:45	3.4	2.5	3.1	2.4	3.0
5:45- 6:00	3.2	1.8	2.4	1.8	2.7
6:00- 6:15	2.1	1.4	2.0	1.4	2.5
6:15- 6:30	1.7	1.0	1.7	1.1	2.2
6:30- 6:45	1.4	1.0	1.4	0.9	2.0
6:45- 7:00	1.0	0.8	1.2	0.7	1.8
7:00- 7:15	0.7	0.7	1.1	0.6	1.9
7:15- 7:30	0.4	0.6	0.8	0.5	1.5
12-hr. %	100.0	100.0	100.0	100.0	100.0
12-hr total	89,700	137,600	67,780	146,800	80,660
12-hr av. per sidewalk location	89,700	34,400	5,650	36,700	40,300

Source: Regional Plan Association

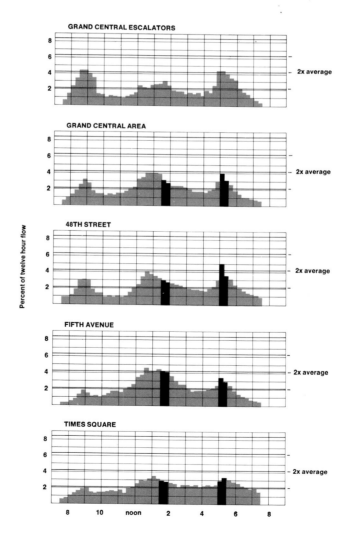

Figure 2.3
Two-way daily peaking patterns on walkways

approach twice the average rate and stay at slightly over 3 percent of the 12-hr total during both the midday and evening peaks.

The general conclusion to be drawn from the outdoor cyclical counts is that the peak 15-min flow rate seldom exceeds twice the average 15-min flow rate, and if so then by very little. However, it approaches this level sufficiently often to warrant accepting twice the average 15-min flow rate, on a 12-hr 7:30 to 7:30 basis, as the critical value for design purposes for outdoor walkways similar to those in Midtown Manhattan. The critical flow generally occurs either from 12:30 to 1:30 P.M., if an area is shopping oriented, or from 5:00 to 5:30 P.M., if an area is office-building oriented. As can be seen from Table 2.9, between 14 and 18 percent of the 12-hr flow occurs during the hour of highest flow.

A comparison with cyclical counts on outdoor walkways in downtown Seattle[8] suggests that in smaller cities the relative importance of the morning and evening peaks for pedestrian movement is less than in Midtown Manhattan, because trips to work account for a smaller share of downtown travel and, in addition, are quickly absorbed by short walks to the automobile. However, the prominence of the midday peak is very similar to that of Manhattan: between 13 and 20 percent of the 12-hr daytime flow in Seattle was found during the hour of highest flow at midday. A similarly strong midday peak was also found in Salt Lake City.[9] The Seattle counts, performed by automatic

devices, have also recorded nighttime flow: 6 to 13 percent of the 24-hr flow on downtown streets was found to occur between 7 P.M. and 7 A.M.

Directional Distribution
A matter related to the daily cycle concerns the directional distribution of trips. As shown in Table 2.10, directional imbalance at the entrance to an office building can be rather extreme. Thus, during the peak 15-min period, between 93 and 98 percent of the flow at the two office buildings investigated occurs in the predominant direction. Similarly, at the Grand Central escalators, 93 percent of the flow at 8:45 A.M. and 88 percent of the flow at 5:00 P.M. occur in the predominant direction. Just as peaks are more attenuated on outdoor walkways, directional distribution outside buildings also tends to be more balanced: two-thirds to three-quarters of the peak flow occur in the predominant direction. The greatest imbalances occur during the morning peak and are followed by the evening peak. Midday, by contrast, is split rather evenly by direction. Also, walkways connecting office buildings to transit stations tend to have highly directional flow, whereas the movement pattern in shopping districts is more ubiquitous. These relationships are illustrated in the lower part of Table 2.10.

Directional distribution in pedestrian design is generally less important than in the design of mechanical systems: a walkway has more flexiblity in accommodating varying directional flows than a reversible lane or a reversible track can ever achieve. More-

over, as will be seen later, the capacity of a walkway is about the same whether 100 percent of the flow is moving in one direction, or whether the movement is split 50-50. The only troublesome condition that can arise is when there is a significant minor flow against the predominant direction of movement. The resulting turbulence can reduce capacity and speed and be psychologically unpleasant for both the minority and majority. This condition should be borne in mind when designing for the morning and evening peaks, especially at constricted locations such as doors and stairways.

Weekly and Seasonal Cycles
A discussion of cyclical variation would be incomplete if no reference were made to weekly and seasonal variation in pedestrian flow. The weekly cycle mostly reflects the influence of the weekend but is also affected by local customs, such as Wednesday theater matinees or late shopping nights on Mondays and Thursdays. To explore its influence on office trip generation, five 12-hr counts were made in the course of a week at one of the office buildings in Midtown Manhattan. The highest daily volume was registered on a Wednesday, with Tuesday and Thursday about 2 percent lower, and Monday and Friday about 4 percent lower. No single day of the week could be considered strictly "average," but the difference in the critical peak volume generated by an office building from day to day appears rather minor.

By way of contrast, the Seattle study referred to earlier[10] found downtown sidewalks busiest on

Mondays and Fridays, with a low point on Wednesdays and Thursdays; the variation was somewhat greater than at the Manhattan office building—roughly between plus 8 and minus 8 percent of the average weekday. In downtown Braunschweig, West Germany, the weekly pattern was found to be similar to the Manhattan office building, with Wednesday 5 percent above average, Tuesday and Thursday 2 to 3 percent above average, and Monday and Friday about 5.2 percent below average. The sharper variation reflects the behavior of a retail shopping area.[11]

The seasonal cycle reflects many countervailing influences: the departure of employees for vacations but an influx of tourists during the summer, increased shopping in December but less pleasure walking during the winter, and so on. An adequate depiction of the seasonal cycle would have required an amount of data collection which was beyond the scope of this study. Thus, evidence for seasonal variation can be only indirect. Since most pedestrians walking in the Manhattan Central Business District arrive there by subway, and since most subway riders are destined for the CBD, the seasonal variation in subway patronage can serve as indirect evidence. Transit Authority data show that the number of weekday revenue passengers reaches a peak in May and June, at about 103 percent of the annual average weekday, and a trough in July and August, at about 95 percent. Clearly, the two figures are not very far apart. November closely approximates the "aver-

age" month. Thus, seasonal variation may be stronger than weekly variation, but their combined effect on pedestrians seems unlikely to be much in excess of 10 percent. Of course, much greater variation occurs on particular days for particular functions, such as Christmas shopping. The Braunschweig study does document the incidence of unique peaks, showing that perhaps two or three times of the year (Easter, winter sale, summer sale) midday hourly volume during a week can somewhat exceed twice the annual average value on a shopping street.

Seasonal variation in strictly pedestrian movement on sidewalks and in plazas or parks, as opposed to the total accumulation of people in a downtown area (which is measured to some extent by subway and shopping counts), is strongly influenced by weather. That particular subject will be touched on at the end of this chapter in connection with the cost of walking.

Trip Length and Purpose: Building Entrances
Having ascertained the number of pedestrian trips produced by different building types and having examined how this number varies in the course of a day, a week, and the seasons, we can proceed to the second dimension of travel demand, namely, trip length. Trip length, as we have indicated, is a very important dimension, because the amount of space that has to be provided for a given number of trips depends on how long those trips are. Trip length, or in this case walking distance, varies according to the characteristics

of the person making the trip and of the trip itself. To determine some of these relationships for pedestrians in Midtown Manhattan, interviews were conducted, intercepting persons entering or leaving a building or a transit station. They were asked where they walked to or from, for what purpose, and what other mode of travel, if any, they used on their trip; the interviewer also recorded their sex and apparent age group. A sample of 4,055 pedestrians was interviewed, representing a universe of 63,000 persons (the sampling rate varied, depending on location and time of day, from 2 percent to 50 percent).

Of most interest are the results of 1,400 interviews that represent about 17,000 pedestrians entering or leaving two major office buildings, one at Sixth Avenue and 50th Street, the other at Park Avenue and 46th Street, analyzed with regard to their trip generation and cyclical patterns in previous tables. Starting with the characteristics of the persons making the trips, Table 2.11 shows that the pedestrians intercepted at the two office buildings were predominantly either males twenty-five to fifty years of age or females under twenty-five. The average walking distance for all groups was found to be 1,720 ft (524 m) but varied from a low of 1,244 (379 m) for females over fifty to a high of 2,044 ft (623 m) for males twenty-five to fifty. In and of itself, the average walking distance column in Table 2.11 offers few surprises: most men walk farther than women and, generally, younger people walk farther than older people.

Table 2.10
Examples of Directional Distribution of
Pedestrian Travel

	Percentage of flow in the predominant direction		
	8:45-9:00 A.M.	12:45-1:00 P.M.	5:00-5:15 P.M.
1. Building Entrances			
Office, flat peak	93	60	85
Office, sharp peak	98	54	98
Department store	—	68	60
Restaurant	—	73	88
Residence	88	55	56
2. Walkways			
Grand Central escalators	93	56	88
Grand Central area	82	50	70
48th Street	74	58	71
Fifth Avenue	70	51	61
42nd Street at Times Square	60	52	63

Source: Based on counts shown in tables 2.7 and 2.9.

Table 2.11
Walking Distance by Age and Sex
at Two Office Buildings

Group	% of trips	Av. walking distance ft	(m)	Estimated av. net walking time min.
Males, under 25	10.2	1,502	(458)	4.70
Males, 25-50	35.1	2,044	(623)	6.83
Males, over 50	6.5	1,711	(522)	6.50
Females, under 25	28.8	1,608	(490)	5.80
Females, 25-50	14.6	1,443	(440)	5.47
Females, over 50	4.8	1,244	(379)	5.59
All males	51.8	1,900	(579)	6.37
All females	48.2	1,520	(463)	5.67
Total (16,740 trips)	100.0	1,720	(524)	6.03

Source: Regional Plan Association.

However, there seems to be a noteworthy explanation for this pattern, offered in the third column of Table 2.11, which estimates the average time these trips took. In a study in downtown Washington, D.C., Littleton MacDorman calculated average pedestrian speeds (exclusive of waiting time and other delays) for age and sex combinations similar to those in Table 2.11.[12] At the extremes, he found that young men walk at 320 ft (97.5 m) per minute as contrasted with older women at 222 ft (67.7 m) per minute. Applying the speeds from that study to the average distances shown in Table 2.11, one finds that most of the groups seem to allocate a similar amount of time to the walking portion of their trips. *On the average, the net time spent walking* (exclusive of delays, waiting time, or window shopping) *appears to be about 6 min,* and most of the range is between 5.5 and 6.8 min. Only the youngest male group stands out, with a disproportionately short travel time of 4.7 min, a result of short trip distance and high speed. With this one exception, most of the groups seem to be economizing on time in a similar manner, but those who walk faster cover more distance in the same time, and it is to a large extent this difference in speed which accounts for the different walking distances.

Turning now to the characteristics of the trips themselves, we will focus on trip purpose and mode of travel as factors affecting walking distance. Trip purpose varies widely in the course of a day. During the morning peak in a central business dis-

trict, virtually all travel is journeys to work. In midmorning, business calls and deliveries became important; at midday, eating, shopping, and business trips predominate; in the early afternoon, trips home become significant and increase to an overwhelming proportion of all travel during the evening rush.

The sampling procedure used at the two office buildings where interviews took place did not make it possible to draw a statistically accurate profile of trip purposes by time of day or a summary for the entire day. However, the general impression gained is that trips either coming from home or going home account for between 50 and 60 percent of the total trips in and out of the office buildings. The rest are nonhome based and represent the kind of swirling activity an urban center is built for. This is in marked contrast to vehicular travel in the Region as a whole, which is approximately 90 percent home based.

Of the trips that are predominantly nonhome based, eating trips are most numerous and amount to perhaps 33 percent at the two office buildings studied. They are followed by business calls, shopping trips, pleasure trips, and deliveries, in that order. The high rate of business calls suggests that there is, indeed, intensive face-to-face communication going on between people in different office buildings, which is presumed to be one of the major reasons why businesses cluster in an office center. In that connection, many of the eating trips could also be added to the business trips. Further, it

is interesting that the number of pleasure trips seems to rival that of shopping trips.

The trip purposes referred to represent those at the end of a journey; they take no account of intermediate stops along the way, which are significant in a central business district. A question asked to ascertain the number of these multipurpose trips received poor response (more than a third of those asked did not answer); of those who did answer, about 16 percent indicated stopping for one intermediate purpose and another 4 percent, for two or more purposes. Thus, at least 20 percent of all trips involved was probably multipurpose. This probably excludes many short stops, such as picking up a newspaper or window shopping. The reader might be taken aback by our unfulfilled desire to consider such minor stops as trip purposes, but we can refer to Morton Schneider's definition of trips as "segments of a person's total travel trajectory that lie entirely on minimum paths," with "those points at which departures from minimum paths occur" being "necessarily trip ends."[13]

As for the mode of travel, close to 26 percent of all trips intercepted at the two office buildings was exclusively walking trips; for the rest, walking represented but the initial or final link in a journey by one or several types of vehicles. As one would expect, the interviews revealed that the most walking-oriented trip purpose is eating (about 87 percent of trips to eat was walk-only trips); shopping follows (72 percent walk only); and business calls and pleasure trips come next (55 to 50 percent walk only). With respect to walking to work, it is known from the census that 3.7 percent of the initial trips to work in the Manhattan CBD is made on foot; the Regional Plan Association interviews registered a much higher percentage because they included return trips from eating, shopping, and other pursuits.

We can now examine the influence of purpose and mode on walking distance. For any category of trips, walking distance can be measured in several ways. The *average* walking distance (the sum of all distances divided by the number of trips) is useful for measuring total travel demand but gives no indication of how many people actually walk the "average" distance. The *median* distance is that which is exceeded by 50 percent of the people walking. Finally, a *cumulative distribution* of trip distances shows exactly what percentage of all trips are shorter (or longer) than a series of distances given.

Table 2.12 and Figure 2.4 present the cumulative distribution of walking distances for all trips at the two office buildings studied and then single out five specific trip purposes. Table 2.12 further shows the average and the median for all trips and for the five trip purposes. It is evident that 50 percent of the pedestrians interviewed at the two office buildings walk less than 1,070 ft (326 m), equivalent to about four north-south blocks in Manhattan. About 94 percent walk less than 1 mi (1.6 km) and virtually all walk less than 2 mi

(3.2 km). However, the average walking distance is 1,720 ft (525 m), about one-third of a mile, and much higher than the median, because of the weight of the small proportion of very long trips.

It is further evident from Table 2.12 that trips to eat have the shortest walking distances, with 50 percent of the people walking less than the equivalent of three north-south blocks. Business calls have the longest median walk, the equivalent of almost five and a half north-south blocks. Shopping trips have the longest average walk. Trips to work, which include return trips from other purposes, are similar to all trips. Pleasure trips have about the same median as work trips but a shorter average, suggesting that trips at the long end of the distribution are not made voluntarily. Theoretically, these differences can be explained if one views the walking distance as a price paid for reaching an opportunity. The scarcer the opportunity, the longer the distance. Eating establishments are ubiquitous in Midtown Manhattan, and people tend to choose one close at hand. The destinations of shopping trips or business calls are more unique, and it is plausible that more effort is expended to reach them.

In practice, the walking distance figures indicate, for example, that a restaurant will impose a smaller burden on nearby sidewalks than its trip generation rate would imply, because trips to eat are short. Retail floor space, by contrast, will impose an above-average burden on adjacent sidewalk space and will

make its presence felt in a wide radius, because walking trips to shop are long.

Since almost three-quarters of the pedestrians studied do not walk all the way to their destination but change to various mechanical modes of travel, a closer look at walking distances in relation to the vehicular mode is in order. In Table 2.13, the trips to work (which include return trips from other purposes at the two office buildings studied), taken from Table 2.12, are broken down by mode of travel. The cumulative walking distance distributions shown are presented graphically in Figure 2.5. It is clear that walking distance varies much more according to the vehicular mode than to the purpose of travel.

The important message in Table 2.13 is the ranking of the different modes, with taxicabs, quite plausibly, having the shortest access distances, followed by local buses and then subways, and the commuter rail and bus terminals having the longest access distances—again, a function of the relative scarcity of opportunities (there are only two rail terminals in Midtown, whereas taxicabs or buses are quite ubiquitous). Interestingly, those who drive to work in the two office buildings studied are willing to walk even farther than people on exclusively pedestrian trips because of the high price of parking space in the vicinity. We should emphasize, though, that while the ranking of the walking distances in Table 2.13 is of interest, the exact distances do not have general validity, as they are strongly influenced by the location of the

Table 2.12
Cumulative Walking Distance Distribution by Purpose of Trips by All Modes at Two Office Buildings

Walking distance		Percentage of trips shorter than the indicated distance					
ft	(m)	All trips	To eat	To work	Pleasure	To shop	Business
250	(76)	7	5	9	5	4	8
500	(152)	13	22	16	19	12	14
750	(229)	27	45	27	29	22	23
1,000	(305)	45	64	42	42	36	35
1,250	(381)	61	78	55	54	50	45
1,500	(457)	67	83	64	62	57	54
1,750	(533)	74	88	71	69	65	61
2,000	(610)	76	90	73	71	68	65
3,000	(914)	83	96	78	82	78	82
4,000	(1,219)	86	97	82	92	82	94
5,000	(1,524)	93	97	91	96	89	98
(1 mi.)	(1,609)	94	98	94	98	89	98
6,000	(1,829)	95	98	95	99	89	98
7,000	(2,134)	96	99	97	99	89	99
8,000	(2,438)	97	99	99	99	90	99
9,000	(2,743)	98	99	100	100	92	100
10,000	(3,048)	99	100	–	–	95	–
(2 mi.)	(3,219)	99	–	–	–	96	–
Av. Walk (ft)		1,720	1,073	1,880	1,666	2,253	1,737
(m)		524	327	573	508	687	529
Median Walk (ft)		1,070	810	1,120	1,130	1,250	1,405
(m)		326	247	341	344	381	428
No. of Trips		17,306*	1,118	7,294†	669	640	955

Source: Regional Plan Association.
*Trips to home, delivery trips, other trips, and those with an unreported purpose totaling 6,630 are included in this figure but not shown separately.
†Trips to work in the two-way definition include return trips to office buildings from other purposes.

Figure 2.4
Cumulative walking distance distribution by purpose at two Manhattan office buildings

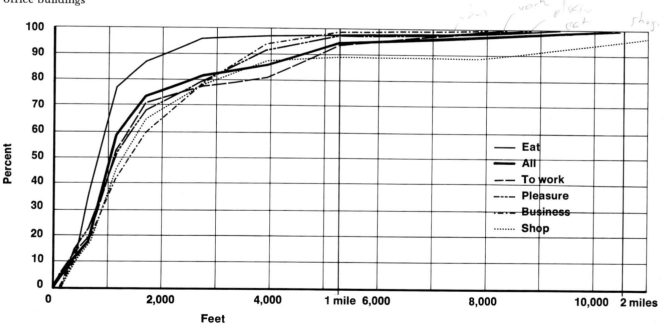

Table 2.13
Cumulative Walking Distance Distribution of Trips to Work at Two Office Buildings, by Mode

Walking distance		Percentage of trips shorter than the indicated distance						
ft	(m)	Taxi	Local bus	Subway	Walk only	Auto	Rail	Commuter bus
250	(76)	50	18	3	10	5	0	0
500	(152)	70	20	8	25	15	0	0
750	(229)	77	35	23	39	21	0	0
1,000	(305)	79	62	50	47	26	23	0
1,250	(381)	81	81	69	52	36	33	0
1,500	(457)	83	90	80	55	51	36	0
1,750	(533)	85	97	88	58	62	39	0
2,000	(610)	86	98	89	61	66	40	0
3,000	(914)	89	99	93	76	76	51	0
4,000	(1,219)	91	100	95	83	78	90	5
5,000	(1,524)	95	—	97	90	91	98	60
(1 mi.)	(1,609)	96	—	98	92	94	100	74
6,000	(1,829)	97	—	98	94	96	—	82
7,000	(2,134)	98	—	99	98	98	—	92
8,000	(2,438)	100	—	99	100	100	—	100
9,000	(2,743)	—	—	99	—	—	—	—
10,000	(3,048)	—	—	100	—	—	—	—
(2 mi.)	(3,219)	—	—	—	—	—	—	—
Av. walk (ft)		892	926	1.330	2,001	2,090	3,231	4,975
	(m)	272	282	405	610	637	985	1,516
Median walk (ft)		160	890	1,010	1,100	1,490	2,970	4,820
	(m)	49	271	308	335	454	905	1,469
No. of trips		347	641	2,827	807	409	1,057	228

Source: Regional Plan Association.

Figure 2.5
Cumulative walking distance distribution by mode at two Manhattan office buildings

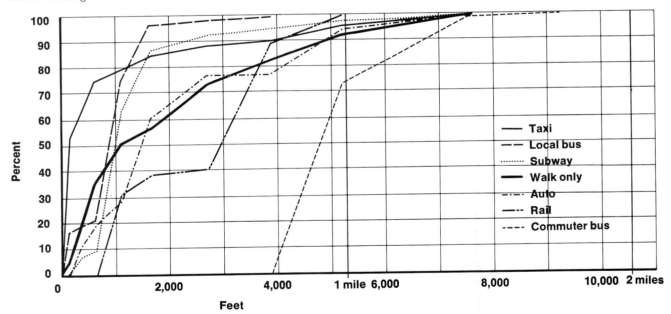

two office buildings and by the disposition of other facilities around them. This is particularly true of subway stations, parking garages, and commuter terminals.

It may also be that walk-only trips in Manhattan are not necessarily longer than access trips to other modes of travel, contrary to what Table 2.13 shows. Walk-only trips from the two office buildings (as opposed to trips toward the buildings, as shown in Table 2.13) were not longer than access trips to other modes of travel, nor was any significant difference between the two trip types revealed by interviews at four residential buildings on the East Side of Manhattan. At this latter location, both types of trips averaged about 1,210 ft (370 m).

Trip Length and Purpose: Outdoor Walkways
To obtain a more generally applicable measure of walking distances to subway stations and parking facilities in Manhattan, additional interviews were conducted, with the results shown in Table 2.14 and in Figure 2.6. Measured at stations, the walking distance to subways averages 1,155 ft (352 m) in Midtown and about 1,450 ft (442 m) on the sparsely served East Side, and the respective medians are 900 and 1,380 ft (274 and 421 m). There is no significant difference between trips to work and trips for all purposes at these stations. Assuming an average walking speed of 285 ft (87 m) per minute, as derived from Table 2.11, the net walking time to the Midtown stations averages about 4 min, to the East Side station, 5.1 min.

The walking distances for trip-to-work parking, if measured at the place of parking, have an average of about 1,800 ft (549 m) and a median of about 1,200 ft (366 m). Both distances are about 500 ft (152 m) shorter for short-term parkers. This is much more than the average of 800 ft (244 m) and the median of 730 ft (223 m) reported by the Bureau of Public Roads for parkers at off-street pay facilities in cities over half a million in population.[14]

This leads to a broader question: How do the Manhattan walking distances compare with those of other places? Available data from other places are sparse, approximate, and often not directly comparable, so the reader should, once more, view the comparison merely as an illustration. Eight sets of cumulative walking distance frequency distributions for six cities are shown in Table 2.15, along with average and median walking distances. Five of them are displayed graphically in Figure 2.7. It seems clear that walking distances in the central business districts of smaller cities are substantially shorter.

Columns 1 and 3 of Table 2.15 show two sets of figures for downtown Seattle, the first representing walks from parking facilities, the second representing walk-only trips between buildings. In smaller cities, walks to parking facilities consistently tend to be shorter than walk-only trips, and such is the case in Seattle, with the median walk to a parked car being 400 ft (122 m) and the median walk between buildings, 725 ft (221 m). The reason these two sets of figures

for Seattle are shown is because they frame the median walking distance in several downtowns for which data are available: Edmonton, Denver, and Dallas.[15] Of these, only Edmonton, which has the shortest trips, is shown in the table. Its walks for all purposes are about the same as walks to parked automobiles in Seattle, roughly half as long as comparable walks in Manhattan. However, there is some evidence of rather short walking distances even from downtown areas much larger than that of Edmonton. A survey of trips to lunch in downtown Washington, D.C., shows a median and an average that are about 40 percent of those for the trips to eat in Manhattan shown earlier in Table 2.12.[16] A study of walking distances to buses in downtown Washington indicates a median roughly 40 percent of that shown in Table 2.13; walking distances to buses at the residential end of the trip are greater than to buses downtown but still shorter than those in Manhattan.[17]

While walking distances in Midtown Manhattan seem to be roughly twice as long as those in the smaller downtowns enumerated, it is by no means clear that they exceed all urban walking distances by the same margin. The only comprehensive data available are for Chicago (Table 2.15, column 4): they cover the entire metropolitan area. If one corrects for the straight line distance definition used and expands walking distance by 15 percent, the average and the median become very similar to those at the Manhattan office buildings (column 6) and longer than those in a residential area of

Table 2.14
Cumulative Walking Distance Distribution at Selected Subway Stations and Parking Facilities

Walking distance		Percentage of trips shorter than the indicated distance			
ft	(m)	Three CBD stations*	77 Lex IRT	Parking short-term	Parking long-term
250	(76)	17	7	19	9
500	(152)	31	16	46	16
750	(229)	44	27	49	23
1,000	(305)	56	36	55	37
1,250	(381)	64	46	65	47
1,500	(457)	69	56	70	56
1,750	(533)	74	64	75	61
2,000	(610)	80	70	80	68
3,000	(914)	95	92	88	82
4,000	(1,219)	98	100	98	92
5,000	(1,524)	99	–	99	97
(1 mi.)	(1,609)	99	–	99	97
6,000	(1,829)	100	–	100	99
7,000	(2,134)	–	–	–	100
8,000	(2,438)	–	–	–	–
9,000	(2,743)	–	–	–	–
10,000	(3,048)	–	–	–	–
(2 mi.)	(3,219)	–	–	–	–
Av. walk (ft)		1,155	1,449	1,198	1,780
(m)		352	442	365	543
Median walk (ft)		900	1,380	700	1,220
(m)		274	421	213	372
No. of trips		32,611	6,336	31[†]	64[†]

Source: Regional Plan Association.
*53rd-Lex; 50th-6th; 42nd-6th IND stations.
[†]Observations, not expanded.

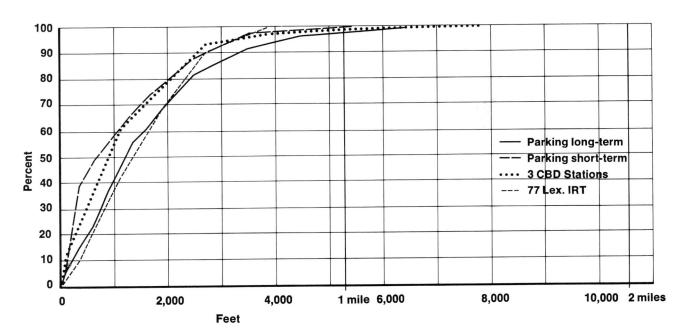

Figure 2.6
Cumulative walking distance distribution at parking lots and subway stations.

Walking distance ft	(m)	Percentage of trips shorter than the indicated distance							
		Seattle CBD parking only	Edmonton, Alberta CBD all modes	Seattle CBD walk only	Chicago Area walk only	Manhattan Res. 4 bldgs. all modes	Manhattan offices 2 bldgs. all modes	Southwest Washington res.‡	London walk to work only
250	(76)	35	31	20	9	22	7	8	5
500	(152)	60	60	40	30	38	13	15	12
750	(229)	74	70	52	42	48	27	22	17
1,000	(305)	82	79	60	53	60	45	30	22
1,250	(381)	87	84	68	60	71	61	37	28
1,500	(457)	92	89	75	67	78	67	44	34
1,750	(533)	94	91	80	73	83	74	55	40
2,000	(610)	97	93	85	78	84	76	69	47
3,000	(914)	98	97	92	89	88	83	86	64
4,000	(1,219)	99	99	95	95	93	86	87	75
5,000	(1,524)	100	99	98	97	96	93	89	80
(1 mi.)	(1,609)	–	99	n.d.	97	97	94	89	82
6,000	(1,829)	–	100	n.d.	98	98	95	90	85
7,000	(2,134)	–	–	n.d.	99	99	96	92	89
8,000	(2,438)	–	–	n.d.	99	99	97	94	91
9,000	(2,743)	–	–	n.d.	99	99	98	94	93
10,000	(3,048)	–	–	n.d.	99	99	99	95	95
(2 mi.)	(3,219)	–	–	n.d.	99	100	99	96	96
Av. walk (ft)		610	870	1,150	1,580*	1,210	1,720†	2,190	2,640
(m)		184	265	342	482	369	524	668	805
Median walk (ft)		400	400	725	900*	780	1,070†	1,600	2,100
(m)		122	122	221	274	238	326	488	640

Table 2.15
Cumulative Walking Distance Distributions at Office and Residential Buildings in Manhattan Compared with Other Locations

Sources: Columns 1 and 3, Wilbur Smith and Associates, New Haven, Conn. Column 2, Donald M. Hill, John J. Bakker and Bert L. Akers, *An Evaluation of the Needs of the Pedestrian in Downtown*, Traffic Research Corporation, 1964. Column 4, Roger L. Creighton, *Report on the Walking Trip Survey*, Chicago Area Transportation Study, 1961. Columns 5 and 6, Regional Plan Association. Column 7, Gary E. Maring, *Pedestrian Travel Characteristics*, Highway Research Record no. 406, 1972. Column 8, *London Traffic Survey*, vol. 1, chart 6-17, p. 117.
Note: Most of the data were scaled off charts and may not accurately represent the findings of the original sources.
n.d.—no data.
*Airline distance, based on a particular block definition; actual walking distance probably about 15 percent longer.
†Same as in Table 2.12.
‡Predominantly walk-only trips, include 7.3 percent of access trips to other modes with an average distance of 760 ft (232 m).

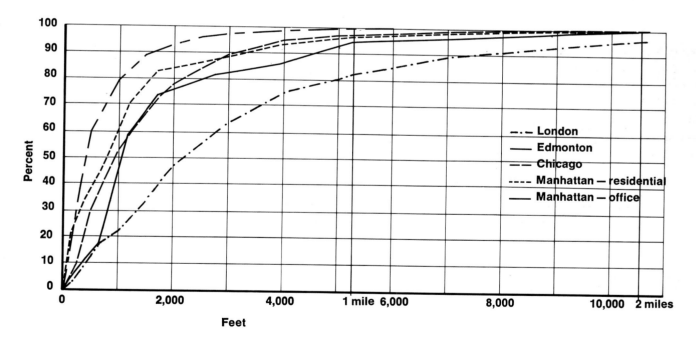

Figure 2.7
Cumulative walking distance distribution in selected cities

Manhattan (column 5). Data for a fairly central residential area in Washington, D.C., show trip lengths substantially in excess of the two Manhattan locations (column 7). However, this is due largely to the extreme underrepresentation in the sample of very short walks to autos, buses, and taxis. The figures for London (column 8) likewise indicate a greater propensity to walk but are also not quite comparable, because they refer to walking trips to work, typically longer than average walking trips. Indications are that in the Tokyo region, where 42.8 percent of all trips in 1968 were walk-only trips, these averaged about 12 minutes (over 3,000 ft or close to 1 km), substantially longer than in any of the North American examples.

In summary, one might surmise that there is an upper limit to the tolerance of walking distances under North American conditions, which the Chicago and Midtown Manhattan figures in Table 2.15 tend to approach.

On the other hand, the downtowns of most medium-sized cities have their intensive trip-generating activities clustered in such a small area—for example, 0.3 sq mi (0.8 km²) in Seattle—that the opportunity for long walks simply does not arise. Much more extensive data on walking distances will have to become available before any firm hypotheses in this area can be tested.

Direct Estimation of Pedestrian Density

The difficulty of assembling a sufficient volume of statistically representative data by means of counts and interviews at individual facilities is by now clear to the reader. For that reason, the primary reliance in this study is not on conventional techniques of travel analysis applied to pedestrians but rather on measures encompassing the entire universe of pedestrians in a selected area.

The area selected for study covers about 1.2 sq mi (3.1 km²) in Midtown Manhattan, from north of 38th Street to south of 61st Street, between Second to Eighth avenues. Practical problems of pedestrian circulation here are acute and urgently require solution. Analytically, the area offers a large sample of pedestrian movement at a reasonable cost. No claim is made that the rates of pedestrian travel determined for this area are universally valid. However, the methodology used can have a wide application, and in the absence of other data the figures derived are useful benchmarks.

Buildings in Midtown Manhattan
The study area represents the core of Manhattan's Central Business District. Its outline is shown in Figure 2.8. About 27 percent of the nonresidential floor space in Manhattan south of 60th Street is located here, representing about 4.75 percent of all nonresidential floor space in the 12,750 sq mi (33,000 km²) New York Region. The concentration of human activities is even higher, since non-residential floor space in Manhattan's Central Business District tends to be more intensively used than elsewhere.

An inventory of the roughly 200 million sq ft (18 million m²) of building floor space in the area is summarized in Table 2.16. The data refer to gross floor space, that is, the area of all floors (including cellars) contained by the outside dimensions of a building. They show that over 60 percent of the gross floor space in the area is occupied by offices; about 15 percent is accounted for by other nonresidential uses, the largest of them being retailing and institutions, such as clubs, schools, or museums. Garages, manufacturing, restaurants, and theaters make up the rest of the other nonresidential uses. Though retail and restaurants together occupy only some 5 percent of total floor space, they exert, as we have learned, a powerful influence on pedestrian movement. About 20 percent of the floor space is in residential use, half of that in hotels. These proportions exemplify the anatomy of a central business district.

Figure 2.8 shows how the 200 million sq ft of floor space are distributed geographically. The shading indicates the density of floor space, by block, where an entire block is occupied by one building, or by sectors within a block, where a block contains many buildings. The density of floor space is measured by the floor-area ratio (FAR), familiar to the reader from the first chapter. Buildings in the lower density range, that is, those with FARs of 10 or less, occupy more

Figure 2.8
Floor-area ratio in Midtown Manhattan

- ■ FAR: 20-30
- ▥ FAR: 10-20
- ▨ FAR: 5-10
- □ FAR: 0- 5

0   500   1,000   2,000 ft

Table 2.16
Gross Building Floor Space in Midtown
Manhattan

Type of use	In 1.2 sq mi. study area		
	sq ft	m²	% of total
Office	123,995,600	11,519,000	63.2
Retail	7,729,900	718,000	3.9
Institutional	7,693,400	715,000	3.9
Garage	4,486,500	417,000	2.3
Manufacturing	4,114,500	382,000	2.0
Restaurant	2,844,200	264,000	1.4
Theater	2,263,200	210,000	1.1
Total Nonresidential	**153,118,300**	**14,225,000**	**78.0**
Private Residences	20,916,200	1,943,000	10.7
Hotels	22,119,400	2,055,000	11.3
Total Residential	**43,035,600**	**3,998,000**	**22.0**
Total Floor Space	**196,153,900**	**18,223,000**	**100.0**

Source: Regional Plan Association.
Note: Floor areas used were scaled off San-
born Fire Insurance maps and the Bromley
Atlas; uses were determined from a field
survey in summer 1969. The data compare
reasonably well with the Tri-State Regional
Planning Commission floor space inventory,
which was not employed directly because of
insufficient detail.

than half the land that is in the building lots in Midtown. The higher density categories, with FARs from 10 to 30, occupy 43 percent of the land but contain 71 percent of the building floor space. The high density concentrations appear in a large cluster around Grand Central Terminal and in two smaller clusters around Rockefeller Center and in the Garment District.

Walkways in Midtown Manhattan

As is evident to any visitor, buildings represent the largest single use of land in Midtown Manhattan. Buildings physically occupy just over half its area. The other half of the land is used to provide light, air, and access to the buildings. Table 2.17 presents the breakdown.

Not counting interior yards and putting public and private areas together, 44 percent of Midtown's surface is devoted to circulation: 26 percent to vehicles, 16 percent to pedestrians, and 2 percent to ornamental space, that is, areas used for planting, fountains, and other amenities. Most of this ornamental space is along the southern edge of Central Park and in Bryant Park. Without these two parks, public ornamental space accounts for only 0.25 percent, and private ornamental space, for 0.33 percent, of the land in Midtown Manhattan. Most of the private ornamental space, as well as the pedestrian pavement in plazas, listed in Table 2.17, were added since 1961 under the provisions of the new zoning law: almost 10 percent of the pavement devoted to pedestrian use is in private plazas. The relative dearth of sidewalk space as well as the new promi-

nence of plazas are illustrated in Figure 2.9, and the ornamental space is shown in Figure 2.10.

Relating the figures on building floor space to those on pedestrian circulation space, we find that the 196 million sq ft (18 million m²) of buildings are served by 5.3 million sq ft (490 thousand m²) of walkways, which works out to an average of 27 units of walkway space for each 1,000 units of building floor space. The average, however, is deceptive, given the large variation in building density in Midtown Manhattan.

While building floor space per unit of land area varies greatly, the supply of walkway space stays pretty well fixed. This leads to the large discrepancies in the relationship between buildings and walkways demonstrated earlier in Table 1.5. To arrive at a balanced relationship between building space and walkway space, we have to proceed with our analysis and investigate how both buildings and pedestrian circulation space relate to pedestrian travel.

An Aerial Count of Pedestrians

Pedestrians visible on the surface of the entire Midtown Manhattan study area were counted twice from aerial photographs: during midday and during the evening rush hour. At an instant after 1:30 P.M., a total of 37,510 pedestrians could be seen in the 1.2 sq mi (3.1 km²) of Midtown, of whom 33,280 were in sidewalks, 1,680 in streets, 1,620 in plazas, 690 in parks, and 240 in other places, such as yards, roofs, and construction sites. During the evening period the total was somewhat lower. Re-

ferring back to the outdoor cyclical counts, we can see that the time of the aerial count (indicated in the darker shade in Figure 2.3) is on the slope of the midday peak. Thus, during the peak of the peak, the number of pedestrians outdoors may have been some 15 percent higher, on the order of 43,000. This excludes people walking through covered passageways or otherwise concealed from view. The aerial photographs were taken from a helicopter provided by the Port Authority of New York and New Jersey.*

The counts from the aerial photographs were tabulated by block face and sections of blocks. The number of pedestrians per block face varied widely. On avenues, it ranged from 7 to 170; on streets, from 5 to 140. The lowest avenue counts were on portions of Second Avenue, the lowest street counts on streets just south of Central Park on the West Side of Manhattan. The highest were, predictably enough, in areas with the highest concentration of floor space, particularly on Fifth Avenue. The midday and evening

---

*The midday photographs were taken on several weekdays between April 29 and May 21, 1969, at times ranging from 1:28 to 1:59 P.M.; the evening photographs, between May 1 and June 4, 5:02 to 5:30 P.M. They were taken with a Hasselblad camera on 70 mm high-speed color film (Kodak Ektachrome 5257 ER Daylight, ASA 160), using a 1/200 sec exposure at f 16, from a helicopter at an altitude of about 2,000 ft, flying at a speed of 50 mph. The camera was held by hand. To interpret the film, a Nikon microscope was used with a 10x diameter enlargement. The technique proved highly successful except in the case of some evening shots, which could not be interpreted due to deep shadows; as a result, only two-thirds of the evening counts were used.

Table 2.17
Surface Use in Midtown Manhattan

	Sq ft	m²	% of total land area
Public Area	13,187,670	1,225,134	40.0
Vehicular pavement	7,789,880		
Pedestrian pavement in sidewalks	4,539,100		
Pedestrian pavement in parks*	222,865		
Ornamental space†	635,825		
Private area (within property line)	19,709,610	1,831,023	60.0
Vehicular pavement	70,150		
Pedestrian pavement (plazas)	497,660		
Ornamental pavement (plazas)	103,900		
Area covered by buildings‡	17,421,200		
Private yards	958,000		
Vacant	61,900		
Parking lots	596,800		
Total area	**32,897,280**	**3,056,157**	**100.00**
Total devoted to vehicles	8,456,830	785,639	25.7
Total devoted to pedestrians	5,259,625	488,619	16.0
Total covered by buildings	17,421,200	1,618,430	53.0
Total ornamental	739,725	68,720	2.2
Vacant and yards	1,019,900	94,749	3.1

Source: Regional Plan Association.
*Includes 43,500 sq ft along the south rim of Central Park, 119,100 in Bryant Park.
†Includes 356,400 sq ft along the south rim of Central Park, 193,350 in Bryant Park.
‡Includes 170,025 sq ft in arcades under buildings, which are not included in the figures on pedestrian space.

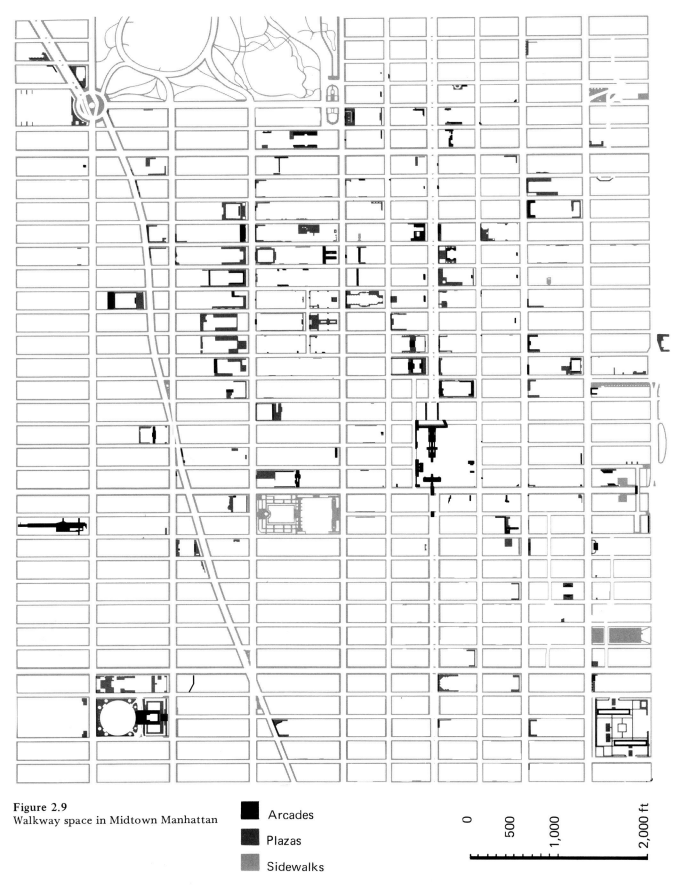

Figure 2.9
Walkway space in Midtown Manhattan

■ Arcades

▨ Plazas

▧ Sidewalks

0   500   1,000   2,000 ft

58 Pedestrian Travel Demand

Figure 2.10
Ornamental space in Midtown Manhattan

◼ Water

▨ Greenery

Note: Street trees and greenery in private yards not shown.

0   500   1,000   2,000 ft

59 Estimation of Pedestrian Density

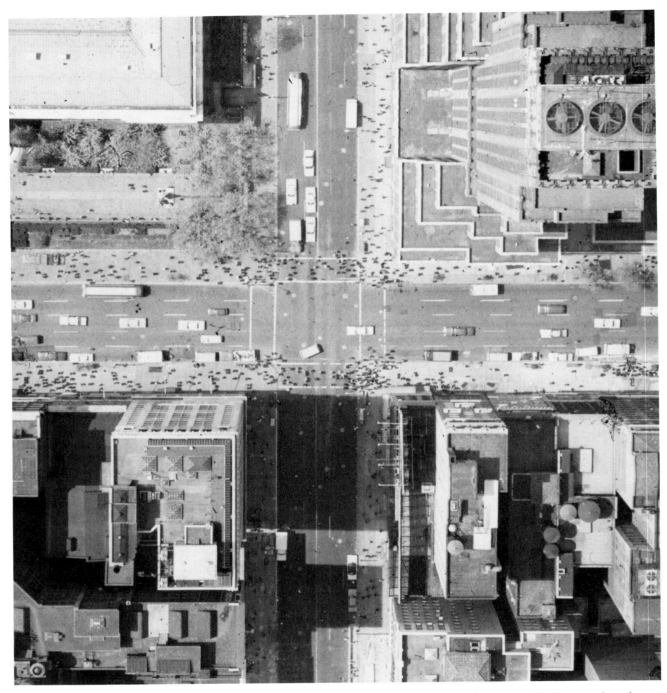

Helicopter aerial photography—the basis for equations (1) through (4), estimating the presence of pedestrians. The picture, one of more than 900 taken by the Port Authority over Midtown Manhattan, is enlarged 3 X from the original color film. It shows the intersection of Fifth Avenue and 42nd Street looking west (top of view), with the New York Public Library in the upper left hand corner. A total of 680 pedestrians and 39 motor vehicles can be seen in the view, taken at midday.

counts translated into hourly flow rates (pedestrians passing per hour on one sidewalk) are shown in figures 2.11 and 2.12. The highest flow rate, on the west side of Fifth Avenue at 47th Street, was found to be 12,000 pedestrians per hour. This location happens to be very near the centroid of Midtown floor space. Sections of Madison, Lexington, and Third avenues had sidewalk flows around 6,000 per hour, and 42nd Street, up to 5,000 per hour during midday, with a higher flow in the evening.

Flows in the middle range of those encountered in Midtown Manhattan are not uncommon in the downtowns of other large cities. Thus, flows up to 5,000 per hour can be encountered in Chicago[18] and Toronto; Market Street in San Francisco carries up to 3,000 per hour on each sidewalk. In smaller cities, such as Seattle, peak hour flows on the order of 1,500 are more common, comparable to many cross-town streets in Midtown.

The magnitude of flow in itself, of course, tells us nothing about comfort unless we know how wide the sidewalks are, that is, how much space the pedestrians have available for walking. On the average, the 33,280 pedestrians found on sidewalks in Midtown at midday had 136 sq ft (12.6 m²) of walkway each. But as we have seen before, averages can be misleading. An examination of individual sections of blocks shows that sidewalk space per pedestrian ranged from a low of 28 sq ft (2.6 m²) on portions of Lexington, Madison, and Fifth avenues, to about 500 sq ft (46.5 m²) per person on portions

of Second Avenue, to some 2,000 sq ft (186 m²) on lightly used cross-town streets south of Central Park. We will turn to evaluating these space allocations in Chapter 3. But first we must see how we can link the pedestrians found on a block to the building floor space and the walkway space on that block so that we can make some reasonable predictions as to how many pedestrians one could expect to find on the walkways of a building of any given size and use.

Equations Relating Pedestrians to Buildings and Walkways

The tabulation of the aerial pedestrian count by block sectors, which matched the inventory of building and surface use, made it possible to statistically relate pedestrians to building floor space and walkway space at two points in time at each of some 600 block sectors. The statistical technique employed, known as *multiple correlation*, uses an empirical equation to explain the variation in the average value of one variable by the variations in the average values of several other variables. In this case, the number of pedestrians visible on any block sector was the dependent variable, or the variable to be explained, while the walkway area as well as the floor space in each of the ten building use categories listed in Table 2.16 were assumed to be the independent variables, that is, the factors that would hopefully explain the variation in pedestrian travel.

Early in the analysis it became apparent that of the ten building uses inventoried only office, retail, and restaurant floor space

appeared to be significantly associated with the presence of pedestrians. Even when treated together, rather than individually, the seven other building uses could not contribute to a more precise explanation of the dependent variable because of their relatively low trip generation rates. So, only office, retail, and restaurant use, plus the walkway area available for pedestrian circulation, were retained as significant variables affecting the presence of pedestrians on a block sector at midday. For the evening an added factor seemed important, namely, the proximity to transit facilities, such as subway stops. After different measures of proximity were tested, certain functions of the distance to the nearest transit entrance proved best and were accepted as independent variables.

Another refinement that proved necessary was the differentiation between streets and avenues. Using the same equation for both tended to overestimate pedestrians in streets and underestimate pedestrians on avenues. The reason for this difference lies in the peculiar geometry of the Manhattan street grid. For every 5,000 units of land width there are about 300 units of sidewalk width on the north-south avenues and about 600 units on the east-west streets. On the assumption that pedestrians have an equal desire to walk north-south as they do east-west, the street sidewalks should have about half the pedestrian density as the avenue sidewalks. This relationship was borne out by the helicopter counts, which found about 53 percent of the

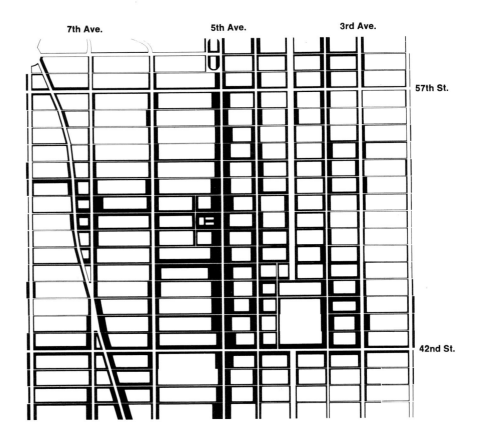

Figure 2.11
Midday hourly pedestrian flow rate in Midtown Manhattan

Hourly flow rate

▮ 15,000	—	1,000
▪ 10,000	—	500
▪ 5,000	—	100

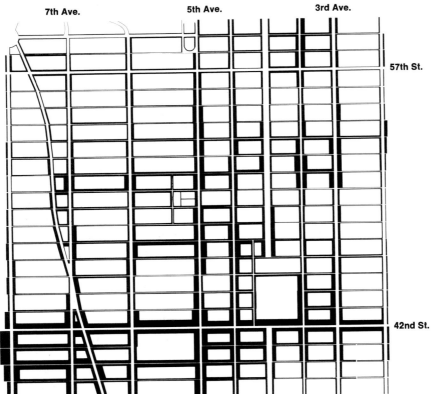

Fig. 2.12
Evening hourly pedestrian flow rate in Midtown Manhattan

Hourly flow rate

▮ 15,000	—	1,000
▪ 10,000	—	500
▪ 5,000		100

pedestrians walking north-south and about 47 percent walking east-west, with the latter having more than twice as much room to themselves as the former.

The final result of the multiple correlation analysis is four equations, shown in Table 2.18, for estimating the number of pedestrians on any block sector at an instant after 1:30 P.M. and after 5:00 P.M. on an avenue and on a street. The simple relationship of the avenues having about twice the pedestrian density of streets is not directly apparent from the equations because most "avenue" block sectors include portions of street sidewalks near the corner.

In the light of our spot measurements of trip-generation rates shown earlier, the equations in Table 2.18 make good sense. For example, equations (1) and (2) tell us that at midday the number of pedestrians on a block sector depends on the amount of office space, retail space, and restaurant space, uses that obviously generate pedestrian trips during lunchtime, as well as as on the amount of surface available for pedestrians to walk on. They also say that retail uses generate 2 to 7 times the pedestrian trips that offices do per unit of floor space and that restaurants generate 13 to 25 times the trips of offices during the noon hours. Comparing the avenue with the street equation, we see that equal increases in pedestrian space produce about equal increases in pedestrians and that the same is true of office floor space. However, retail uses on avenues attract about three times as many pedestrians as retail uses on streets, a finding that helps

explain why ground floor rents on avenues are much higher than those on streets. The main indication of the more intensive use of the avenues is the constant term at the end of the equations, which seems to indicate that there will be an average of 26 additional pedestrians per block on an avenue, regardless of sidewalk or building space.

Equations (3) and (4) likewise include office space. Since most pedestrians during the evening rush hour are leaving office buildings, this is quite plausible. Retail floor space is significant on the avenues but substantially less attractive during the evening rush hour than at midday: fewer people are shopping. Retail space on streets ceases to be significant. Pedestrian space on streets is just as important during the evening rush hour as it is at midday but ceases to be statistically significant on the avenues. This anomaly can be interpreted to mean that during the more leisurely lunch hour pedestrians probably will seek out areas with more elbowroom and distribute themselves in relation to the available sidewalk space, whereas during the evening peak they tend to rush along the avenues irrespective of available space. As for restaurant space, it ceases to be statistically significant during the evening rush hour and does not appear in either the avenue or the street equation. However, a new factor, the distance to the nearest transit entrance, emerges in the evening equations.

The distance to transit entrances must be considered in conjunction with the constants at the end of the equation. At 100 ft

(30.5 m) from a transit entrance, the avenue equation produces, on the average, −2.0 + 56.7 = 54.7 pedestrians, in addition to those generated by office and retail uses. There is a constant drop-off of about 2 pedestrians for every additional 100 ft (30.5 m) of distance from the transit entrance. Quite a different pattern prevails on streets. At 100 ft (30.5 m) away, a transit entrance produces 46.1 + 2.2 = 48.2 pedestrians on the sidewalk of a street, but this concentration drops off very rapidly, inversely to the cube of the distance, and becomes about 2.5 pedestrians at 500 ft (152 m). In other words, transit entrances do not strongly affect volumes on street sidewalks beyond a 500 ft radius in Midtown. As can be seen from the evening pedestrian flows shown in Figure 2.12, the street blocks leading to transit facilities are indeed much busier than other streets, while the flow on avenues stretches out in a more uniform pattern.

Evaluating the Equations

Even though the relationships portrayed in Table 2.18 appear intuitively plausible, the significance of the equations has to be evaluated by more rigorous, statistical measures. The most common such measure is the multiple correlation coefficient R. If $R = 1.0$, then a perfect fit exists and all variation in the dependent variable can be explained by the independent variables. If $R = 0$, then the independent variables explain nothing. The perfect condition, possible in the physical sciences, is extremely unlikely in the social sciences. The correlation coefficient squared represents the fraction, or the percentage, of the variation that is explained. These R^2 values for the four equations are given in the first column in Table 2.19: the street equations explain 61 to 52 percent of the variation in the presence of pedestrians, and the avenue equations, 36 to 23 percent. In both cases the midday equations explain more of the variation than the evening ones. An interpretation of this pattern is in order.

The values any correlation equation produces are averages, not actual observations. The spread of the actual observations around the average is measured by the standard error S_e, likewise indicated in column 1 of Table 2.19. The probability is about 68 percent that the actual value lies within plus/minus one standard error and about 95 percent that it lies within two standard errors of the average produced by the equation.

A major reason for the wide spread of observed values around the calculated average in our case is that the observed values are based on instantaneous photographs. There is a considerable variation in pedestrian flow from instant to instant because of the phenomenon of platooning. More will be said about it later; suffice it to say here that platooning is caused, to a large extent, by changes in traffic lights and affects avenues more than the longer street blocks: this is one reason for the greater accuracy of the street equations.

The extent to which the standard error is affected by platooning is best illustrated by a numerical example. Let us assume that a block sector facing an avenue

has 10,000 sq ft ($929 m^2$) of walkway, 1 million sq ft ($92,900 m^2$) of office space, and 10,000 sq ft ($929 m^2$) each of retail and restaurant use. Inserting these values into equation (1) we see that the block sector should have an average of 122 pedestrians at a midday instant. However, the standard error of equation (1) from Table 2.19 is 43.5. Multiplying that by two and adding it to or subtracting it from 122, we can say with a 95 percent confidence that the actual number of pedestrians on the block will be somewhere between 35 and 209. This appears to be a large spread: the high value is 1.7 times the average value. However, if one looks at manual counts of the minute-to-minute variation in pedestrian flows of a comparable magnitude during any 15-min period, one can see that the highest minute is easily 1.2 to 1.5 times the average minute. While the evidence is indirect—no helicopter counts of a block sector at 1-min intervals were available—it seems clear that a large portion of the standard error is due to the short-term pulses. For purposes of establishing design standards, we are not so much interested in the average number of pedestrians on a block at a particular instant as we are in insuring, with a stated probability, that space allocations do not fall below a certain level. The equations provide this yardstick if one makes use of their standard errors as given in Table 2.19.

Of course, there are other sources of error besides the short-term fluctuations due to platooning. For the evening equations, which generally per-

form more poorly than the midday ones, a major source is the large-scale pattern of pedestrian flow toward the major terminals, such as Grand Central and the Port Authority Bus Terminal, evident in Figure 2.12. The factor of proximity to the nearest transit entrance alone cannot take care of that error, since transit stations vary widely in the volumes they attract: during the evening peak hour 50,000 passengers enter the Grand Central subway station, while only 3,000 enter the Seventh Avenue stop at 53rd Street.

A related factor, operative both at midday and in the evening, is the influence of adjacent blocks. We stated earlier that it is not essential to consider the influence of neighboring areas on an area in question if no abrupt changes in land use occur. But, when abrupt changes do occur, the standard error of the estimating equations would have been reduced by including a measure of this aspect of accessibility. For example, pedestrian flow on the block that contains St. Patrick's Cathedral is affected by the presence of 400,000 sq ft ($37,160 m^2$) of retail floor space across the street at Saks Fifth Avenue; of two blocks with identical-size buildings on Third Avenue, the one closer to Grand Central has higher pedestrian flow; and so on. This phenomenon, most pronounced on avenues, is only partially handled by the constant term at the end of the equations, which shows ambient pedestrians present because of the high floor space density in the area.

Table 2.18
Equations Relating the Presence of Pedestrians to Building Use and Walkway Space

(1) Avenues, midday
$$P = 2.97 \text{ walkway} + 0.05 \text{ office} + 0.35 \text{ retail} + 1.22 \text{ restaurant} + 26.66$$

(2) Streets, midday
$$P = 3.12 \text{ walkway} + 0.06 \text{ office} + 0.12 \text{ retail} + 0.74 \text{ restaurant} - 4.01$$

(3) Avenues, evening
$$P = 0.06 \text{ office} + 0.20 \text{ retail} - 1.98 D + 56.70$$

(4) Streets, evening
$$P = 3.17 \text{ walkway} + 0.04 \text{ office} + \frac{46.12}{D^3} + 2.17$$

Source: Regional Plan Association.
Note:
P = number of pedestrians at an instant in time on the sidewalks, plazas, and in the vehicular roadway of a block sector.
walkway = sidewalk and plaza space on the block sector, in thousands of square feet (92.9 m^2).
office, retail, restaurant = gross office, retail, and restaurant floor space, respectively, in the block sector, in thousands of square feet (92.9 m^2).
D = distance from the centroid of the sidewalk and plaza space to the nearest transit entrance, in hundreds of feet (30.5 m).

Table 2.19
Statistical Measures of Equations in Table 2.18

Equation	Variable	Coefficient (not rounded)	Standard error of coefficient	t-value
(1) Avenues, midday				
$R^2 = 0.36$	walkway	2.97	0.439	6.8
$N = 344$	office	0.0485	0.0089	5.5
$S_e = 43.5$	retail	0.35	0.061	5.7
	restaurant	1.22	0.370	3.3
(2) Street, midday				
$R^2 = 0.61$	walkway	3.12	0.430	7.3
$N = 261$	office	0.0575	0.0076	7.6
$S_e = 31.6$	retail	0.12	0.039	3.1
	restaurant	0.74	0.277	2.7
(3) Avenues, evening				
$R^2 = 0.23$	office	0.0622	0.0086	7.2
$N = 228$	retail	0.20	0.062	3.3
$S_e = 39.0$	D	−1.978	0.6212	3.2
(4) Streets, evening				
$R^2 = 0.52$	walkway	3.17	0.567	5.5
$N = 179$	office	0.0388	0.0102	3.8
$S_e = 34.6$	$1/D^3$	46.121	9.9240	4.6

Source: Regional Plan Association
R^2 = correlation coefficient squared.
N = number of observations (block sectors).
S_e = standard error.

Next, one should mention some purely idiosyncratic factors, which could not possibly be accounted for by the equations. The number of pedestrians window shopping in the diamond district on 47th Street is substantially underestimated, as is the number of those loitering in front of peep shows on 42nd Street between Seventh and Eighth avenues. People congregating in front of the New York Public Library are likewise underestimated. Even leaving aside these extremes, it is clear that the intensity of use varies inevitably within particular categories of buildings—no two retail stores are exactly alike. Besides, residential and other uses that could not be registered by the statistical technique employed also generate pedestrians.

Last but not least, both difficulties of definition and measurement inaccuracies (such as the timing of the helicopter flights) contribute their share to the unexplained variation. As previously discussed, the aerial photographs, taken between 1:30 and 2:00 P.M., underestimate the true midday peak; the degree of the underestimate varies by location (see Figure 2.3). The evening peak is captured more accurately, but there is a considerable difference in flow between the first and the second 15-min time period during that count, which also contributes to the unexplained variation.

Analysis of the standard error is useful not only with respect to the equations as a whole but also in reference to particular coefficients. The coefficients of the equations in Table 2.18 are listed in column 3 of Table 2.19 (without rounding), and their respective standard errors are listed in column 4. Thus, in the case of avenues at midday, we can estimate that the addition of 1 million sq ft (92,900 m^2) of office space on a block will produce 48.5 additional pedestrians, with a 95 percent confidence that the actual value will be between 30.7 and 63.3 pedestrians. Similarly, the addition of a quarter-million sq ft (23,225 m^2) of retail space on an avenue block sector will add 88 ± 15 pedestrians. It is evident that the standard errors of the individual coefficients are relatively much smaller than those of the equations as a whole.

The t-value, given in column 5 of Table 2.19, represents the ratio of the coefficient to its standard error; the greater this number, the greater the relative significance of the variable. Walkway space in all equations, retail space on avenues, and office space at midday are the variables that have the highest t-values, or the smallest standard error.

Finally, one last technicality. The validity of a correlation equation can be undermined if the independent variables are related to each other. Tests revealed that, in most cases, the relationships among the five independent variables are sufficiently weak so as not to affect the outcome of the analysis. For example, no significant correlation was found among the three building uses; in fact, the amount of retail and restaurant use has a slight tendency to be negatively related to the amount of office space—an indication of office buildings displacing small establishments. Proximity to transit entrances is completely unrelated to the amount of building floor space—a sad comment on past planning of Midtown Manhattan. The amount of walkway space is unrelated to the floor space in retail and restaurant establishments but shows some positive correlation with office space, due, in part, to the new plazas. In the evening avenue equation, the relationship of walkway space to floor space in offices is sufficiently strong (because counts of block sectors with deep shadows were not available) so as to delete walkway space as an independent variable.

The Cost of Walking

The demand for travel by any mode is strongly influenced by the cost of travel. That cost typically includes expenditures of money as well as of time and exposure to various kinds of inconvenience. Generally, people try to minimize the sum total of these costs. In some cases part of the cost may be ameliorated by the pleasure of the trip: some people may enjoy driving, or reading on the train. An analysis of how people perceive and trade off these various cost components is essential for understanding the reasons for travel demand by various modes and for an assessment of investment decisions in transportation. Moreover, if some forms of travel impose costs on society or on the environment which are not paid for by the traveler, then achieving shifts in behavior towards less-damaging forms of travel likewise requires an understanding of the value structure that underlies existing behavior.

Walking is no exception to these general principles. While its direct cost in money is only the cost of wear on shoes, its cost in time for any but short trips is high and so is its cost in inconvenience, primarily in physical effort. These high costs are ameliorated somewhat by the intrinsic rewards of walking, such as physical fitness, esthetic pleasure, opportunities for socializing, and a minimal impact on the environment. But in pointing these out, one should not lose sight of the fact that, on balance, the cost of walking remains very high, which is why journeys on foot are shorter than those by any other mode.

The thrust of this book is to reduce some unnecessary costs of walking—specifically, the aggravation of walking in downtown congestion and the unpleasantness of walking in a drab environment. In this section we will also touch briefly on two aspects of inconvenience pertaining to weather conditions which can be ameliorated by physical design. But the two major components of the cost of walking—time and physical effort—are rather irreducible, and knowing how they fit into people's value structure will help to maintain a sense of realism in design.

To understand the values of people who are engaged in travel and the full cost of a particular trip to the traveler, it is useful to bring the various components of cost to a common denominator, such as dollars. Money equivalents of time and inconvenience can be established by observing how much people are willing to pay when they have a choice to avoid a certain time loss or a certain amount of physical effort. A considerable amount of research has been done on the value of time in travel but without much attention to the time spent walking.

There is wide agreement that time spent traveling while at work can be valued at the prevailing hourly wage or salary rate. It has also been suggested, on theoretical as well as empirical grounds, that time spent traveling during nonworking hours is valued at a lower rate. Exactly how much lower has been the subject of studies that so far have failed to produce a consistent picture. For example, economists

from the British Ministry of Transport have concluded that 25 percent of the hourly income is a reasonable value for in-vehicle time spent by commuters; they stress, though, that values for walking and waiting time may be more than twice as high.[19] A widely cited American study for the Bureau of Public Roads,[20] based on time savings from the use of toll roads instead of free roads, has come up with an average value of in-vehicle time which represents about 50 percent of the respondents' hourly income, or about 5 cents per minute saved, in 1970 prices. Several other American researchers have arrived at values in the 3- to 5-cent range, but the higher values have been subject to criticism.[21] A major study of trans-Hudson commuter behavior, based on 1964 data (when the price index was about 22 percent below the 1970 level), indicated that peak-hour riders to the Manhattan Central Business District valued their time at about 7.3 cents per minute in an auto, 4.4 cents per minute by rail, and 4.0 cents per minute by bus. Off peak, the value of time in an auto rose to 18.3 cents per minute but dropped below peak-hour levels for bus and rail riders. The inconvenience of changing trains was found to be equivalent to a 3.9 min time loss during peak hours.[22] However, the trans-Hudson study did not distinguish the value of time by income level nor did it distinguish between in-vehicle time and time spent waiting or walking. We cannot pretend to give a full view of the complex topography of these values here but will merely show a few suggestive examples, focusing on the value of avoiding walking and peripherally on the value of time savings due to the avoidance of walking.

Prices Paid to Avoid Walking

Parking facilities in Manhattan represent one situation in which the choice of walking less is available at a price. The common sense supposition that lower-priced parking, located at the edge of the Central Business District, also involves longer walking distances is confirmed by the interviews at the four parking lots cited previously in this chapter. Table 2.20 shows the average distances walked from these parking lots by all-day parkers, mostly commuters, related to the daily parking fee. The fees paid by short-term parkers could not be determined. Hence, the value that short-term parkers placed on avoiding walking is unknown.

Based on figures in Table 2.20, one can calculate that long-term parkers at the higher-priced lots paid an average of $1.30 for the convenience of not walking an extra 1,000 ft (0.3 km) one way, or, since every walk involves a return trip, 65 cents for every extra 1,000 ft of walking both ways, in 1969 prices. At an average speed of 250 ft (76 m) per minute, which includes delays due to traffic signals, walking that distance takes 4 min. Given the vehicular congestion in Midtown Manhattan, with peak-hour speeds in the 6- to 9-mph range (9.6 to 14.4 km/h), and given that car-handling delays at the more centrally located parking facilities are typically greater than on the periphery, the net time saved due to not walking

might be as little as 2 to 2.7 min for every 1,000 ft (0.3 km), suggesting a value of time in the range of 24 to 32 cents per minute. This is so far above the other values of time shown that avoiding the effort of walking, rather than saving time, clearly emerges as the dominant motive for paying high parking fees. One might add that a parking study in Los Angeles found mean values of walking to parking lots in the range of 36 to 48 cents per 1,000 ft, which is not too far from the 65 cents shown above.[23]

Nevertheless, auto commuters to Manhattan are a very atypical group. They represent only about 10 percent of all peak-hour arrivals, and their income is about 40 percent above the level of subway riders, who form the majority of pedestrians in Midtown Manhattan. Unfortunately, the kind of direct data available for parkers could not be obtained for subway riders or other users of public transit. Therefore, we must resort to evidence that is more circumstantial. This consists of the trade off between walking and paying a fare in two situations: to the Port Authority Bus Terminal in Midtown Manhattan and to subway stations in three low-income neighborhoods in New York City outside Manhattan.

Data on the modes of travel which passengers use to get to the bus terminal from various parts of the City are available from periodic surveys conducted by the Port Authority of New York and New Jersey. The surveys also indicate the area, or "zone," where each passenger

starts his trip, so that an approximate distance can be assigned to the group of travelers from each zone. In Table 2.21 the proportion of travelers arriving at the bus terminal on foot from each of eighteen areas is shown, along with the estimated distance to each zone. The data include all bus passengers and cover a 17-hr weekday period in 1972.[24] A curve of averages is hand fitted to the eighteen points, in Figure 2.13.

The curve shows that at distances greater than 16,000 ft (roughly 3 mi or 5 km) virtually none of the passengers walk. Almost all take some mechanical means of travel—subway, bus, taxi, or auto. At a distance of roughly 8,000 ft (2.4 km) the proportion of walkers rises to about 8 percent. However, these long-distance walkers represent only 4 percent of all those who walk to the Bus Terminal. At a distance of about 4,500 ft (1.4 km) the proportion of walkers is 50 percent. At distances of less than 1,000 ft (0.3 km) almost everybody walks. Since the cheapest alternative to walking is a bus or subway ride to the bus terminal, which at the time of the survey cost 35 cents, we can conclude that the riders valued not walking at a price of anywhere from 2 cents to 35 cents for every 1,000 ft (0.3 km).

To look at the trade offs in greater detail, we single out the Grand Central area. Its distance to the bus terminal can be assumed to be 5,740 ft (1.7 km). By taking the subway, one can cut 3,800 ft (1.2 km) off that distance, by taking the crosstown bus, 4,300 ft (1.3 km). Some 14 percent of the riders did the former and some 36 percent the latter, paying, in effect, 9 cents and 8 cents, respectively, for the ability not to walk 1,000 ft (0.3 km). However, the net time gain was barely 5 min by subway and 4 min by bus, indicating that half the travelers were willing to pay between 7 and 9 cents per net minute saved. Again, avoiding the effort of walking, not pure time saving, seems to have been the dominant consideration.

While the 45 percent of the travelers who did walk on this route clearly considered both prices excessive, there was 5 percent who chose to take a cab. For $1.40 (including tip) they escaped almost all walking and saved about 10 min. To them, riding alone and not walking were worth 24 cents for every 1,000 ft (0.3 km), and the time saved was worth 14 cents per minute. One might add that after a citywide, 47 percent taxi fare increase in New York in 1971, taxi trips of three-fifths of a mile (1.0 km) declined by 62 percent, trips of four-fifths of a mile (1.3 km) by 22 percent, indicating that to these percentages of taxi riders, paying an additional 25 to 30 cents per 1,000 ft (0.3 km) of walking avoided appeared excessive.[25]

Taxi riders in Manhattan generally belong to the upper-income groups; it is instructive to see what happens at the lower end of the income range. Data on the split between walking and taking a bus to subway stations for workers traveling to work from three low-income neighborhoods of New York City outside Man-

hattan are available from an earlier study by Regional Plan Association.[26] They are presented in Figure 2.14 and Table 2.21 in a form similar to the Port Authority data. Each data point represents a residential area of relatively few blocks, so that the average distances in this case are more accurate than the distances from zone centers in the bus terminal example. However the samples from some areas are very small, and in this sense the data on low-income groups are less reliable. Just as in Figure 2.13, there is a scatter of points around the line of averages, which reflects the varying convenience of transit in different areas.

The curve in Figure 2.14 shows, once more, that everybody walks for distances of less than 1,000 ft (0.3 km), but here the similarity with the bus terminal curve ends. The curve in Figure 2.14 falls off more sharply: the precentage walking drops to 50 at a distance of about 2,500 ft (0.76 km) and to about 10 at a distance of 5,000 ft (1.5 km). Observations for substantially longer distances were not available. The break-even point between walking and taking the bus suggests that half the low-income workers, who paid 30 cents for the bus at the time of the survey in 1971, valued not walking at 12 cents or more for every 1,000 ft (0.3 km), a figure higher than that for users of the bus terminal. Moreover, considering the facts that at prevailing speeds it takes a bus at least 3.5 min. to traverse 2,500 ft (0.76 km) and that walking to and waiting for the bus may take close to 5 min., the time saved

by not walking 2,500 ft to a subway stop is minimal, and the implicit value of time, extremely high, is close to that of the taxi rider. One may add that the wages of the workers in question averaged about $3.30 an hour.

Based on our knowlege of pedestrian trip length in general, the choice of walking versus taking a bus shown for the low-income areas is much more typical than the highly unusual pattern of long walking trips to the Port Authority Bus Terminal. The pattern also raises the question of how meaningful it is to measure the reluctance to walk in terms of time savings. For one can readily visualize situations in which people prefer to lose time rather than to walk. Such a condition, in fact, prevails at escalators that parallel fairly high stairways, as we will show in Chapter 3. With respect to the value placed on avoiding walking distance, we can conclude that 10 cents per 1,000 ft (0.3 km), in 1970-72 prices, is a conservative figure, which may go to three times that level for transit riders and six times that level for auto users.

Environmental Influences
An important factor in the cost of walking is weather. The data presented so far refer to fairly good weather conditions. The weather, of course, is not always good: if we accept, for the sake of simplicity, temperatures below freezing as being "too cold" and temperatures of 80° F (+ 27° C) or higher as being "too hot," then, according to Table 2.22, Manhattan has uncomfortable temperatures for 22 percent of the daytime hours of the year.

Table 2.20
Average Walking Distance at 4 Manhattan
Parking Lots Related to Parking Fee, 1969

Average walking distance of all-day parkers (one-way)		
ft	(m)	All-day parking fee
703	(214)	$4.25
740	(226)	3.50
2,022	(616)	2.25
2,540	(774)	1.50

Source: Regional Plan Association.

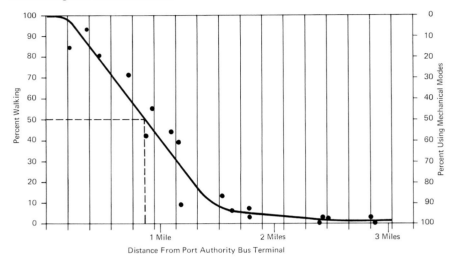

Figure 2.13
The trade off between walking and
riding to the Port Authority Bus
Terminal

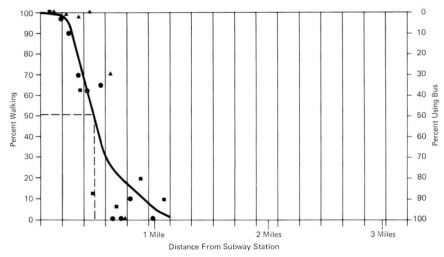

Figure 2.14
The trade off between walking and
riding to subway stops in low-income
areas

■ South Jamaica

● East Tremont

▲ Bushwick

Table 2.21.
Choice of Walking by Distance

Area	Estimated distance		% of all travelers walking
	ft	m	
To Port Authority Bus Terminal			
38th-42nd St. West	1,040	317	83.8
34th-38th St. West	1,850	564	92.7
42nd-50th St. West	2,420	738	79.9
25th-34th St. West	3,770	1,149	70.9
50th-29th St. West	4,570	1,393	42.4
34th-42nd St. East	4,850	1,478	54.8
Grand Central Area	5,740	1,750	44.5
23rd-34th St. East	6,080	1,853	39.1
14th-25th St. West	6,150	1,875	8.4
50th-59th St. East	8,110	2,472	13.7
North of 59th St. West	8,600	2,621	5.7
14th-23rd St. East	9,300	2,835	7.4
Greenwich Village	9,400	2,865	3.3
Canal-Houston West	12,600	3,840	0.3
North of 59th St. East	12,800	3,901	3.6
East Village	13,000	3,962	2.1
Lower East Side	15,000	4,572	3.2
Chambers-Canal West	15,200	4,633	0.3
To Subway Stops in Three Low-Income Areas			
Jamaica	480	146	100.0
Bushwick	620	189	100.0
East Tremont	950	290	96.8
Bushwick	1,250	381	98.5
East Tremont	1,300	396	89.6
Bushwick	1,700	518	97.0
East Tremont	1,700	518	68.2
South Jamaica	1,750	533	64.3
Bushwick	2,250	686	100.0
East Tremont	2,250	686	61.1
South Jamaica	2,370	722	11.1
East Tremont	2,750	838	63.7
Bushwick	3,120	951	70.0
East Tremont	3,370	1,027	0.0
South Jamaica	3,480	1,061	5.6
East Tremont	3,800	1,158	0.0
Bushwick	3,850	1,173	0.0
East Tremont	3,900	1,183	9.0
South Jamaica	4,650	1,417	18.7
East Tremont	5,120	1,561	0.0
South Jamaica	5,740	1,750	9.0

Source: The Port Authority of New York and New Jersey and Regional Plan Association.

Table 2.22.
Daytime Weather Conditions in Manhattan

| | % of hrs between 8:00 A.M. and 8:00 P.M. during which | | |
	Temperature is 80° F (27°C) or more	Temperature is 32° F (0°C) or less	Precipitation occurs
January	0.0	34.3	14
February	0.0	39.2	13
March	0.0	6.1	12
April	1.2	0.0	14
May	7.4	0.0	11
June	39.6	0.0	7
July	43.7	0.0	10
August	45.0	0.0	8
September	14.0	0.0	10
October	1.8	0.0	7
November	0.0	2.7	15
December	0.0	24.9	15
Year	12.7	9.3	11.3

Source: Calculated from U. S. Environmental Science Services Administration, *Local Climatological Data*, 1965-1969.

Typical good-weather occupancies of Paley Park (left) and Greenacre Park (above) in Midtown Manhattan. Available space in each case is on the order of 30 sq ft (2.8 m^2) per person. As will be pointed out subsequently, sitting requires much less space than walking. Some 74 percent of the Paley Park occupants, and 67 percent of the Greenacre Park occupants walked more than 500 ft (152.4 m) to get to the park. Photographs by Paul Cardell.

The temperature of enclosed non-air-conditioned pedestrian spaces, such as the subways, is uncomfortably high for a much longer time than that.

Given the present lack of choice of temperature conditions, the effect of temperature on walking behavior is rather subtle, and no effort was made to measure it in any general way. However, a series of counts was made over a two-year period at Greenacre Park on East 51st Street, with the intent of determining the effect of temperature on park attendance and, indirectly, on pleasure walking in general. The observations, made at lunchtime, fail to show any neat statistical pattern but do seem to fall roughly into three distinct groups. At temperatures below the freezing point lunchtime accumulation of visitors did not exceed 10 people, with the majority seated under a protective canopy equipped with radiant heat. At temperatures between 32° and 55° F (0° and 13° C) lunchtime accumulation was in the range of 10 to 75 people. At temperatures between 55° and 80° F (13 and 27° C) accumulations ranged from 40 to as many as 260 people on one day in spring. The latter number corresponds to about 24 sq ft (2 m²) per visitor, above comfortable seating capacity of the tiny park. It represents about 13 times greater density than the the average density encountered in plazas, as Table 4.19 will show later. This can be attributed to the availability of seating in the park, the presence of a snack bar, and the exquisite landscape design of the space. Another interesting aspect of these counts

is the seeming importance of a temperature around 55° F (13° C) as a threshold above which a significant amount of pleasure walking begins to occur.

The existence of this threshold is confirmed by studies by Jan Gehl[27] of the Stroget, the pedestrianized main shopping street of Copenhagen. These studies emphasize the difference between the amounts of necessary walking and pleasure activities which is evident with changing temperature. As temperature rises from –8° C in January to +20° C in July, the pedestrian flow doubles. However, declining average speed of the walking stream (from 318 ft [98.8 m] per minute to 232 [70.6 m] per minute) and an influx of standing and sitting pedestrians cause the number (and hence the density) of people present in the Stroget to increase fourfold.

While outdoor temperature has a strong effect on seasonal variation, particularly where voluntary pedestrian activities are important, on a day-to-day basis a more disruptive effect is caused by precipitation. One of the counts reflected in Table 2.9 earlier was also repeated during a period of heavy rain from 5:00 P.M. to 6:00 P.M. Depending on the intensity of the rain, there was a reduction in pedestrian flow on the sidewalk of 42nd Street during particular 15-min intervals that ranged from 24 to 55 percent. Most of it appears to be due to diversion to public transit: thus, the 42nd Street Shuttle and the Flushing Line in Manhattan as well as their underground access corridors are notoriously overcrowded in

rainy weather by people who prefer to walk in good weather. Some of the reduction in sidewalk flow is also due to trips foregone, postponed, or reduced in length.

An effort was made to measure the effect of rain on walking distance. Limited data collected at one of the office buildings where interviews took place suggest that during the period of 9:30 A.M. to 12:00 noon, when 0.57 in. (1.45 cm) of rain fell, average walking distance of people entering and leaving the office building was reduced by 25 percent. This can be interpreted to mean that on walk-only trips with optional destinations a closer destination was chosen, as long as it minimized the walking distance in the rain. No reduction in walking distance was observed during the morning rush hour. These observations are roughly in scale with observations in Seattle, which report a 5 percent reduction in pedestrian flow with more than 0.05 in. (0.13 cm) of precipitation. This reduction represents the combined effect of shorter walking distances and fewer walking trips. Counts made in New York during the thirties indicated that rainy weather reduced pedestrian traffic volume in strictly shopping areas by as much as 60 percent and in local neighborhood areas, by 40 percent.[28]

Table 2.22 suggests that not to design for rainy days in Manhattan means to design a transportation system that is only 88.7 percent reliable. By all norms accepted in transportation practice, this is a poor standard of reliability. While the standards of comfort for 11.3 percent of the time can be lower than those for the remaining 88.7 percent of the time, relatively smooth accommodation of pedestrian travel demand during the inclement weather should be assured either by providing sheltered walks of adequate capacity in the main travel corridors or by designing public transportation facilities and their access walks with sufficient ability to handle the overflow in bad weather.

While the effects of rain clearly argue for more sheltered space, more interesting, in many ways, from the viewpoint of design is the positive influence of a pleasantly designed environment and the degree to which it can encourage walking.

Equations (1) and (2) and (4) cited earlier in this chapter clearly show that walkway space, whether in sidewalks or in plazas on private property, in and of itself attracts pedestrians. This is somewhat akin to what is known in traffic engineering as "induced" travel, which occurs in response to improvements in transportation. In the case of pedestrian movement, given two Manhattan streets with the same building floor space, the one with wider sidewalks has more pedestrians: 1,000 sq ft (93 m^2) more sidewalk results in an average of 3 more pedestrians at any moment during peak periods. That extra walkway space actually induces more people outdoors was illustrated by the experimental closing of Madison Avenue to vehicles in 1971. Even during the second week, when the novelty had largely worn off, the number of persons on the avenue was two times larger than normal without any drop in pedestrians on Fifth Avenue. The increase represented up to 13 pedestrians per 1,000 extra sq ft (93 m^2) of space.

The earlier comparison of the attractiveness of Greenacre Park and average plazas suggests that a large "induced" pedestrian use of a Madison Avenue mall could be quite permanent, given proper landscaping and amenities. The induced use is accounted for by a greater number of people sitting and standing, by a greater frequency of walking trips, and by greater trip length. Thus, Olof Lovemark claims that pleasant pedestrian environments encourage an up to 30 percent greater walking distance.[29] Unfortunately, a closer investigation of this topic had to remain outside the scope of this study. More light on it will be shed by the findings of the "Street Life" study by William H. Whyte,[30] which is striving to define some of the design features that attract pedestrians to relax outdoors. Just as walkway space is important for walkers, sitting space for sitters is important among these features.

1. For an effort to extract walk links of trips by mechanical modes from the data files of a traditional home-interview survey, see William F. Fort, *Walk Time from Vehicle to Final Destination,* Highway Research Board, Highway Research Record no. 439 (Washington D.C., 1973).

2. Roger L. Creighton, *Report on the Walking Trip Survey,* Chicago Area Transportation Study, (Chicago, 1961).

3. David Emmons, *The Pedestrian Count,* American Society of Planning Officials, ASPO Planning Advisory Service Report 199 (Chicago, 1965). See also Vincent J. Hubin, "Pedestrian Traffic Counts," *The Appraisal Journal,* American Institute of Real Estate Appraisers, July 1953.

4. Herbert S. Levinson, *Modeling Pedestrian Travel* (New Haven: Wilbur Smith and Associates, 1971. The report, dealing primarily with downtown Seattle, was done as a part of the 1968 Center City Transportation Project, sponsored by the U.S. Department of Transportation, Urban Mass Transportation Administration. Other cities covered by the Project studies included Atlanta, Dallas, Denver, and Pittsburgh.

5. U.S. Bureau of Public Roads, *Parking Guide for Cities* (Washington: United States Government Printing Office, 1956), see esp. pp. 28-29 and 116-120.

6. The assumptions lean to a great extent, on auto occupance figures apparent from the U.S. Census Journey to Work data as well as on Federal Highway Administration, *Nationwide Personal Transportation Study;* Report no. 1, *Automobile Occupancy* (Washington, D.C., 1972) and "Trip Generation Study . . . ," *Traffic Engineering,* March 1974, p. 28.

7. For a more systematic exposition, see Tri-State Regional Planning Commission, *Residential Trip Generation,* Interim Technical Report 4234-4424 (New York, 1971).

8. Ronald M. Cameron, *Mechanical Measurement of Pedestrian Volumes* (Seattle: City Traffic and Transportation Division, 1973), p. 15.

9. "Pedestrian Traffic Patterns in Salt Lake City," *Utah Economic and Business Review,* September 1962, p. 4.

10. Cameron, *Mechanical Measurement of Pedestrian Volumes,* p. 14.

11. Claus Heidemann, "Ueber Gesetzmaessigkeiten des Fussgaengerverkehrs einer Einkaufsstrasse" (Concerning Regularities of Pedestrian Traffic on a Shopping Street), in *Strassenverkehrstechnik* (Heft, 1967),pp. 55-60. This is a statistically rigorous study of weekly and seasonal variation, based on regular counts in the course of three years on a shopping street in downtown Braunschweig.

12. Littleton C. MacDorman, "An Investigation of Pedestrian Travel Speeds in the Business District of Washington, D.C." (Ph.D dissertation, School of Engineering and Architecture, Catholic University, 1967).

13. Morton Schneider, "Access and Land Development," *Urban Development Models* (Washington: Highway Research Board, 1968), p. 167.

14. U.S. Bureau of Public Roads, *Parking Guide for Cities,* p. 119.

15. Herbert Levinson, *Modelling Pedestrian Travel,* Wilbur Smith and Associates (New Haven, 1971).

16. Robert Morris and S. E. Zisman, "The Pedestrian, Downtown, and the Planner," *Journal of the American Institute of Planners* 28, no. 3 (August 1962), pp. 152-158.

17. Stephen G. Petersen, *Walking Distances to Bus Stops in the Residential Areas of Washington, D.C.,* Alan M. Voorhees & Associates publication reprint (Washington, D.C., 1968).

18. City of Chicago, Pedestrian Mall Task Force, Subcommittee on Pedestrian Movements. *Chicago Loop Pedestrian Movements Study.* 2 vols. (December 1973).

19. For an excellent review of studies on the value of time, see A. S. Harrison and D. A. Quarmby, *Theoretical and Practical Research on an Estimation of Time-Saving;* Report of the Sixth Round Table on Transport Economics, European Conference of Ministers of Transports (Paris, 1969). See also: *Behavioral Demand Modeling and Valuation of Travel Time.* Special Report 149, Transportation Research Board, Washington, D.C. 1974.

20. Stanford Research Institute, *The Value of Time for Passenger Cars: An Experimental Study of Commuters' Values,* Prepared for the Bureau of Public Roads, U.S. Department of Transportation (Menlo Park, Calif., 1967).

21. Creighton, Hamburg Inc., *Alternative Multimodal Passenger Transportation Systems,* National Cooperative Highway Research Program Report 146 (Washington, D.C., 1973), pp. 37-40.

22. Eugene J. Lessieu, and Jeffrey M. Zupan, *River Crossing Travel Choice: The Hudson River Experience,* Highway Research Board, Highway Research Record, no. 322 (Washington, D.C., 1970).

23. Terrence W. Austin, *Allocation of Parking Demand in a CBD,* Highway Research Board, Highway Research Record no. 444, (Washington, D.C., 1973).

24. The Port Authority of New York and New Jersey, unpublished printouts of the 1972 PABT survey, indicating mode of arrival of short-haul, medium-haul, and long-haul passengers.

25. James M. Freiband, "Pedestrian Travel as a Function of Taxi Fare Rates" (paper for New York University Graduate School of Public Administration, 1971).

26. Regional Plan Association, *Transportation and Economic Opportunity,* A report to the Transportation Administration of the City of New York. (New York, 1973), p. 182.

27. Jan Gehl, "Mennesker til fods" [People on Foot] , *Arkitekten,* no. 20 (Copenhagen, 1968).

28. The Real Estate Board of New York, *The Seventh Annual Pedestrian Traffic Survey of Retail Store Locations in Manhattan* (New York, 1941).

29. Olof Lovemark, "New Approaches to Pedestrian Problems," *Journal of Transport Economics and Policy* (London, January 1972).

30. William H. Whyte, "Street Life Project" (forthcoming). For a popular summary, see "The Best Street Life in the World," *New York Magazine,* July 15, 1974.

Chapter 3

Pedestrian Space Requirements

The confusion that has existed concerning the meaning of many terms used in traffic engineering practice has contributed . . . to the wide differences of opinion regarding the capacity of various . . . facilities. In fact, the term which is perhaps most widely misunderstood . . . is the word "capacity" itself.

Transportation Research Board, *Highway Capacity Manual*

Space Related to Speed and Flow

Having dealt with the magnitude and the characteristics of pedestrian travel demand, we can now look at the capacity of pedestrian facilities. *Capacity* usually means the maximum possible ability to accommodate a flow. However, more often than not in traffic design, operation at maximum capacity is undesirable. For example, in highway design, flow at or near maximum capacity is unstable and can easily grind to a standstill. So as not to establish imminent congestion as a design standard, *levels of service* have been defined to characterize the quality of traffic flow at various fractions of maximum capacity. Generally, the lower this fraction, the less interference each participant in the traffic stream experiences from others and the more room there is for him to select his own path and his own speed. Similar relationships are characteristic of pedestrian movement as well. Thus, several pedestrian levels of service can be objectively defined by indicating what kind of behavior is possible—or impossible—at various degrees of spaciousness or crowding. The selection of any particular level of service as a desirable design standard is, of course, to a large extent, a matter of judgment and policy.

Standing Room

Average-size human bodies in a vertical position, pressed together with virtually no ability to move, can occupy as little as 1.0 sq ft (0.09 m^2) per woman and 1.5 sq ft (0.14 m^2) per man. But, to avoid touching each other, standees require about 2.4 to 2.8 sq ft (0.22 to 0.26 m^2) per person and prefer a "body buffer zone" of 4 to 9 sq ft (0.27 to 0.84 m^2) to avoid emotional discomfort in the presence of strangers. Emotional considerations aside, there are purely practical ones. For example, a woman's opened umbrella, with a 30 in. diameter, covers an area of 4.9 sq ft (0.46 m^2). A man's opened umbrella, with a 43 in. diameter, covers an area of 10.1 sq ft (0.94 m^2). In establishing the dimensions of outdoor spaces for pedestrians, practical considerations of this type can be of controlling importance if we do not want circulation to break down when it rains.

The point that psychologists make about human space requirements is essentially twofold. First, people need enough room to perform whatever physical tasks they are doing without interference from objects or from other people. Thus, bumping into an object, or making a violent maneuver to avoid it, is an indication of crowding. Second, and on a more subtle level, people, if they have a choice, adopt different distances from other people depending on the intensity with which they are communicating with them. This interpersonal distance varies from culture to culture, depending on social conventions and taboos, and also from individual to individual, depending on psychological characteristics. On the whole, however, if one's personal sphere reserved for close acquaintances is invaded by a stranger, stress sets in and various defensive postures are adopted. A classification of interpersonal distances based on the North American experience and suggested by anthropologist Edward T. Hall[1] is shown in Table 3.1.

At an intimate distance, parts of two bodies can touch each other; one is aware of odors and even of thermal radiation. At a personal distance, one has to reach out to touch another person; odor becomes less important and the visual perception of the other person's face is most clear. At a social distance, one is beyond an "arm's length" of the other person, that is, beyond the limit of possible physical contact. This is a distance commonly used by people who work together. The full figure of the other person can be brought into view at the far end of the social distance. At a public distance, recognition of an acquaintance is no longer mandatory, evasive action can be taken in case of danger, and speech patterns become more formal and impersonal.

If it were of overriding importance to express the level of personal involvement in the allocation of space, one would dimension circulation facilities in such a way that those who want to be intimate have a chance to be intimate while those who have no business being together have adequate room to stay a public distance apart. The latter, of course, is not always possible, because of the economics of such things as elevators and subway cars, nor is it, perhaps, always desirable. Yet, even if considerable compression of the public distance is unavoidable in some cases, there is still plenty of opportunity to improve space standards.

There are many situations in which the space available around standing pedestrians is of importance. These include queuing areas before ticket windows, elevator lobbies, subway platforms, and waiting areas at street crosswalks. In a recent study of pedestrian design standards, John J. Fruin described the characteristics of five levels of pedestrian density in these stationary situations,[2] which are shown in Table 3.2.

People waiting in queues and having unrestricted space available will select, according to Fruin, an area of roughly 8 to 9 sq ft (0.74 to 0.84 m^2) for themselves, regardless of whether or not they have baggage. People converging upon an escalator will compress themselves more tightly, with 3 to 5 sq ft (0.28 to 0.46 m^2) per person, while people riding elevators will tolerate as little as 2 sq ft (0.19 m^2) per person for short periods of time. Other studies have found about 5 sq ft (0.46 m^2) per person as the average space in groups waiting for a traffic light, while space allocations at mass rallies have been found to range from about 6 sq ft (0.56 m^2) in dense crowds to 10 sq ft (0.93 m^2) in loose crowds.

The selection of an appropriate service level has to be related to the function of each particular facility. Train platforms, for example, should allow enough room for circulation between waiting standees. Reservoir spaces, or standing room for movie theater queues, to the extent that they do not conflict with sidewalk flow, can get by with less room, perhaps 8 sq ft

(0.74 m^2) per person, and still less room is required for short-term queues at signalized intersections. But if avoidance of physical contact between strangers is a desirable goal, space allocations must not be allowed to drift below 3 to 4 sq ft (say 0.35 m^2) per person. Thus, to abolish inhuman subway crowding, which we depicted in Chapter 1, the New York City Planning Commission in 1965 proposed 3.2 sq ft (0.3 m^2) per standee as a goal of rapid transit expansion.[3] In 1975, Regional Plan Association recommended 5 sq ft (0.46 m^2) of net in-vehicle space per passenger, seated or standing. Close to 2 sq ft (0.2 m^2) per person may be permissible in elevators; with this amount of space, standees are touching each other, but are not physically pressed together.

Walking Room
Human locomotion, quite naturally, requires more room than standing, to allow for the physical act of pacing, for a buffer zone large enough to anticipate potential collisions, and for taking evasive action. For example, because of the angle the human eye encompasses, another person has to be at least 7 ft (2.1 m) away to be seen from head to toe so that his speed and direction of movement can be accurately judged. Pedestrians have been found to take evasive action anywhere from 2 to 17 ft (0.6 to 5.2 m) ahead of a stationary or moving obstacle. The longer the distance, the less violent the maneuver necessary, and the less likely the possibility of a collision. The spacing between pedestrians, just as the spacing between vehicles, is re-

Table 3.1.
Interpersonal Distances

	Distance, face to face		Area required per person	
	ft	(m)	sq ft	(m²)
Intimate	Less than 1.5	(0.5)	Less than 3 sq ft	(0.3)
Personal	1.5-4	(0.5-1.2)	3-13 sq ft	(0.3-1.2)
Social	4-12	(1.2-3.7)	13-110 sq ft	(1.2-10)
Public	More than 12	(3.7)	More than 110 sq ft	(10)

Source: Hall, *The Hidden Dimension.*

Table 3.2
Levels of Service for Standing Pedestrians

	Spacing		Area per person		
Quality	ft	(m)	sq ft	(m²)	Description
UNIMPEDED	over 4	(1.2)	over 13	(1.2)	Circulation between pedestrians is possible without disturbing them.
IMPEDED	3.5-4.0	(1.0-1.2)	10-13	(0.9-1.2)	Circulation between standing pedestrians is somewhat restricted.
	3.0-3.5		7-10	(0.7-0.9)	Comfortable for standing without being affected by others, but walking between standees possible only by disturbing them ("excuse me").
CONSTRAINED	2-3	(0.6-0.9)	3-7	(0.3-0.7)	Standing pedestrians do not touch each other but are uncomfortably close together, circulation through the group is severely restricted, and forward movement is possible only as a group.
CONGESTED	Under 2	(0.6)	2-3	(0.2-0.3)	Contact with others is unavoidable, circulation through the group is impossible.
JAMMED	0		Under 2	(0.2)	Standees are pressed together, no movement is possible.

Source: Fruin, *Designing for Pedestrians*

lated to the speed at which they are moving: the faster the movement, the more space is required. The relationships among space requirements (or density), speed of movement, and rates of flow in pedestrian streams have been studied by a number of investigators. Among the more recent ones are Detlef Oeding, S. J. Older, Francis P. D. Navin and R. J. Wheeler, and Fruin.[4] Their findings are generally consistent with those of several other researchers.[5]

The traditional equation describing traffic flow[6] is

(5) flow = speed × density,

where flow represents the number of moving objects crossing a unit of channel width in a unit of time, speed indicates how many units of distance they pass in a unit of time, and density represents their number per unit of channel area. When the units by which channel area is measured are relatively small, such as square feet or square meters, density becomes an inconvenient concept, forcing us (in this case) to deal with fractions of pedestrians. Moreover, a density scale shrinks rapidly precisely in that range in which we are most interested—where varying degrees of comfort prevail, with less than 0.1 pedestrians per sq ft (less than 1.0 per sq m). Therefore, the reciprocal of density, or *available space per pedestrian,* is a more useful unit for trying to arrive at comfort criteria. With that in mind, and adding dimensions, we can rewrite equation (5) as follows:

(6) space $\dfrac{\text{ft}^2}{\text{ped}} = \dfrac{\text{speed (ft/min)}}{\text{flow (ped/min/ft)}}$.

First we will look at the relationship between speed and flow. It can be approximated by a parabolic curve, familiar from motor vehicle flow analysis. Top speed can be reached when there is no one else on the road or on the walkway, that is, when flow is near zero, as in the upper-left-hand corner of Figure 3.1. As flow increases (moving toward the right across the diagram), each participant in the traffic stream is more and more affected by others and speed declines. At a certain point, typically about half the average top speed, flow is at a maximum (the apex of the parabola), often described as "capacity." As speed drops below this point, flow can no longer increase and begins to decline, as well. Finally, as speed reaches zero, flow is, quite naturally, also zero, as in the left-hand corner of Figure 3.1. The diagram shows a family of five speed-flow curves, abstracted from measurements by the investigators cited previously and converted to common units.

The first curve, based on the work of Older in England, represents shoppers (mostly on Oxford Street in London), and the second one, based on Fruin, represents commuters in two-way flow at the Port Authority Bus Terminal in New York.

Both curves show averages derived by statistical methods. The third curve is hand fitted to the data collected by Oeding in various urban situations in West Germany. In his original study, Oeding goes into considerable detail distinguishing pedestrian flows among manufacturing plants, general business traffic,

sports events, and shopping streets. Generally, the performance of the traffic stream declines in that order: workers leaving manufacturing plants attain high volume of flow at high speeds, whereas shoppers are the most inefficient walkers and attain perhaps only two-thirds of the flow at three-quarters of the speed. For the sake of simplicity, this kind of detail has been omitted, and the curve shown is an average aggregating all of Oeding's observations. To give the reader a notion of the extremes observed by Oeding, the outer boundary of his data is indicated by a dotted line in Figure 3.1. The remaining curve, hand fitted to the data collected by Navin and Wheeler, shows the average of their observations on the campus of the University of Missouri. Over 99 percent of Navin and Wheeler's data points and about 97 percent of Older's data points fall within the outer boundary of Oeding's observations; this dotted line can thus be viewed as an approximate limit of pedestrian behavior under normal conditions.

The formula for the parabolas in Figure 3.1 is a quadratic equation:

(7) speed $= \dfrac{A \pm \sqrt{A^2 - 4B\text{ flow}}}{2}$

where A and B are constants. These constants can be statistically calculated for any set of observations by means of the least squares technique or estimated by inspection on a plot of speed versus density. Plotting density, rather than space per pedestrian, is useful in this case because the resulting relation-

Table 3.3
Coefficients of Pedestrian Flow Equations

Type of flow and source	A (theoretical maximum speed at free flow)		B	B/A (theoretical minimum space per pedestrian at zero speed)	
	(ft/min)	(m/min)		(sq ft)	(m²)
1. Shoppers, Older (average)*	258	(78.6)	714	2.77	(0.257)
2. Commuters, Fruin (average)*	267	(81.4)	722	2.70	(0.251)
3. Mixed traffic, Oeding (average)†	295	(89.9)	835	2.83	(0.263)
4. Students, Navin & Wheeler (average)†	320	(97.5)	1,280	4.00	(0.372)
5. Mixed traffic, Oeding (outer boundary)†	400	(121.9)	1,132	2.83	(0.263)

Sources: See footnote 4.
Note: Extreme observations by Older suggest a minimum space allocation of 2.1 sq ft (0.2 m²) per pedestrian at zero speed.
*Calculated. †Estimated.

Table 3.4
Maximum Pedestrian Flow

Type of flow and source	Maximum flow, peds. per unit of walkway				Mean speed at maximum flow			
	Calculated av.		Observed extreme		Calculated av.		Observed extreme	
	per ft	(per m)	per ft	(per m)	ft/min	(m/min)	ft/min	(m/min)
Shoppers, Older	23.3	(76.4)	33.0	(108.3)	129	(39.3)	170	(51.8)
Commuters, Fruin	24.7	(81.0)	n.d.	—	134	(40.8)	n.d.	—
Mixed traffic, Oeding	26.1	(85.6)	34.0	(111.5)	148	(45.1)	246	(75.0)
Students, Navin & Wheeler	20.0	(65.6)	26.4	(86.6)	160	(49.8)	240	(73.2)
Close military drill formation	n.d.	—	48.0	(157.5)	n.d.	—	300	(91.4)

Sources: See footnote 4 for observed values; calculated values by Regional Plan Association.
Note: n.d.—no data.

Table 3.5
Space per Pedestrian at Maximum Flow

Type of flow and source	Maximum flow, peds. per min per unit of walkway width		Space allocation per ped. at maximum flow	
	per ft	(per m)	sq ft	(m²)
1. Students, Navin & Wheeler, average	20.0	(65.6)	8.0	(0.74)
2. Shoppers, Older, average	23.3	(76.4)	5.5	(0.51)
3. Commuters, Fruin, average	24.7	(81.0)	5.4	(0.50)
4. Mixed traffic, Oeding, average	26.0	(85.3)	5.5	(0.51)
5. Students, Navin & Wheeler, extreme	26.4	(86.6)	9.1	(0.85)
6. Shoppers, Older, extreme	33.0	(108.3)	5.2	(0.48)
7. Mixed traffic, Oeding, extreme	34.0	(111.5)	7.2	(0.67)
8. Close military drill formation	48.0	(157.5)	6.3	(0.59)

Sources: Same as Table 3.4.

81   Space Related to Speed and Flow

Figure 3.1
Speed-flow relationships

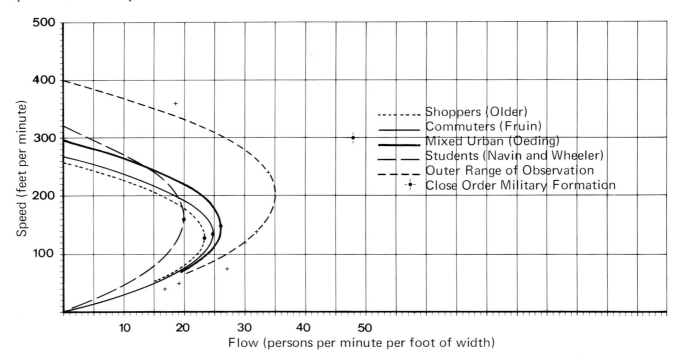

Figure 3.2
Speed-density relationships

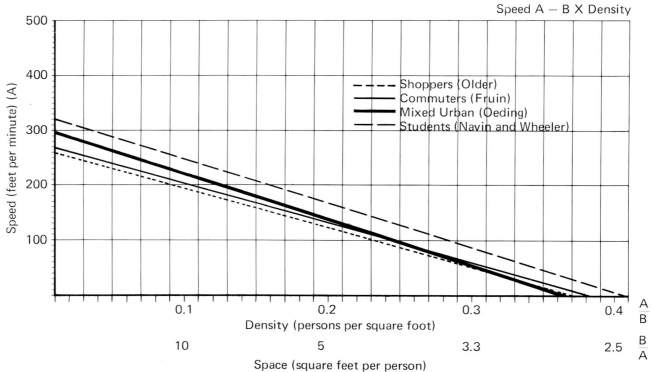

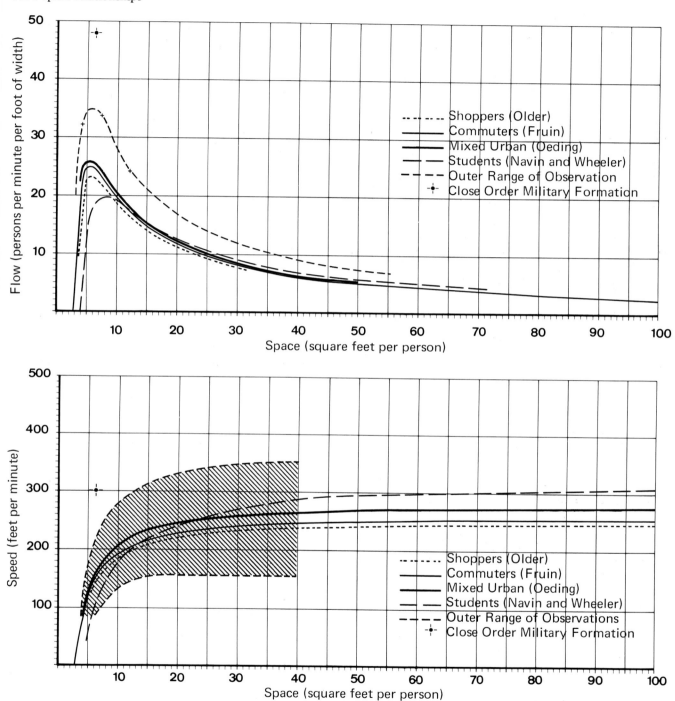

Figure 3.3
Flow-space relationships

Figure 3.4
Speed-space relationships

ship can be represented as a linear one. The straight-line form, though in some ways not ideal, has been shown to represent a reasonable approximation of reality.[7] It takes the form of equation

(8) speed = $A - B \times$ density.

A represents the intercept on the y axis (speed in this case) and B, the slope of a straight line, or the rate at which speed declines with density, as shown in Figure 3.2. The meaning of these two constants can be also interpreted as follows: A represents the theoretical speed attained by a traffic stream under conditions of completely free flow, with an unlimited amount of space per pedestrian; B is a factor that, divided by A, yields the theoretical minimum space allocation per pedestrian at a point where all movement in a traffic stream grinds to a halt and speed is zero. The constants A and B for the curves in Figures 3.1 and 3.2 are given in Table 3.3.

To determine what the maximum, or capacity, pedestrian flow is and at what speed it occurs, all we have to do now is to find the maxima on the curves defined by equation (7). These calculated maxima are listed in Table 3.4, along with the extreme observations encountered empirically by the different investigators.

It is evident that the findings of Older, Oeding, and Fruin concerning maximum pedestrian flow are in very close agreement. In fact, Fruin's calculated maximum of 24.7 pedestrians per minute per foot of walkway width (81 per

meter of width) at a speed of 134 ft (40.8 m) per minute falls exactly halfway between the maxima derived from Older and from Oeding. The extremes observed by Older in England and Oeding in Germany are also in close agreement, though the speeds differ. These extreme flow rates are very high and begin to come somewhat close to those attainable in highly organized military formations, shown in the bottom line of Table 3.4. The behavior of Navin and Wheeler's student population is different, with greater spacing between individuals and an accordingly lower flow at comparable speeds. One may speculate that the higher interpersonal distances adopted by the students are more representative of a comfortable situation than the close spacing found in forced downtown flows by Older, Oeding, and Fruin.

To be able to make an evaluation from the viewpoint of comfort, we must take a look at the relationship between flow and space per pedestrian.

Following equation (6), if we take the speed at any point on the curves in Figure 3.1 and divide it by the flow at that point, we obtain the amount of space available per pedestrian at that point. For example, at a speed of 200 ft per minute and a flow rate of 20 pedestrians per minute, the average space allocation is 10 sq ft per pedestrian. In this manner, the speed-flow diagrams in Figure 3.1 are converted into flow-space diagrams in Figure 3.3. The formula for the flow-space curves is

(9) flow = $\dfrac{A \times \text{space} - B}{\text{space}^2}$,

where A and B are the constants previously described and listed in Table 3.3. The space available per pedestrian at maximum flow is shown in Table 3.5.

It is apparent from Figure 3.3 and Table 3.5 that all the different observations of maximum flow previously listed fall in a very narrow range of density— that in which space allocation per pedestrian varies between 5.2 and 9.1 sq ft (0.48 and 0.85 m²). As space is reduced to less than 5 sq ft (0.46 m²) per pedestrian, the flow rate declines precipitously; all movement comes to a standstill at space allocations between 2 and 4 sq ft (0.2 to 0.4 m²), as Table 3.3 has shown. The latter figures are quite comparable to the minimum standing room referred to in the beginning of this chapter.

Thus, if our objective is to maximize pedestrian flow, regardless of speed or comfort, the space allocation per pedestrian should be between 5.2 and 9.1 sq ft (roughly 0.5 to 0.9 m²). Letting space allocations drift below that level will lead to a crush, with the crowd growing in size as long as the number of incoming pedestrians is greater than what the bottleneck can release.

On the other hand, increasing space allocations above 10 sq ft (0.9 m²) per capita will lead to declines in flow. It can be deduced from Figure 3.3 that at 40 sq ft (3.7 m²) per pedestrian, the flow rates are, depending on which curve one chooses, between 24 and 32 percent of maximum flow. At 100 sq ft (9.3 m²) per pedestrian, the flow rates are down to about 10 percent of maximum flow. Our concern is, of course, with the quality of flow, not with its sheer quantity. This leads us to look at the average speed in relation to space per pedestrian.

Going back to equation (6), if we multiply the flow at any point of Figure 3.1 by the space per pedestrian at that point, we obtain the speed at which the flow is occurring. Thus, the flow-space diagram in Figure 3.3 can be transformed into the speed-space diagram in Figure 3.4. Accordingly, the equation of the speed-space curve is

$$(10) \quad \text{speed} = A - \frac{B}{\text{space}},$$

where A and B are the constants from Table 3.3. The form of equation (10) makes clear why A equals B divided by the space allocation at zero speed. It also makes clear that, as space per pedestrian increases toward infinity, speed increasingly approaches A, previously defined as the theoretical maximum speed at free flow for a given type of traffic stream.

Thus, for example, at 100 sq ft (9.3 m²) per pedestrian, the average speed is between 96 and 97 percent of the theoretical speed at an infinite space allocation per pedestrian. At 40 sq ft (3.7 m²) per pedestrian, average speed drops to between 90 and 93 percent of this theoretical level. From then on the reduction becomes sharper, and, at 11 sq ft (1 m²) per person,

average speed is down to between 64 and 75 percent of the theoretical maximum. In the range where flow is maximized, approximately between 9 and 5 sq ft (0.9 to 0.5 m²) per person, speed drops drastically to between 27 and 50 percent of its theoretical level and then keeps declining to reach zero at space allocations between 2 and 4 sq ft per person.

Reductions in average speed come about because, as available space per pedestrian shrinks, fewer people have the freedom to select their own desired rate of movement due to the interference from others in the traffic stream. The fastest walkers are slowed down first, but eventually even slow walkers are affected. Thus, the range of observed speeds shrinks as space per pedestrian is reduced. Some indication of this is given by the dotted lines in Figure 3.4, which portray the upper and the lower limit of speeds observed by Oeding.

Service Levels

Studies concerning the distribution of pedestrian speeds under conditions of free choice have been carried out by numerous observers, among them, Mac-Dorman, Fruin, and Gehl, previously cited, as well as L. A. Hoel.[8] L. F. Henderson in Australia has advanced the intriguing proposition that the distribution of speeds of individual pedestrians in a crowd under different density conditions is analogous to the distribution of the speed of molecules in a gas.[9] He obtained reasonably good agreement with physical theory, though males and females clearly behaved as two different popula-

tions. We need not pursue this analogy here except to reiterate that as space per pedestrian increases, the range of freely chosen speeds expands.

However, there are biological limits to both how fast and how slowly people will walk. The different investigators are in agreement that virtually nobody will voluntarily select speeds higher than 400 ft per minute (122 m per minute, or 4.5 mi per hour) or lower than 145 ft per minute (44 m per minute, or 1.6 mi per hour). Fruin in New York found that 99.7 percent of walkers select speeds in this range under totally unobstructed conditions. Gehl in Copenhagen found maximum speed to be 410 ft (125 m) per minute and minimum speed to be 143 ft (43.8 m) per minute. The latter was attained by a patrolling policeman, who clearly trained himself to walk with all deliberate slowness, even more slowly than parents with children and oldsters.

Generally, speeds above the indicated range necessitate running. (The technical difference between walking and running is that in walking one foot at all times touches the ground, in running both feet for short instances are off the ground). Speeds below that range can be classified as shuffling (both feet touch the ground some of the time). Oeding, citing other authors, points out that speeds in the shuffling range do not occur under unobstructed conditions because they require cramped movements, which are unnatural in terms of body balance.

On this basis we may note, first of all, that average speeds on all the curves in Figure 3.4 are depressed into the unnatural shuffling range of less than 150 ft (46 m) per minute at space allocations between 6 and 8 sq ft (0.56 and 0.74 m^2) per person. Second, those who choose to (or have to) walk at the minimum speed of about 150 ft (46 m) per minute when space per walker is ample cannot maintain even that speed when space shrinks below 15 to 18 sq ft (1.4 to 1.7 m^2). The fast walkers lose the ability to maintain their chosen speed as space drops below 30 to 40 sq ft (2.8 to 3.7 m^2) per person.

There are other indicators of congestion besides the inability to maintain a freely selected speed. An important one is the inability to choose one's path freely across the traffic stream. Fruin studied pedestrian crossing conflicts in relation to available space per pedestrian. He defined conflicts as "any stopping or breaking of the normal walking pace due to a too close confrontation with another pedestrian" requiring adjustments in speed or direction to avoid collision. He found such situations inevitable when flow is dense, with less than 15 sq ft (1.4 m^2) per person. As the gaps between pedestrians widen, crossing movements become easier and the probability of conflict drops to between 65 and 50 percent. However, the probability of conflict does not drop to zero until the space allocation per pedestrian reaches about 45 sq ft (4.2 m^2).

A related indicator is the ability to pass slow-moving pedestrians,

which Oeding found to be relatively unrestricted at space allocations of more than 36 sq ft (3.3 m^2) per walker. He found the ability to pass to be considerably restricted in the range between 18 and 36 sq ft (1.7 to 3.3 m^2) per person. At lower space allocations, he found passing to be possible only (unless there was a fortuitous gap) by physically pushing the slow-walking person aside.

Finally, an important consideration is the ability to maintain flow in the reverse direction. All of the data presented here—with the exception of some extreme observations by Oeding—refer to bi-directional flow. The performance of bi-directional flow is not substantially different from that of one-directional flow as long as the directional distribution is relatively balanced. Pedestrians spontaneously form directional streams that minimize conflict with the opposing flow; each stream occupies a share of the walkway which is proportional to its share in the total flow, and the reduction in speed or capacity is minimal: Fruin found it to be less than 6 percent under maximum flow conditions. However, Navin and Wheeler have shown that the reduction in capacity increases as directional imbalance increases. Thus, for directional distributions of 25-75 or better, the reduction in capacity approaches 10 percent; for a 10-90 distribution, it rises to 14.5 percent, given a space allocation of 10 sq ft per pedestrian. As space allocations are reduced, maintaining a small flow in the opposite direction becomes more difficult (a problem acute on

some subway stairways), and the effect on capacity becomes more pronounced. A summary of the different kinds of pedestrian behavior possible or impossible at different densities is presented in Table 3.6, based on the work of Oeding and Fruin.

Though the lines of demarcation between the ranges of density shown in Table 3.6 are necessarily blurred and somewhat subjective, the two authors who have attempted to formulate pedestrian service levels so far are not far apart in evaluating them. Thus, Fruin brands space allocations of less than 5 sq ft (0.5 m^2) and Oeding those of less than 7 sq ft (0.66 m^2) completely unacceptable.

Both authors agree that space allocations below 10 or 11 sq ft (say, 1 m^2) can easily lead to stoppages of flow and a buildup of crowds; pedestrians should not be required to endure this "most difficult" degree of congestion. Yet, it is at this level that the maximum flow of 25 to 28 pedestrians per foot (82 to 92 per meter) per minute, frequently accepted as design capacity, occurs. Oeding and Fruin point out, however, that such crush loads can, on occasion, be difficult to avoid in short-term bulk situations, such as when a crowd leaves a sports stadium.

Oeding calls space allocations between 18 and 36 sq ft (1.7 and 3.3 m^2) per pedestrian "tolerable." Fruin subdivides the range between 15 and 35 sq ft (1.4 and 3.3 m^2) into two service levels, "B" and "C," which he conditionally recom-

Table 3.6

Pedestrian Behavior Related to Available Space

Approximate average area per person		
sq ft	(m²)	
2-5	(0.2-0.5)	Flow: erratic, on the verge of complete stoppage Average speed: shuffling only Choice of speed: none Crossing or reverse movement: impossible Conflicts: physical contact unavoidable Passing: impossible
5-7	(0.5-0.7)	Flow: attains a maximum in traffic streams under pressure Average speed: mostly shuffling Choice of speed: none, movement only with the crowd Crossing or reverse movement: most difficult Conflicts: physical contacts probable, conflicts unavoidable Passing: impossible
7-11	(0.7-1.0)	Flow: attains a maximum in more relaxed traffic streams Average speed: about 70% that of free flow Choice of speed: practically none Crossing or reverse movement: severely restricted with collisions Conflicts: physical contact probable, conflicts unavoidable Passing: impossible
11-15	(1.0-1.4)	Flow: 65 to 80 percent of maximum capacity Average speed: about 75% that of free flow Choice of speed: restricted, constant adjustments of gait necessary Crossing or reverse movement: severely restricted with conflicts Conflicts: unavoidable Passing: rarely possible without touching
15-18	(1.4-1.7)	Flow: 56 to 70 percent of maximum capacity Average speed: about 80% that of free flow Choice of speed: restricted except for slow walkers Crossing or reverse movement: restricted, with conflicts Conflicts: probability high Passing: rarely possible without touching
18-25	(1.7-2.3)	Flow: roughly 50 percent of maximum capacity Average speed: more than 80% that of free flow Choice of speed: partially restricted Crossing or reverse movement: possible, with conflicts Conflicts: probability high Passing: difficult without abrupt maneuvers
25-40	(2.3-3.7)	Flow: roughly 33 percent of maximum capacity Average speed: approaching free flow Choice of speed: occasionally restricted Crossing or reverse movement: possible, with occasional conflicts Conflicts: about 50 percent probability Passing: possible, but with interference
Over 40	(Over 3.7)	Flow: 20 percent of maximum capacity or less Average speed: virtually as chosen Choice of speed: virtually unrestricted Crossing or reverse movement: free Conflicts: maneuvering needed to avoid conflicts Passing: free, with some maneuvering

Sources: Fruin, *Designing for Pedestrians;* Oeding, *Verkehrsbelastung und Dimensionierung von Gehwegen* (see footnote 4).

mends for transportation terminals and similar heavily used facilities. Fruin's levels "B" and "C" represent volumes of flow up to 10 and 15 pedestrians per foot (33 and 49 per meter), respectively, of walkway per minute. Oeding cites similar volumes of flow, 14 pedestrians per foot (45 per meter) per minute for shoppers and 18 per foot (60 per meter) per minute for commuters, as the upper limit of his "tolerable" range.

While tolerable on occasion in tight circulation areas, space allocations of 15 to 35 sq ft (1.4 to 3.3 m²) per person still impose serious restrictions on pedestrian flow, as evident from Table 3.6.

Both Oeding and Fruin characterize space allocations only greater than 35 or 36 sq ft (3.3 m²) per pedestrian as permitting free flow. Stramentov, on the basis of observations in Moscow, suggests, in effect, a similar range, between 25 and 55 sq ft (2.3 and 5.1 m²). Thus, 40 sq ft (3.7 m²) per pedestrian, corresponding to a flow rate of 6 persons per minute per foot (20 per meter) of walkway width, can be reasonably accepted as a threshold beyond which pedestrian behavior is no longer physically constrained by the traffic stream.

One should note, however, that a space allocation of 40 sq ft (3.7 m²) per person, while allowing a relatively free choice of speed and direction of movement, does not really represent an uncrowded situation. The lateral spacing adopted by people under conditions approaching free flow was found by Fruin

to be roughly 3.5 ft (about 1 m); assuming this, the longitudinal spacing on the threshold of Oeding's and Fruin's "comfortable" density is a little over 11 ft (3.5 m). At such close spacing, people, while able (most of the time) to avoid physical collisions or restrictions in speed, are acutely aware of others in the traffic stream and must continuously interact with them.

For example, Michael Wolff and Verena Hirsch[10] point out that at distances of less than 15 ft (which represents a space of at least 60 sq ft, or 5.6 m²) people normally do not walk behind each other but rather walk in a checkerboard pattern, looking "over the shoulder" of the person in front. Thus, if any person in a group of walkers changes his lateral position, he forces others to accommodate to maintain the checkerboard spacing. A similar phenomenon can also be observed in the lateral direction: people prefer not to walk side by side with a stranger for any length of time and either accelerate or slow down if someone else is walking alongside. Navigating in the fluid situation of a dense pedestrian stream thus requires constant attention and interaction with others. Psychologists suggest that it is this kind of effort that makes walking in crowded places tiresome, especially if the other walkers are uncooperative, as shoppers with bags tend to be.

Exactly what density is sufficiently sparse so as not to induce stress in the presence of other pedestrians on a walkway is a good subject for further study. Only fragmentary pieces of evi-

dence are available. Thus, Wolff and Hirsch show that the distance at which evasive action is taken in the face of an imminent collision increases from about 2 ft (0.6 m) at a space allocation of 40 sq ft (3.7 m²) per pedestrian to an average of about 7 ft (2.1 m) at 100 sq ft (30 m²) and then stays constant, suggesting that evasion at that distance may be sufficiently smooth. However, they caution that the latter distance may have been foreshortened by the conditions of the experiment. They found 16.5 ft (5 m) to be the distance at which evasive maneuvers with respect to fixed objects were initiated.

Another method for analyzing the quality of flow in the lower-density range, into which neither Fruin nor Oeding ventured, is the *maximum pedestrian technique*: the pedestrian sets out to walk as fast as he humanly can and observes both his speed and the number of conflicts—sharp evasive maneuvers or near-collisions—which he encounters at different flow rates. In one experiment, on Fulton Street in Brooklyn,[11] the maximum pedestrian was generally unable to walk faster than 300 ft (91 m) per minute, at a flow of about 5 people per foot (16 per meter) per minute, the threshold of Oeding and Fruin's "comfortable" density, and encountered an average of 12 conflicts per 250 ft (76 m) of walking distance. With average hourly flow declining to less than 3 people per foot (10 per meter) per minute, the number of conflicts declined linearly to about 4, and the maximum possible speed increased to 380 ft (116 m) per minute, at an average space allocation on the order of

90 sq ft (8.4 m²) per person in the traffic stream.

Qualitative observations made as a part of this study, both in transit corridors and on outdoor walkways, suggest that a space allocation on the order of 130 sq ft (12 m²) per person may be a reasonable minimum limit for truly unimpeded walking, with only negligible influence from the traffic stream. That corresponds to Hall's "public" range of interpersonal distances and represents a flow rate of 2 persons per foot (6.5 per meter) of walkway per minute, a rate that feels comfortable but retains a busy appearance. However, involuntary bunching, or platooning, a subject that will be discussed later, still occurs at this flow rate and does not disappear until flow falls below 0.5 persons per foot (1.6 per meter) per minute and space allocation increases to roughly 500 or 600 sq ft (say 50 m²) per pedestrian. With space allocations beyond this range (a density of about 6 people per typical Manhattan block front), one can no longer talk about pedestrian flow but only about isolated pedestrians.

At this point the question can be asked, When does space allocation become excessive? The question is not totally idle. On occasion, monumental buildings cannot generate enough pedestrians to fill the monumental spaces around them. Or residential streets may have excessively wide pedestrian pavements, which could be put to better use as landscaped areas or playgrounds.

Needless to say, answers to the question of how much walkway

space is too much are highly relative and depend on prevailing densities in an area and on such requirements as minimum sidewalk width necessary for voluntary groups of people to pass each other, even if infrequently. As we will show later, pedestrian flows are so sparse in most non-downtown situations that designing for any reasonable space allocation per moving pedestrian is meaningless, and the minimum walkway width becomes a function of the size of voluntary groups of walkers which one desires to accommodate. On the other hand, in downtown situations, where competition for space is acute, a space allocation in which the auto becomes a more efficient user of space than the pedestrian might be one of the criteria for maximum walkway width.

Before we complete the discussion of the characteristics of average flow and proceed to look at short-term pulses within the traffic stream, an important definitional issue must be settled; What is walkway width?

By analogy with highway design, some sources in the past have used the concept of a pedestrian *lane,* defined occasionally as a strip as narrow as 22 in. (56 cm).[12] However, the lane is irrelevant to capacity calculations even for autos on local streets (capacity being a continuous, rather than stepped, function of street width), and this also holds true for the even more versatile pedestrian. The lane can be meaningful only if one wishes to calculate how many people can walk abreast— or pass each other simultaneous-

ly—along a walkway of a given width, and here, according to Oeding and the observations of this study, the lateral spacing to avoid interference with a passing pedestrian is at least 30 in. (75 cm). Pedestrians who know each other and are walking together will walk as close as 26 in. (65 cm) center-to-center; at this distance there is considerable likelihood of touching the other person. Lateral spacing of less than 24 in. (60 cm) between strangers occurs, as Fruin has shown, only under jammed conditions, with less than about 5 sq ft (0.5 m²) per person, or in rather contorted evasive maneuvers on narrow stairs, where, if necessary, people can squeeze by in about 20 in. (50 cm) of space. Under normal conditions, even the 2.5 ft (0.75 m) lateral spacing is tolerated only momentarily, to pass a person or to walk alongside a person through a stairway. Otherwise, a spacing of 3 to 4 ft (0.9 to 1.2 m) or more is adopted by walking in a checkerboard pattern.

Multiples of about 2.5 ft (0.75 m) can be used to calculate clear walkway width for a given number of people to walk abreast in a voluntary group and to be able to pass a group, but the term *clear walkway width* deserves more emphasis. People will shy away from walking along the very edge of a curb and they will not press themselves against building walls, and therefore dead space along the edges of a walkway must be excluded from its effective width when calculating design flow. Also excluded must be strips preempted by physical obstructions, such as light poles, mail boxes, and

JAMMED FLOW. Space per pedestrian in this view is about 3.8 sq ft (0.35 m^2). This is representative of the lower half of the speed-flow curve, where only shuffling movement is possible and even the extremely un-comfortable maximum flow rate of 25 people per min per ft (82 per m) of walkway width cannot be attained due to lack of space. Photograph by Louis B. Schlivek.

The threshold of CONGESTED FLOW. The first eleven people in the view have about 16 sq ft (1.5 m^2) per person, corresponding to a flow rate of about 15 people per min per ft (49 per m) of walkway width. The beginnings of congestion are evident in bodily conflicts affecting at least three of the walkers, and in blocked opportunities for walking at a normal pace.

The onset of CROWDED FLOW, with an average of about 24 sq ft (2.2 m^2) per person, or a flow rate of about 10 people per min per ft (33 per m) of walkway width. Choice of speed is partially restricted, the probability of conflicts is fairly high, passing is difficult. Voluntary groups of two, of which two can be seen in the picture, are maintained, but cause interference. Note also some overflow into the vehicular roadway in the background.

The midpoint of the CONSTRAINED FLOW range, with about 30 sq ft (2.8 m^2) per person, or a flow rate of about 8 people per min per ft (26 per m) of walkway width. The choice of speed is occasionally restricted, crossing and passing movements are possible, but with interference and with the likelihood of conflicts. The man in the dark suit seems to be able to cross in front of the two women in the foreground quite freely, but in the background near the curb people are having difficulty with passing maneuvers.

The borderline between IMPEDED and UNIMPEDED FLOW, with about 130 sq ft (12 m²) per person, or a flow rate of about 2 people per min per ft (6.5 per m) of walkway width. Individuals as well as couples visible in this view have a choice of speed and direction of movement. This rate of flow is recommended for design of outdoor walkways in office districts and other less dense parts of downtown areas.

The uneven nature of UNIMPEDED FLOW. While the people walking in the plaza—which is 17 ft (5.2 m) wide, compared to 23 ft (7 m) in the preceding picture—have almost 130 sq ft (12 m²) per person on the average, the space allocation for the eight individuals in the foreground is closer to 70 sq ft (6.4 m²). Thus, indirect interaction with others is still quite frequent in the upper range of UN-IMPEDED FLOW.

The midpoint of the IMPEDED FLOW range, with about 75 sq ft (6.9 m²) per person, or a flow rate of about 4 people per min per ft (13 per m) of walkway width. Physical conflicts are absent, but pedestrian navigation does require constant indirect interaction with others. This rate of flow is recommended as an upper limit for the design of outdoor walkways in shopping districts and other dense parts of downtown areas.

Lower range of UNIMPEDED movement, approaching OPEN FLOW. About 350 sq ft (32.2 m²) per person, or a flow rate of less than 1 person per min per ft (3.3 per m) of walkway width. Complete freedom to select the speed and direction of movement; individuals behave quite independently of each other. For a design standard based solely on pedestrian density, this amount of space can be considered excessive.

parking meters, though their exact effect on pedestrian flow has not been sufficiently investigated. Lastly, the area preempted by standing pedestrians is not available for walking.

In a study of shopping walkways in Leeds, England, Coleman O'Flaherty and M. H. Parkinson found that a speed-density relationship calculated on the basis of curb-to-wall sidewalk width could not be meaningfully converted into a flow-space relationship because of a large number of standing pedestrians, who occupied space but did not contribute to flow.[13] Only by subtracting the space occupied by the standees from the total sidewalk space could a meaningful relationship be obtained. They found that the width preempted by window shoppers was between 1.6 ft (0.5 m) and 2.5 ft (0.75 m) and the width preempted by standees at a bus stop, about 3.6 ft (1.1 m). The implicit space allocations per window shopper were roughly between 5 and 7 sq ft (0.5 to 0.7 m^2). These findings are in agreement with the lateral clearances from building walls suggested by Oeding. The clearance from the curb suggested by him is 1 to 1.5 ft (0.3 to 0.5 m).

On the basis of these observations we can now proceed to summarize the characteristics of pedestrian flow at different levels of spaciousness. This is done in Table 3.7, which goes beyond the range investigated by Oeding and Fruin. The boundaries of the various conditions are slightly adjusted for arithmetical convenience. The data in Table 3.7 assume that the pedestrian flow

is even, or homogenous, in time. The flow rate is expressed in terms of one minute and should not be extrapolated to longer periods of time until the considerations presented in the next section are fully taken into account.

Movement at a rate of less than 0.5 pedestrians per foot (1.6 per meter) of walkway width per minute is characterized as OPEN FLOW: essentially no interaction among pedestrians occurs at that level. Movement at a rate of less than 2 per foot (6.5 per meter) is called UNIMPEDED: while some bunching begins to occur, an individual is generally not influenced by others in the traffic stream, and walking is carefree. However, the next level of flow, up to 6 people per foot (20 per meter) per minute, is IMPEDED, because progress is possible only in constant interaction with the movement of others. At the CONSTRAINED level, up to 10 people per foot (33 per meter) of walkway width per minute, interaction turns into physical restrictions on the freedom of movement, speed is limited, and conflicts occur. The next higher level, up to 14 people per minute per foot (46 per meter), can already be termed CROWDED. It is rarely reached, only for short periods of time on urban sidewalks, and is more typical of very heavily used transportation terminals, where movement may still be fluid but with a lot of friction and at a depressed speed. A flow of up to 18 per minute per foot (60 per meter) is, by common consensus, CONGESTED. Finally, flow near the maximum possible level is JAMMED.

Space for Platoons

To have defined the possible flow rates at different levels of pedestrian comfort does us little good unless we know to what time spans these rates should be applied. A flow rate of 10 pedestrians per minute does not necessarily equal 600 pedestrians per hour, because flow is very uneven. We portrayed one aspect of this unevenness in Chapter 2, by showing cyclical variation in 15-min intervals. Such intervals are usually large enough to mask the other aspect —short-term bunching—to which we alluded when explaining the seemingly large errors of the trip generation equations.

The Platoon Effect
A good picture of minute-by-minute variation can be obtained from data collected by Rai Okamoto and Robert Beck in their time-lapse photography studies of two walkways in Lower Manhattan.[14] Shown in Figure 3.5, the data cover the morning rush hour on Nassau Street and at the entrance to the Chase Manhattan Plaza as well as the lunch hour at the latter. The maximum 15-min flow rate at the Nassau Street location averaged about 10 people per minute per foot (32.8 per m) and at the Chase Plaza entrance, 1.4 and 1.9 per minute per foot (4.6 and 6.2 per m) during the hours when the measurements were taken.

However, the diagrams indicate that flow during one minute can, on occasion, be more than twice as high as during the next minute, particularly when the overall volume is low. Even during the peak 15-min periods, differences of one and one half times from

How wide is a pedestrian "lane"? Left view shows a 48-in. (122 cm) stairway, which allows 24 in. (61 cm) per person. It is evident that two persons passing have to twist their arms to avoid contact. Nevertheless, an even smaller "lane width" of 22 in. (56 cm) is frequently accepted in traffic engineering literature. Right view shows 27 in. (69 cm) per person, which allows a freer body position, aided by the fact that everyone is walking in the same direction, with checkerboard spacing. About 30 in. (76 cm) is recommended by this study as a minimum width necessary for two people to pass each other without disturbance. The notion of a "lane" is generally inapplicable to pedestrian design, except in constricted situations, such as stairways.

Figure 3.5
Minute-by-minute variation in pedestrian flow

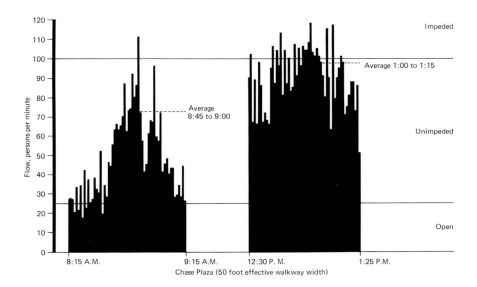

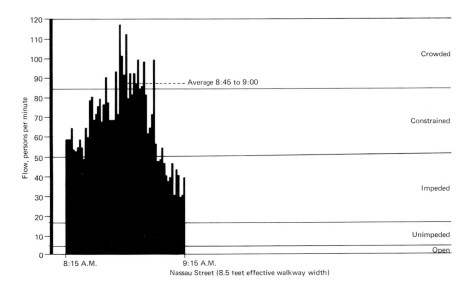

Table 3.7
Characteristics of Pedestrian Flow in a
Homogeneous Stream

Quality of flow	Space per person		Flow rate, persons per min per unit of walkway width	
	sq ft	(m²)	ft	(m)
OPEN	over 530	(50)	under 0.5	(under 1.6)
UNIMPEDED	530-130	(50-12)	0.5-2	(1.6-6.5)
IMPEDED	130-40	(12-3.7)	2-6	(6.5-20)
CONSTRAINED	40-24	(3.7-2.2)	6-10	(20-33)
CROWDED	24-16	(2.2-1.5)	10-14	(33-46)
CONGESTED	16-11	(1.5-1.0)	14-18	(46-60)
JAMMED	2-11	(1.0-0.2)	0-25	(0-82)

Source: Regional Plan Association.

Figure 3.6
Flow in platoons related to average
flow

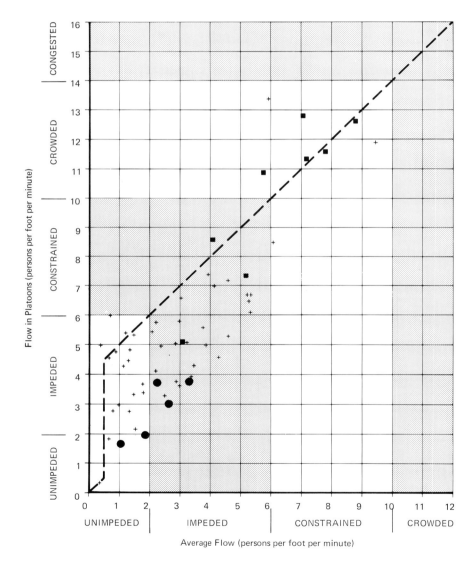

94 Pedestrian Space Requirements

one minute to the other do occur, both in what would appear to be, on the average, an UNIMPEDED flow to the plaza and CONSTRAINED flow on Nassau Street. Relating the scatter in the diagrams to the 15-min average, we find that the highest minute within a 15-min period exceeds the average by at least 20 percent and, on occasion, by up to 75 percent. The third highest minute exceeds the average by at least 10, and up to 30 percent. Even the seventh highest minute can be up to 20 percent higher than average. In general, at least 6 and up to 9 min of every 15-min period have an above-average rate of flow. As a result, more than half, and up to 73 percent of the people walk during minutes when flow exceeds the 15-min average. For them, the flow on Nassau Street is no longer CONSTRAINED, but CROWDED, and the noon-time flow in the Chase Plaza entrance is not UNIMPEDED but IMPEDED.

These findings are supported by manual minute-to-minute counts in Midtown Manhattan, which fall in the same range. It is clear that any facility designed for the average flow in a 15-min period will be underdesigned for a sizable portion of the pedestrians using it. At the same time, it would be extravagant to design for one peak minute that may be 150 percent of the average but which may only occur with a 1 or 2 percent probability. To resolve that dilemma and to find a relevant time period, a closer look at the short-term fluctuation is necessary.

Short-term fluctuation is generally present in any traffic flow that is not effectively regulated by a schedule, and its underlying cause is that the participants in a traffic stream arrive on a given spot at random. Thus, due purely to the laws of chance, one minute a section of sidewalk may receive many pedestrians, whereas the next minute it may receive very few. In an urban situation this random unevenness is exaggerated by three additional factors. First, if passing is impeded because of insufficient space, faster pedestrians will slow down behind slow-walking ones, and a random bunch of pedestrians soon snowballs into what can be called a *platoon*. Second, subway trains and, to a lesser extent, elevators and buses release groups of people in very short intervals of time, with pauses during which no flow may occur at all. Until they have a chance to dissipate, these groups proceed more or less together as a platoon. Finally, and most importantly, traffic signals release pedestrians in groups, which tend to proceed as groups along a sidewalk.

Platoons represent involuntary groupings of pedestrians and as such should be distinguished from groups that walk together by choice. Of course, a voluntary group of people strolling leisurely together and chatting can cause a platoon to form, when opportunities for passing are limited.

One of the reasons platoons have been neglected by previous researchers may be that they are phenomena hard to define. In this exploration two definitions— one positive and one negative— were tried. In the positive definition, platoons were timed and counted when it appeared to the observer that a wave of above-average density was swelling up in the traffic stream. In the negative definition, by contrast, gaps in flow were timed and the stragglers walking during these lulls were counted; then the nonplatoon time and flow were subtracted from total time and flow to determine performance in platoons. The total time of an observation was generally 5 to 6 min except at subway exits, where hourly counts were taken. The platoons were timed in seconds to avoid the arbitrary mixing of periods of flow with periods of no flow which results from choosing longer units of time. Some fifty-eight observations are summarized in the scatter diagram in Figure 3.6.

The duration of platoons defined either positively or negatively ranges from 5 to 50 sec, but the average time in platoons is shorter under the positive definition. Accordingly, by the positive definition, 53 percent of the flow was found to occur in platoons during roughly 20 percent of the time and by the negative definition, 84 percent of the flow occurred in platoons during 63 percent of the time. The flow rate in platoons is, in the positive definition, about 2.5 times greater than the average flow rate and, in the negative definition, about 1.3 times greater than the average flow rate. There is a tendency for platooning to be more pronounced during the morning and evening rush hours than during midday.

The most important influence on platoons at the street surface is traffic signals, and platoons generally follow their cycle with a longer duration along avenues (50 secs of green time in Manhattan) and a shorter one along streets (30 secs of green time). To explore a different situation, counts were also taken during the morning arrival period at eight subway station exits. With a tight definition of platoons, it was found that 75 percent of the flow occurred in platoons during 47 percent of the time, a platoon flow rate about 1.6 times the average flow rate. A more loose definition of platoons found 95 percent of the flow in platoons during 60 percent of the time, likewise a platoon flow rate about 1.6 times the average flow rate. The subway exit observations are indicated separately in Figure 3.6.

It is clear that an average flow rate, even if it refers to a period as short as 1 min, is of little relevance to defining the condition of the majority of pedestrians in a traffic stream. To the pedestrian caught in a platoon it is small consolation that, a few seconds prior to his arrival, the section of walkway on which he is now bumping into others was virtually empty. The time period *truly relevant for design* appears to be not 15 min, 1 min, or any other arbitrary time span but rather *that period during which flow in platoons occurs*. Since this time in platoons is composed of short spans of variable length, the most convenient way to deal with it is to take a time interval that is appropriate from the viewpoint of cyclical variation, say 15 to 30 min, and then design not for the average but for the platoon flow rate during that period.

Revised Service Levels

Thus, our task becomes to show what flow rates in platoons occur at what average flow rates so that the characteristics listed in Table 3.7 can be applied to platoons. A comprehensive way of going about this would have been to plot distributions for a range of pedestrian densities, by type of facility and time of day, showing what percentage of the people have to walk at densities exceeding the average by what amount. Then a cutoff level could have been chosen to serve a specified percentage of the walkers at a specified level of service. This detail could not be attained and a shortcut method was used.

In Figure 3.6 a line was drawn approximating the upper limit of all the platoon observations, covering 51 out of the 58 cases. Above it are three observations typifying small platoons during periods of light flow, an observation showing extreme conditions on an approach to the Port Authority Bus Terminal shortly after 5:00 P.M., and three out of the eight observations at subway exits. The equation of this line relating maximum platoon flow to average flow is

(11) platoon flow (peds/min/ft) = 4 + average flow (peds/min/ft).

Application of this equation shows that an average flow rate of 6 to 10 pedestrians per minute per foot (20 to 33 per meter) of walkway width, which we have previously described as CONSTRAINED but tolerable, can actually result in a CROWDED flow of 10 to 14 per minute per foot (33 to 46

per meter) in platoons. Likewise, a flow between 2 and 6 pedestrians per minute per foot (6.5 to 20 per meter), which all preceding authors have unanimously qualified as free and which we have called IMPEDED, can actually result in platoon flows between 6 and 10 persons per minute per foot (20 to 33 per meter), which, by common consensus, are CONSTRAINED.

To ensure a platoon flow rate of less than 6 per foot (20 per meter) or a space allocation of more than 40 sq ft (3.7 m^2) per person in platoons, the average flow rate must drop below 2 (6.5 per meter) and the average space allocation must rise above 130 sq ft (12 m^2) per person. This is especially the case when sidewalks are narrow. There is some evidence to suggest that whereas on 12- to 15-ft (3.7 to 4.6 m) wide sidewalks it takes an average space allocation in excess of 500 sq ft (46 m^2) per person to altogether prevent the formation of platoons (a requirement that would be rather impossible to meet in downtown areas), on wide sidewalks (in excess of 30 ft, or 9 m) platoons do not quite disappear but are very substantially attenuated at average space allocations between 80 and 200 sq ft (7.4 and 18.5 m^2). Five such observations are shown separately in Figure 3.6.

The form that equation (11) takes—a constant added to average flow—indicates that platooning has a relatively much greater impact on light volumes of flow than on heavy ones. Thus, for an average flow rate of 2 persons per minute per foot (6.5 per meter), the additional margin

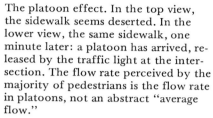

The platoon effect. In the top view, the sidewalk seems deserted. In the lower view, the same sidewalk, one minute later: a platoon has arrived, released by the traffic light at the intersection. The flow rate perceived by the majority of pedestrians is the flow rate in platoons, not an abstract "average flow."

Attenuation of platoons on wide sidewalks. The average space per pedestrian in the top view is 113 sq ft (10.4 m^2), which is in the low range of IMPEDED flow. However, the confluence of three voluntary groups, which are unable to pass each other on the 15-ft (4.6 m) wide sidewalk causes a platoon, where available space is only 25 sq ft (2.3 m^2) per pedestrian, close to being CROWDED. The average space per person in the lower view is 90 sq ft (8.3 m^2), closer to the middle of the IMPEDED range. However, circulation is much freer because the 33 to 41 ft (10 to 12.5 m) sidewalk width illustrated tends to dissipate platoons, and the spacing of pedestrians is fairly even.

Table 3.8
Average Flow Characteristics Related to Flow in Platoons

Average flow			Possible flow in platoons		
Quality	Sq ft per person (m²)	Flow rate pers/min/ft (pers/min/m)	Quality	Sq ft per person (m²)	Flow rate pers/min/ft (pers/min/m)
OPEN	Over 530 (50)	Under 0.5	OPEN	Over 530 (over 50)	Under 0.5 (under 1.6)
UNIMPEDED	530-130 (50-12)	0.5-2 (1.6-6.5)	IMPEDED (except on wide walkways)	60-40 (5.6-3.7)	4.5-6 (15-20)
IMPEDED	130-40 (12-3.7)	2-6 (6.5-20)	CONSTRAINED	40-24 (3.7-2.2)	6-10 (20-33)
CONSTRAINED	40-24 (3.7-2.2)	6-10 (20-33)	CROWDED	24-16 (2.2-1.5)	10-14 (33-46)
CROWDED	24-16 (2.2-1.5)	10-14 (33-46)	CONGESTED	16-11 (1.5-1.0)	14-18 (46-60)
CONGESTED	16-11 (1.5-1.0)	14-18 (46-60)	JAMMED	Under 11 (under 1.0)	Over 18 (over 60)

Source: Regional Plan Association.

Table 3.9
Past Walkway Design Capacity Recommendations

Maximum flow rate, persons per min			
per ft	per m	Note	Application
25	82	Level walkways	New York City Transit Authority
15	49	Without adjustment to reflect surge conditions	World Trade Center, New York
10-15	33-49	Clear width, sub-tracting curbside and wallside space 1.5 to 3 feet	General urban applications, England
14	46	Level walkways	Bay Area Rapid Transit
13.6	45	Level walkways	Washington Metropolitan Area Transit Authority
12.7	42	Level walkways	Grand Central Terminal Study by Wilbur Smith

Sources: Line 1, New York City Transit Authority.
Line 2, Frank N. Caggiano, *Planning for Pedestrians at the World Trade Center,* The Port Authority of New York and New Jersey, December 1972, p. 9.
Line 3, Ministry of Transport, *Roads in Urban Areas,* London HMSO, 1966, p. 396.
Line 4, Wilmot R. McCutchen, "Passenger Design Standards for Bay Area Rapid Transit Stations," in *Man-Transportation Interface,* American Society of Civil Engineers, June 1972, p. 197.
Line 5, Albert J. Roohr, "Design of Pedestrian Facilities for the Washington Metro," in *Man-Transportation Interface,* p. 159.
Line 6, Wilbur Smith and Associates, *Pedestrian Impact Study for the Proposed Grand Central Tower,* 1968, p. 4.

necessary to accommodate platoons is 200 percent; at a flow rate of 10 (33 per meter), it is 40 percent. This pattern is not illogical since gaps between platoons tend to fill up as flow increases. It does point to a design conclusion: when flows are small, there appears to be a need for minimum walkway standards that apply almost irrespective of the actual volume of flow, because there is always the probability of a sudden, large platoon. An example is the entrance to an apartment house, which may be experiencing zero flow for many minutes until an elevator arrives with a platoon. As average flow increases, the space requirements do not grow proportionately but rather at a retarded rate, which is fortunate for the design of such high-intensity pedestrian facilities as shopping malls or transportation terminals. There are clear economies of scale in providing walkway space.

To summarize the discussion of platooning, the correspondence between average flow characteristics and platoon flow characteristics as suggested by equation (11), is listed in Table 3.8.

The messages of Table 3.8 are the following. If the designer wants to attain what Oeding calls "free flow" and what Fruin calls "service level A," not on the average, but in platoons, then 130 sq ft (12 m²) per person is the minimum average space allocation, and 2 people per minute per foot (6.5 per meter) of walkway width is the maximum flow except in the case of very wide walkways or where the absence of platooning can be demonstrated. This is the standard recommended later on in Chapter 4 for most office building sidewalks in Manhattan and one that seems generally applicable to busy outdoor walkways.

If unusual cost limitations are present, as in the case of underground passageways, or if a degree of crowding is desirable, such as in very intensive shopping areas, then the average space allocation can be lowered and the flow rate accordingly raised. Yet, in no case, if overcrowding and congestion in platoons are to be avoided, should the space allocation fall below an average of 40 sq ft (3.7 m²) (that is, below 24 sq ft, or 2.2 m,² in platoons), nor should the flow rate rise above an average of 6 persons per foot per minute (20 per meter), which is 10 persons per foot per minute (33 per meter) in platoons.

These recommended standards are at sharp variance with past engineering practice. Historically, the transit operating agencies in Chicago, London, and New York have accepted values of 28, 27, and 25 pedestrians per minute per foot (92, 89, and 82 per meter), respectively, as the "maximum capacity" of pedestrian passageways in subways. A look back at Table 3.4 will confirm that these flow rates are, indeed, attainable and can even be exceeded, but only under JAMMED conditions. In recognition of this fact, designs made in the 1960-70 decade have raised the standards and lowered the "maximum design capacity" to levels shown in Table 3.9. But, as the above discussion indicates, not nearly enough. Most values in Table 3.9 fall into the range that we have classified as CROWDED, which spells CONGESTED in platoons. This level of flow can be experienced during rush hours in the main concourse of the Port Authority Bus Terminal in New York, which, incidentally, is characterized by unusually low surge conditions, or platooning, in part because of its large width, in part because of the evenly spaced nature of bus arrivals. To what extent this level of flow represents a desirable ideal can best be judged by the users of that facility. Recognizing its inadequacy, the Port Authority itself embarked on a major expansion of the facility in 1975.

Special Requirements

The walkway standards summarized above apply primarily in level terrain but are not invalid for mildly inclined walks and ramps, inasmuch as neither speed nor spacing between pedestrians is affected by small grades. Thus, MacDorman, in his studies in Washington, found grades of less than 6 percent (a 6-ft or 6-m rise in 100 ft or meters of distance) to have no effect on speed. The *Traffic Engineering Handbook*[15] quotes data that confirm this but indicates that a 12 percent grade does result in almost a 30 percent reduction in horizontal speed, according to experience in Pittsburgh. A maximum of 12.5 percent is permitted by the New York City building code. A grade of this magnitude may not have a very pronounced effect on capacity, inasmuch as in uphill movement the reduction in speed is compensated by closer spacing, and in downhill movement the opposite is true. Though much steeper grades—16 to 30 percent —do, on occasion, occur in very hilly cities, these are exceptions and will remain outside our purview.

Stairways

Grades in excess of about 30 percent are usually handled by stairways. Pedestrian behavior on a stairway is fundamentally different from that on a level or inclined walkway. The dimensions of the steps restrict the spontaneous pacing distance and make it short and uniform. This results in a close spacing between pedestrians and reduces the range of freely selected speeds. The restricted pace and the energy needed to overcome or to control

gravity reduce average horizontal speed in ascent to roughly one-third, and in descent to roughly one-half, of that on a level walkway.

The details of how pedestrians perform on a stairway, either in ascent or in descent, depend on how steep it is. Fruin quotes a recent medical study in the United States indicating that an increase in step riser height from 6 in. to 8.25 in. (15.2 to 21 cm) virtually doubled the energy expenditure of a sample of women in ascent and increased it by more than half in descent. Fruin himself shows 11 to 16 percent declines in speed (under free flow conditions) as riser height increases from 6 to 7 in. (15.2 to 17.8 cm). Oeding quotes studies by Lehman and Engelmann (1933) and by Scholz (1952) in Germany which have dealt with the relationship between energy expenditure and speed on stairways to determine optimum steepness. Thus, according to Scholz, the step requiring the least energy expenditure has a riser of 5.7 in. (10.5 cm) and a tread of 13.4 in. (34 cm), or a 42.6 percent incline. Inclines up to 50 percent do not seem to tax the human body greatly, but beyond that energy expenditure rises sharply. *Time Saver Standards,*[16] an accepted manual of American building practice, states that "for exterior stairs, riser should not exceed 6 inches and treads should not be less than 12 inches," which is within the 50 percent grade criterion.

However, stairways inside American buildings are much steeper, usually between 58 and 70 percent incline. Occasioned per-

haps by the real estate developer's desire to minimize the unrentable space that stairways occupy and perhaps by the widespread use of elevators in taller buildings, where interior stairs serve only emergency purposes, these steep inclines have not been subjected to any experimental evaluation in terms of human psychology in the United States, although recently some work in this area was commenced.[17] The occasionally complex formulas for proportioning steps recommended by architectural handbooks do not have any substantive basis in human behavior. Following convention, public staircases that are often "exterior" in nature and carry more pedestrians than any other, namely, the staircases between the street and subway mezzanines and platforms, are also uncomfortably steep. The traditional Transit Authority design in New York City is based on a step with a 7 in. (17.8 cm) riser and an 11 in. (27.9 cm) tread, or an incline of 63.6 percent. There seems to be no question that a reduction of this grade would increase not only comfort but also speed and flow.

A rigorous speed-flow analysis of stairways was performed by Fruin. Based on measurements at the Staten Island Ferry terminal in Manhattan and at Shea Stadium in Queens (both of which have the same riser and tread as most Transit Authority stairs), Fruin derived flow-space and speed-space curves of a form described by equations (9) and (10) earlier, in which the coefficients are

for ascent: $A = 111$, $B = 162$,
for descent: $A = 128$, $B = 206$.

These yield a maximum theoretical flow of 18.9 pedestrians per minute per foot (62 per meter) of width ascending and 20.0 (65.6) descending in strictly one-directional flow. Fruin's *actual* observations did not exceed 16 or 17 pedestrians per minute per foot (52.5 or 55.8 per meter) of stairway width. Only under exceptional circumstances (a fast surge over a previously empty stairway) did this study observe a flow as high as 20 per minute per foot (65.6 per meter). It was attained by agile commuters at the PATH World Trade Center station, and similar values have been reported at some railroad stations in Germany.

Under more usual conditions, Fruin's work shows that movement on stairways begins to approach free flow at 8.7 pedestrians per minute per foot (28.5 per meter) of stairway width up and 7.6 per foot (24.9 per meter) down, at space allocations of some 11 and 15 sq ft (1 and 1.4 m^2), respectively. The horizontal component of the speed at these flow rates is about 100 ft per minute (30.5 m/min) up and 120 ft per minute (36.5 m/min) down. Measured along the incline, speed would be approximately 20 percent higher. Fully free flow in one direction, with adequate opportunities for passing slow pedestrians, is attained, according to Fruin, at space allocations of about 20 sq ft (1.9 m^2) per person, which corresponds to a flow rate of 5 to 6 persons per minute per foot (16.4 to 19.7 per meter) of stairway width.

Oeding's findings, though not as systematic as Fruin's, present a similar picture. Oeding's maximum observed flow was 16.7 pedestrians per foot (55 per meter) of stairway width in one direction, a condition under which heavy queuing occurred.

On stairways in downtown areas, Oeding found that flows of about 6.0 to 7.6 persons per minute per foot (20 to 25 per meter) of width represent "practical" capacity. These occurred at space allocations between 15.5 and 20 sq ft (1.4 and 1.9 m^2) per person and at speeds of about 120 ft (36.5 m) per minute. Oeding notes that "with this load, the freedom of movement of the individual pedestrian is considerably restricted, i.e., passing in comfort and without mutual interference is no longer possible . . . nor is the free choice of speed."

To obtain additional data on stairway performance with a particular emphasis on the incidence of queuing, counts were made at eight subway stairways between the mezzanine and the street in Manhattan. Individual observations from two of these counts are listed in Table 3.10. They show that the maximum upward flow rate was 16.2 persons per minute per foot (53.1 per meter) of stairway width, very similar to the maxima observed by Fruin and Oeding. However, heavy queuing occurred at that flow rate at the bottom of the stairway.

No queuing occurred at flow rates of less than 12 persons per minute per foot (about 40 per meter) of stairway width, if the flow was exclusively in the upward direction and nobody tried to make his way down. With an occasional reverse movement, that figure dropped to 11 (36 per meter). With heavy reverse flow (more than 3 downward pedestrians per upward platoon, which averaged 56 people), even a flow of 7.6 pedestrians per minute per foot (25 per meter) of width resulted in queuing on the narrow stairway. If one descending pedestrian blocks roughly half the stairway width, only upward flows of less than 6 pedestrians per minute per foot (20 per meter) of width can be free of queues, assuming 12 per foot (40 per meter) as the queueless platoon capacity of a stairway with a purely one-directional movement.

The precise conditions under which this assumption holds true are not clear. Some of the observations made as a part of this study found queuing to commence at platoon flows as low as 9 people per minute per foot (30 per meter), even on wide stairways with no reverse flow. Table 3.11 gives a general idea of the incidence of queuing related both to flow in platoons and to average flow on eight subway stairways. It is evident that to avoid platoon flow rates at which queuing sets in, average flow rates during the peak hour or half-hour have to be at or below about 5 or 4 people per minute per foot (16 or 13 per meter) of stairway width.

Queuing in front of stairways, often neglected by previous researchers, is emphasized here because it indicates objectively that the space allocation on a stairway is at a minimum level—about 7.5 sq ft (0.7 m^2)—beyond which

Table 3.10
Platoon Flow Rates Related to Queuing at Two Subway Stairways

No Reverse Flow			Light Reverse Flow			Heavy Reverse Flow		
Upward flow pedestrians per min per ft	Queuing	Stair width, ft	Upward flow pedestrians per min per ft	Queuing	Stair width, ft	Upward flow pedestrians per min per ft	Queuing	Stair width, ft
14.4	yes	4.8	16.2	yes	5.8	10.4	yes	4.8
14.2	yes	5.8	15.2	yes	5.8	9.4	yes	4.8
13.8	yes	4.8	14.1	yes	5.8	9.3	yes	4.8
13.8	yes	4.8	13.9	yes	5.8	7.6	yes	4.8
12.7	yes	5.8	13.4	yes	4.8			
12.7	yes	4.8	13.0	yes	4.8			
12.0	no	5.8	12.7	yes	5.8			
11.5	no	4.8	12.0	yes	5.8			
11.0	no	4.8	11.6	yes	4.8			
10.8	no	5.8	11.2	no	5.8			
10.5	no	5.8						
9.3	no	5.8	9.9	no	4.8			
6.6	no	4.8	9.2	no	4.8			
			8.8	no	4.8			

Source: Regional Plan Association.
Note: Light reverse flow defined as 1 to 3 persons per platoon walking in the reverse direction; heavy reverse flow, more than 3.

Table 3.11
Incidence of Queues Related to Average and Platoon Flow of Exiting Pedestrians at 8 Subway Stairways

	Average flow, pers/min/ft	Platoon flow, pers/min/ft	% of platoons* with queues	Stair width, ft
1.	8.7[†]	12.7	69	5.8
2.	7.8	11.6	34	6.0
3.	7.2	11.3	47	11.6
4.	7.1	12.8	39	5.0
5.	5.8[†]	10.9	59	4.8
6.	5.2	7.3	0	11.1
7.	4.1[†]	8.6	0	10.0
8.	3.1	5.1	4[‡]	9.9

Source: Regional Plan Association.
Note: Lines 1 and 5 represent stairways shown above in Table 3.10; line 7, the stairway shown in Table 3.12.
*The number of platoons observed ranged between 23 and 33 per hour.
[†]Represents half-hour counts; all other counts hourly.
[‡]One queue due to coincidence of two train arrivals.

people will not compress themselves so as not to step on other people. It also represents a breakdown of movement and an irritating source of delay. A prime condition of adequate capacity on a stairway should be the absence of queuing.

While necessary, this condition, of course, is not sufficient to ensure truly comfortable movement. As an example, Table 3.12 lists detailed notes about the operation of the stairway listed in line 7 of Table 3.11, which had an average outbound flow of 4.1 people per minute per foot (13.5 per meter) during a half-hour at the peak after 5:00 P.M. This would seem to be a comfortably low flow rate, free of queuing. The stairway, formerly severely congested and suffering from extremely long queues during the home-bound rush period, was one of four at that particular station, recently rebuilt to double its capacity. The count was taken to evaluate how the reconstruction was functioning.

Only exiting traffic was counted and only while platoons were in progress. It takes about 1 min to clear the platform after each arriving train at that station, and most platoons lasted about that long; a total of 1,236 persons left through the 10-ft wide (3 m) stairway during 30 min, in 15 platoons that lasted 14 min, 25 secs in toto.

It is evident that on 7 out of the 15 occasions the stairway was cleared with no delay, though one must note that walking at 6 to 10 people per foot (20 to 35 per meter) per minute is dense, shoulder to shoulder, with many

people touching each other. On 4 occasions there was turbulence (people bumping into each other) because the platoon coincided with a group of people descending the stairway in reverse flow. On another 4 occasions there were clear signs of incipient queuing (people shortening their pace and bunching up). For short moments, the queue became 3 or 4 people long, as flow exceeded the previously defined threshold of 12 people per minute. Generally, the exit functioned *at the edge of discomfort,* in large part because of reverse flow.

In summary, people need less room on stairways than on level walkways because their movement is inherently *impeded.* In fact, their speed of movement is so much lower that the stairway tends to have a smaller capacity than a level or inclined walk of equal width when flow rates are high. However, in the range of flow that can be considered for design, that is, in the IMPEDED and CONSTRAINED service levels, the capacities of a stairway and a level walkway are remarkably similar. Three basic modes of operation of a stairway are shown in Table 3.13.

Only stairway flows of less than 6 people per minute per foot (20 per meter) offer an adequate level of comfort, with some choice of speed, the ability to bypass slower-moving pedestrians, and without significant conflict with reverse flow.

Flows in the 6 to 12 people per minute per foot (20 to 40 per meter) range are severely constrained, without the ability to bypass slower-moving walkers

and with turbulence and delay due to reverse flow. Space per pedestrian can fall below 10 sq ft (0.9 m), walking is shoulder to shoulder, and the onset of queuing is possible.

Flows in excess of 12 people per minute per foot (40 per meter) mean, as a rule, that a queue is present and hence are characterized as CONGESTED.

These flow rates must, of course, be applied to flow in platoon, not to average flow. The degree and the character of platooning on stairways vary greatly, depending on conditions. A railroad train pulling into a terminal may bring a platoon of 1,000 people, with no one else using the stairway perhaps for the next half-hour. Stairways at subway exits are also most heavily taxed by exiting platoons caused by train arrivals, while entering pedestrian traffic is generally more even. Detailed station design requires simulation of the relevant flows,[18] which no general rules of thumb can adequately replace. Merely for purposes of illustration, the last two columns in Table 3.13 indicate what kind of average flow would correspond to the flows in platoons if the design platoon flow were twice the average rate. This assumption is generally in scale with the data in Table 3.11. Flow in particular platoons exceeds twice the average flow rate in 10 out of 15 cases for the stairway in line 7, in 6 out of 17 cases for the stairway in line 5, and not at all for the stairway in line 1.

The suggested standards for platoons, which actually can mean average flow rates less than half

Table 3.12
Example of Outbound Flow on One Subway Stairway

Flow in Platoons			
No. of people	Duration in min	Pedestrians per ft per min	Notes
128	1:00	12.8	Slowdown, incipient queue 3 to 4 people long
105	1:00	10.5	Slowdown, incipient queue
101	1:00	10.1	No delay
116	1:15	9.3	No delay
91	1:00	9.1	Slowdown
120	1:20	9.0	Slowdown, incipient queue
88	1:00	8.8	No delay
87	1:00	8.7	Some turbulence due to reverse flow
70	0:50	8.4	Reverse flow turbulence
55	0:40	8.3	Reverse flow turbulence
76	1:00	7.6	Reverse flow turbulence
68	1:00	6.8	No delay
54	0:50	6.5	No delay
44	0:45	5.9	No delay
33	0:45	4.4	No delay

Source: Regional Plan Association.
Note: Observations based on 30-min period after 5:00 P.M. and shown in rank order, not in order of occurrence.

Table 3.13
Stairway Service Levels

Quality of flow	Space per person on stairway (in platoons)		Maximum flow, persons per min per unit of stairway width (in platoons)		Maximum av. flow *assuming* platoon flow at twice av. flow rate	
	sq ft	(m²)	per ft	(per m)	per ft	(per m)
IMPEDED	Over 17	(1.6)	Under 6	(under 20)	Under 3	(under 10)
CONSTRAINED	17-7.5	(1.6-0.7)	6-12	(20-40)	3-6	(10-20)
CONGESTED	7.5-5.0	(0.7-0.5)	12-17	(40-56)	6-8.5	(20-28)

Source: Regional Plan Association.

that level, depending on conditions, differ again from those accepted by current practice. For example, while the Bay Area Rapid Transit District recognizes 12 people per minute per foot (40 per meter) as a limit for design, a recent consultant report on the capacity of Grand Central Terminal[19] accepted 13.3 pedestrians per foot of stairway width as a "practical capacity," with no consideration given to platoons. New York City Transit Authority standards accept the value of 16.7 which accurately reflects maximum observed one-way flow but was intended for application to an average 15-min peak, making no reference to platooning, to the formation of queues (which are inevitable at that rate of flow), or to the accommodation of reverse flow. The existence of both reverse flow and a distinct group of very slow-walking pedestrians (the elderly and the physically handicapped) can strongly affect movement on a stairway[20] and must be recognized in design.

Escalators and Moving Walks
The discomfort and delay involved in climbing stairs have led to the use of mechanical moving stairways, first introduced in 1900. Employed originally to overcome large differences in grade where pedestrian flows could not be handled by elevators, moving stairways are increasingly being used for pedestrian assistance wherever large flows have to ascend or descend, even over differences in grade as small as 10 ft. The new Washington subway has an average of seven escalators per station. Motorstairs or escalators perform in a manner quite different from

that of stairways. Their speed is regulated by the motor setting; users can accelerate their progress by walking, but this in no way increases escalator capacity, which is determined by the dimensions of the entrance and the rate at which people enter. The latter, in turn, depends on (1) the arrival rate of users, which (unless they are waiting in a queue) is either random, with unavoidable bunches and gaps, or determined by train arrivals or other platoon-forming events; (2) the agility of the users, who may hesitate longer or shorter before stepping on the escalator; and (3) the users' preference for more or less room on the escalator, depending on whether or not they want to avoid touching other people.

Because of these human factors, the maximum capacity of an escalator, as rated by the manufacturers (50 persons per minute per foot of tread width, or 167 per meter or per escalator unit[21]), cannot be achieved in practice. What can be achieved are essentially two levels of service: a random arrival pattern, without a queue, and a force-fed operation from a waiting queue. Oeding suggests maximum flow on a wide escalator (with steps designed for two people) to be about 18 persons per minute per foot (60 per meter) of tread width, with free arrivals and only occasional bunching, and up to 27 (90) under pressure from a waiting queue. Based on measurements at the Port Authority Bus Terminal, Fruin found 31 persons per foot (103 per meter) of tread width per minute to be the maximum achievable capacity with a long queue. With the most

frequently used tread width (40 in. or 1 m), the flow per meter of width represents, in effect, the flow on one escalator. These values are confirmed in a recent study by Robert O'Neil,[22] who found 103 pedestrians per minute on a wide escalator to be maximum observed flow under crush conditions in subway stations, and he recommends 90 per minute as the maximum value for design. O'Neil emphasizes that, because of short-term pulses, the 1-min. flow rate is "more realistic" than any hourly extrapolation and should apply to flow fed from a waiting queue, "assuming that short queuing delays at escalators are acceptable."

This still leaves open the question, What is moderate queuing and how acceptable is it to people? With the help of computer simulation, Fruin calculated the maximum queue length at that rate of flow to be about 15 persons, implying about a 10-sec maximum delay, which would seem to be acceptable.

In reality, however, when the approach rate of pedestrians to an escalator averages 90 per minute for any considerable period of time, it will inevitably exceed that level for short periods of time, at which point a queue can build up very quickly. Thus, observation of escalators as a part of this study on rare occasions found no queuing even at a flow rate of 90 persons per minute, if the flow during preceding minutes was much lower than that. If, however, the flow during the preceding minutes was at that level or higher, queues of anywhere from 10 to 90 people could be observed, the latter implying a

1-min maximum waiting time, which is quite obnoxious.

Thus, we return to the statement made at the outset of this chapter, that flow near maximum capacity is undesirable because it can lead to a breakdown of movement. If continuous movement over an escalator is to be insured and no queuing is to be tolerated, flow should not exceed 60 to 70 people per escalator per minute, a finding that confirms the lower figure recommended by Oeding. Only when short, sudden surges are preceded by long periods of very sparse flow is the 90 person per minute rate acceptable.

All the flow rates referred to so far pertain to an escalator with a speed of 120 ft per minute (36.6 m/min), measured along the standard 58 percent grade. Observations by Fruin suggest maximum capacity at a speed of 90 ft per minute (27.4 m/min) to be about 9 percent lower, and there is wide agreement that higher speeds can improve both the efficiency and the comfort of escalators. Following overly conservative safety codes, escalator speeds in the United States are set at either 90 or 120 ft per minute (27.4 or 36.6 m/min), with many installations equipped to operate at either of these speeds. In Europe, on the other hand, speeds in the 128 to 180 ft per minute range (39 to 55 m/min) are customary. The London Transport Board found that flow is maximized at a speed of 145 ft per minute (44.2 m/min) and moved as many as 37 persons per minute per foot of tread width (121 per meter) at that speed, with queuing. Further increases in speed tended to reduce flow because of

boarding difficulties. Aside from the obvious benefit of time saving, higher escalator speeds also give each rider more elbow-room while riding because gaps between entering pedestrians are increased by higher speed. However, such high-speed escalators do require a somewhat different design; for example, it is desirable to extend the moving handrails several feet in front and behind the moving steps so that the adjustments of the hands and the feet to a different mode of movement are separated in time. This design is employed in Moscow, London, and other cities. Higher-speed installations sometimes also extend the number of flat steps at the end of the escalator to give the rider a greater sense of security.

Comparing the performance of escalators to that of stairways, we should note that the entire escalator installation is much wider than its moving treads. An escalator with a 40-in. (1 m) tread width and a "nominal" dimension of 48 in. (1.2 m) at the hip level is, including the heavy balustrades, about 6 ft (1.8 m) wide. At the no-queuing flow rate of 18 people per foot (60 per meter) of tread width, it is really moving people at a rate of 10 per foot (33 per meter) of total width occupied. At the maximum flow rate of 27 per foot (90 per meter) of tread width recommended by O'Neil, it is moving people at a rate of 15 per foot (33 per meter) of total width occupied. Thus, the rate per unit of total width without queuing is very similar to the no-queuing stairway capacity in one-way flow without reverse movement, and the maximum

rate with queuing is similar to the maximum rate with queuing on stairs. The capacity of a given band of space to move people is not increased by replacing a stairway with an escalator. The speed is not much better than walking speed upstairs at free flow, unless people do not stand but rather move up on an escalator or unless the escalator is operated at more than 120 ft (36.6 m) per minute. So, the primary purpose of an escalator is to save the effort of climbing a grade.

Indications are that people value that purpose very highly. Earlier we quoted studies concerning the cost of time and introduced some notions concerning the cost of walking. What is the cost of climbing steps? One way of measuring it is in terms of the time spent to avoid climbing steps. This exchange can be observed in places where there is a choice, where stairs parallel an escalator.

In such circumstances, one encounters a group of pedestrians who avoid the escalator even if no waiting is involved. This group usually includes young people who find the escalator too slow and can gain time by running up or downstairs themselves and sometimes older or infirm people who are not sufficiently sure of themselves to venture on a moving stairway.

In Manhattan, this nonescalator group was found to range from less than 2 percent on the 42nd Street Flushing Line escalators, where the stairway is 50 ft (15 m) high and has a 71 percent slope, to about 12 percent on Penn Station escalators, where the stairway is 18.5 ft (5.6 m) high

Queuing in front of escalators. Top photo, at the PATH World Trade Center platforms in Lower Manhattan. The last person in line will have to wait more than half a minute; a considerable number of people are seen using the stairway, which parallells an escalator hidden from view behind it. Lower photo, at the Port Authority Bus Terminal in Midtown Manhattan. The last person in line has about a 14-second wait; about 14 percent are choosing the stairway. Top photograph by Jerome Posatko.

and has a 59 percent slope. At the Port Authority Bus Terminal, where the height is almost the same—19.8 ft (6 m)—a 70 percent slope has a sufficiently deterrent effect so that only 5 percent walk up the steps when there are no queues at the escalators. However, this figure may be depressed because confirmed stairway users have alternative stairs available, which were not observed. Oeding reports the confirmed walker group to number 7 to 8 percent on pedestrian underpasses in Germany, which have differences in grade of about 13 ft (4 m).

As the escalator approaches the limit of free-flow operation and queuing begins to develop, people who would normally use it begin to use the parallel stairway in order to avoid waiting in line. Approximate measurements of this diversion at two Manhattan locations—Penn Station and the Port Authority Bus Terminal—are shown in Figure 3.7. No diversion could be discovered at the third location—the Flushing line escalators, also shown in the diagram. Because of the great height involved and because the station layout is such that queuing occurs before a choice of riding versus walking is available, the small proportion of people using the stairs stayed constant, regardless of the length of the queue. Also shown in the diagram is a fourth location, at the platform of the World Trade Center PATH station, where a typical 30-sec wait for the escalator leads some 26 percent of the people to walk up 15 ft (4.5 m).

The bus terminal and Penn Station curves in Figure 3.7 show

that, as waiting time increases to 40 secs, more than 30 percent of the people will switch from the escalator to the parallel stairway. The wait has to approach 1 min before close to 50 percent use the stairway in lieu of the escalator. Roughly a 20-ft (6 m) climb of stairs seems to be worth 1 min or more of waiting time to half the people. This reinforces our earlier finding in Chapter 2, that the effort of walking appears more onerous to people than the associated time loss, in spite of the high value placed on time. It also suggests that the latent public demand for escalators is high indeed.

By contrast, level moving walks or passenger conveyors so far have not found much application. This is mostly so because their speed is limited to about the same as that of escalators, some 120 ft per minute (36.6 m/min) in the United States and 150 ft per minute (45.7 m/min) in Europe. The limits are intended to avoid sudden acceleration and loss of balance by people stepping on and off, and the difference reflects a different willingness to initiate liability lawsuits. Still, while the top permissible speed in the case of an escalator is either the same or higher than walking speed on stairways, in the case of a moving walk it is always substantially below normal walking speed, which is, say, 260 ft per minute (79 m/min). Though people could, in theory, walk along a moving walk and thus significantly increase their rate of progress, in practice they do so only at very low rates of flow, when more than 30 to 40 sq ft (2.8 to 3.7 m²) per walker are available. Even then, a signifi-

cant number do not walk because of blocked opportunities for passing, because of baggage, or because they do not value time savings high enough compared to the effort of walking. This further reduces the usefulness of moving walks, unless they help to overcome differences in grade.

In fact, about four out of every five moving walks currently in existence are employed to negotiate grades (generally between 10 and 27 percent) and can really be described as moving ramps, not too different from escalators in purpose.

While we found diversion from stairways to parallel escalators—in the absence of a queue—to be generally in the 98 to 88 percent range, depending on the steepness and the height of the stairs, diversion from walkways to parallel horizontal moving walks is in that range only with very light flow, when walking on the belt is possible. Horizontal walks at the Los Angeles International Airport generally attract about 95 percent of the pedestrians on the route they serve off peak, with a flow of about 10 people per belt per minute. This proportion drops to about 70 percent during peak periods when the belts, at 50 persons per minute, begin to develop capacity constraints.

It might seem that the capacity of a moving walk should be the same as that of an escalator of equal speed and width, if people are willing to step on at the same rate and tolerate the same tread area per person. However, the escalator tread area per person is 6.6 sq ft (0.6 m²) with free

Horizontal moving walks at Los Angeles International Airport, in operation since 1965. Each is 424 ft (129 m) long, has a 36 in. (91 cm) clear width of interlocking metal sections, and operates at a speed of 1.36 mph (2.2 km/h), driven by four 7.5 hp electric motors. Except at flows of less than 10 people per minute, corresponding to 36 sq ft (3.3 m^2) per person, most pedestrians stand on the belt because of insufficient space. Photograph courtesy of Los Angeles Department of Airports.

The Bouladon Integrator, one of several experimental designs for an accelerating moving walk. Horizontally sliding metal sections accelerate pedestrians along a parabolic path from walking speed to 9.3 mph (15 km/h). Pedestrians then step sideways onto a synchronized rubber belt moving at constant speed, and leave via a symmetrical decelerating arrangement. Photograph courtesy of Dunlop Limited.

Figure 3.7
The trade off between walking up steps and waiting in a queue for an escalator

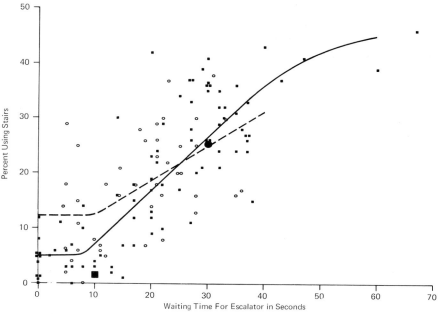

- - - ○ Pennsylvania Station: 18.4 foot rise, 57% grade

——— ▪ Port Authority Bus Terminal: 20 foot rise, 70% grade

▪ Flushing Line 3rd Avenue Exit: 50 foot rise, 71% grade

● World Trade Center: 14 foot rise, 54% grade

arrivals and about 4.4 sq ft (0.4 m²) under moderate pressure from a queue. While these are acceptable for vertical movement, they are, given what we have learned about the space preferences of walking pedestrians, very tight. To the extent that people on a moving walk try to attain more room than that, capacity drops accordingly.

To overcome the main handicap of moving walks, namely, their slow speed, which is conditioned by the pedestrian's vulnerability to sudden acceleration, much ingenuity has been expanded on the design of gradually accelerating moving walks. After nearly a century of false starts, some of the efforts seem to be bearing fruit, and promising designs are in the experimental stage.[23] They could, if successful, accelerate the walker to four or five times the boarding speed and achieve roughly a threefold increase over normal walking speed. This would be competitive not only with downtown bus travel but also with the taxicab in congested traffic. However, an evaluation of the performance and the space requirements of these new devices must wait until they are tested under actual use conditions.[24]

Signalized Intersections

Pedestrian circulation in a downtown area is greatly complicated by conflicts with vehicular surface traffic. Though *separation in space*, such as the pedestrian mall, and *grade separation,* such as the pedestrian underpass, are gaining greater acceptance, the principal means is still *separation in time* at intersections. When intersection flows are so heavy

that random gaps in one stream do not allow safe passage for the other, time must be apportioned among users by traffic signals.

Separation in time means that while one stream of traffic moves through an intersection the other pretenders to its use must wait. The capacity of a traffic channel interrupted by an intersection is thus reduced in relation to the amount of time the intersection is occupied by the conflicting traffic stream.

For example, if the traffic signal shows green on a walkway for only one-third of the time, the crosswalk has to operate at an average of three times the flow rate of the approach walkway to keep up with the incoming pedestrians. This can lead to extreme congestion in the crosswalk. To avoid it, the flow rate at the midblock section of the walkway must be lower than what it could have been with uninterrupted flow.

Nor is congestion in crosswalks the only problem. While people are waiting for the light to change they need standing room, called *reservoir space* in traffic engineering vocabulary. And they are incurring time losses. To date, the most complete analysis of pedestrian flow at signalized intersections has been undertaken by Oeding. He traces several stages of pedestrian progress through an intersection: waiting and formation of platoons, acceleration, interpenetration of the two opposing platoons, and clearing the intersection.

Waiting at the approach to an intersection, pedestrians distrib-

ute themselves at a density that declines as distance from the curb increases. Oeding found that pedestrians at the curb select a space between about 3 and 5 sq ft (0.3 and 0.5 m²) per person, increasing to about 7 sq ft (0.7 m²) per person at a distance 20 ft (6 m) from the curb. This corresponds to Fruin's definition of a *constrained* level of service for standing, as shown in Table 3.2. The short duration of this condition and the fact that all those waiting will move forward as a group are reasons why this level of discomfort is accepted; thus, 5 sq ft (0.5 m²) per standee can be used as an average requirement for reservoir space.

The depth of the reservoir space needed to accommodate the waiting pedestrians can be calculated on the *relative accumulation* at the crosswalk, that is, the number of people per linear unit of curb who wait to cross the roadway during a signal cycle. This is given by the expression

$$(12) \text{ relative accumulation} = \frac{\text{approach flow} \times \text{non-green phase (sec)}}{\text{time of flow (sec)} \times \text{width (ft)}}.$$

For example, with a nongreen time of 1 min and a sidewalk flow of 6 pedestrians per minute per foot (20 per meter), the relative accumulation is 3 persons per foot (10 per meter) of curb, assuming that half the stream is walking in one direction and that turning movements at the intersection balance each other out. With this accumulation, a reservoir space 15-ft (5 m) deep is required at the standard 5 sq ft (0.5 m²) per person. Even at the absolutely minimum allocation of 3 sq ft (0.3 m²) per standee, a 9-ft (3 m) deep reservoir is called for. This depth, of course, could be reduced by making the usable crosswalk wider than the approaching sidewalk. In practice, the problem is handled by pedestrian overflow into vehicular pavement.

Once the waiting group of pedestrians starts moving, the time it will need to clear the roadway is of obvious importance for determining the minimum length of the green phase of the pedestrian signal. This time has two components: the *starting time* needed for the group to get off the curb and the *crossing time* needed to walk to the other side of the roadway. The group waiting for the traffic signal does not start moving instantaneously. Just as in the case of the driver behind the steering wheel, there is a reaction time and an acceleration time involved. Oeding found pedestrians to have an average initial rate of acceleration of 1.1 mi (1.8 km) per hour per second, ranging up to a maximum of 2.2 (3.5 km). This rate declines soon, so that about 5 secs elapse before full speed is attained. Under pressure from a waiting queue, pedestrians step off the curb at an average rate corresponding roughly to 18 persons per minute per foot (60 per meter) of crosswalk width. The total starting time depends on the approach flow, the width of the crosswalk, and the length of the time during which the queue forms, that is, on the relative accumulation as previously defined. On the basis of empirical measurements, Oeding found starting time to vary with relative accumulation as follows:

(13) starting time (secs)
= relative accumulation
(persons/foot) × 1.64 + 4.

Thus, for an accumulation of 3 persons per foot (10 per meter) of crosswalk width, a starting time of about 9 secs is required.

To determine crossing time, pedestrian speed in crosswalks has to be measured. The *Traffic Engineering Handbook*[25] shows the full range of unimpeded pedestrian speeds, from 150 to 400 ft (45.7 to 122 m) per minute, with an average of 250 ft (76.2 m) for women and 270 (82.3) for men as being characteristic of behavior in crosswalks. By contrast, Oeding found very substantial differences in crosswalk speeds, depending on whether the flow is one-directional or bi-directional, and depending on the rate of flow. In one-way flow, he measured speeds as high as 295 ft (90 m) per minute at very tight space allocations of 10 to 15 sq ft (.9 to 1.4 m²) per pedestrian, suggesting that the commuters involved were really in a great rush to clear the intersection. In two-way flow and shopping-type traffic, he measured speeds ranging from a high of 260 ft (79 m) per minute at space allocations of 40 sq ft (3.7 m²) per pedestrian to a low of 130 ft (40 m) per minute at about 5 sq ft (0.5 m²) per pedestrian. The latter figures clearly show a performance depressed by internal friction, a result of the meeting of two opposing streams of pedestrians in the middle of the crosswalk.

The time needed to cross the roadway has three components: the time needed for the two pla-

toons to walk up to each other, the time needed to penetrate each other, and the time needed to walk the rest of the distance to the curb on the opposite side of the street. Oeding shows an analytical procedure for estimating these individual components, which we will not recount in detail. Suffice it to say that, on the average, crosswalk speeds seem to be at or above free-flow levels when the sum of the two relative accumulations is less than 1 person per foot (3 persons per meter) of crosswalk width. As total accumulation rises from 1 to 3 persons per foot (3 to 10 per meter) of width, average crossing speed drops from the neighborhood of 270 to about 200 ft (80 to 60 m) per minute and then stays at that level up to a total accumulation of about 6 persons per foot (20 per meter). This, of course, is valid only for bi-directional flow. When flow is only in one direction and no confrontation of two platoons in the middle of the street occurs, crosswalk speeds are only marginally affected by volume.

The mechanics of the meeting of the two platoons in the middle of the roadway deserves closer attention. As the light turns green, they start walking toward each other at a speed that requires perhaps 15 sq ft (1.4 m²) per pedestrian. As they start interpenetrating, each individual's space allocation (if the platoons are equal in number) is suddenly cut in half. If we remember equation (10) and the speed-space diagram in Figure 3.3, we can see that the average speed also has to fall drastically, perhaps from 230 to 150 ft (from 70 to 46 meters) per minute, given the space allo-

Pedestrian space in crosswalks. Top view in Midtown Manhattan: UN-IMPEDED flow on approaches results in an acceptable space of about 20 sq ft (1.8 m^2) per person on the average in the crosswalk, and about 14 sq ft (1.3 m^2) in the middle. Lower view, in Lower Manhattan. CONSTRAINED flow on approaches results in wall-to-wall people: an estimated 7 sq ft (0.6 m^2) per person on the average in the crosswalk, and less than that in the middle.

The absence of pedestrian reservoir space on narrow sidewalks forces those waiting for the light to change into the vehicular roadway. Without sidewalk widening at intersections, this kind of overspill becomes inevitable when flow on the approaches is in the IMPEDED range, on the average, and becomes critical when approach flow is in the CONSTRAINED range.

The five phases of crossing an intersection. First, led by a few venturesome souls, the waiting platoon of pedestrians is poised at the curb to accelerate. Second, the platoons from both sides of the street start moving toward each other. Third, the platoons meet and interpenetrate. For a short time, available space in the pedestrian stream is cut in half, causing delay. In this view, people compensate for the shortage of space in the crosswalk by walking a wider front. Fourth, the platoons begin to arrive at opposite sides of the street. Fifth, the major platoon flow is over, but stragglers—among them several older people—continue to walk; cars begin to make turning movements. The total time required for the operation depends on the number of pedestrians, their directional distribution, the width of the front in which they are waiting and walking, and on the width of the street to be crossed. Photographs by Paul Cardell.

cation used as an example. If the space allocation is low to begin with, at the time the two platoons meet it can fall below the critical value of about 5 sq ft (0.5 m²) per pedestrian, at which point not only the speed but also the flow rates begin to decline, and movement is jammed. Fortunately, since the time during which the two opposing platoons interpenetrate is not too long, the jam can dissipate fairly quickly. Still, the minimum space per pedestrian at the moment the two platoons meet strongly affects the service level of the intersection. Oeding found this space to depend on the sum of the relative accumulations (accum.₁ and accum.₂) on both sides of the street, in a manner shown below:

(14) minimum crosswalk space (sq ft/ped) =

$$\frac{10.76}{0.25\ (\text{accum.}_1 + \text{accum.}_2) + 0.77}.$$

The equation, generally valid in a range where the sum of the two accumulations is greater than 1 but smaller than 6, suggests that the minimum crosswalk space falls below the critical value of 5 sq ft (0.5 m²) per person when the sum of the two accumulations exceeds 6 pedestrians per foot (20 per m) of crosswalk width.

The three intersection characteristics discussed above—the *minimum pedestrian green time,* the *depth of reservoir space,* and the *minimum space allocation in the crosswalk* at the time the opposing platoons meet—are summarized in Table 3.14 for average flow rates ranging from 0.5 to 10 pedestrians per minute per

foot (1.6 to 33 per m) of sidewalk width; higher flow rates are rarely encountered on sidewalks. In each case it is assumed that the intersection approach flow is half the average sidewalk flow, a condition fairly representative of midday. The roadway widths assumed in the Table 3.14 and the nongreen phase are quite typical of avenues and streets in Midtown Manhattan. The figures represent theoretical values based on the relationships presented above. No field testing of intersection performance was possible as a part of this study.

Table 3.14 confirms our earlier analysis that only average flows of less than 2 persons per minute per foot (6.5 per m) of walkway width are truly UNIMPEDED. Thus, at this flow level, starting times are short, crossing speeds are almost free flowing, the required depth of reservoir space does not preempt more than one-quarter to one-third of the sidewalk width, and the tightest space allocation in the crosswalk the moment two opposing platoons meet is on the order of 10 sq ft (0.9 m²) per person.

Flows of 2 to 6 persons per minute per foot (6.5 to 20) are no longer free but are IMPEDED in various ways. The minimum pedestrian green time does not pose any problems, but the crossing speeds are constrained in varying degree. The required depth of reservoir space goes up to 15 ft (4.6 m) on an avenue and 10 ft (3 m) on a street; since sidewalks typically come in 15- to 20-ft (4.6 to 6 m) widths on avenues and 12- to 15-ft (3.6 to 4.6 m) widths on streets, a substantial spillover of waiting pedes-

trians into the roadway cannot be avoided, because the sidewalk still has to accommodate the perpendicular flow. The minimum space per person in crosswalks at the time the opposing platoons meet drops below the critical level of 5 sq ft (0.5 m²) at flows in excess of 5 (16) in our avenue example and at flows in excess of 8 (26) in our street example. Thus, an undetermined number of seconds of congestion delay (when movement is at a standstill) has to be added to our minimum crossing time in that range, indicated by the question marks in the table (though Oeding observed that pedestrians tend to make up for congestion delay in crosswalks by walking faster once out of the jam).

Finally, at flows of 6 to 10 persons per minute per foot (20 to 33 per meter) of width, the minimum pedestrian green time begins to exceed the actual green time available in our avenue example. The required reservoir space becomes wider than the actual sidewalks available. And the minimum crosswalk space drops to virtually standing-room levels. In reality, of course, people would take various evasive maneuvers under these conditions, such as walking in a much wider front than the painted crosswalk and preempting some of the nongreen time. *In summary, 6 persons per minute per foot (20 per m) of sidewalk width represents the practical capacity of a sidewalk system with signalized intersections,* and *2 persons (6.5) per minute per foot represents a desirable service level.*

Perhaps the most serious problem of intersections from the pedes-

Table 3.14

Examples of Intersection Characteristics at Varying Rates of Pedestrian Flow

Average sidewalk flow, peds./min/ft		Minimum pedestrian green time (starting time + crossing time), secs	Required depth of reservoir space, ft	Minimum crosswalk space, sq ft
Crossing 65-ft roadway with 60 secs nongreen time per cycle				
0.5	OPEN	4.4 + 14.5 = 18.9	1.3	Adequate
1	UNIMPEDED	4.8 + 14.5 = 19.3	2.5	10.5
2		5.6 + 17.0 = 22.6	5.0	8.5
3		6.5 + 20.0 = 26.5	7.5	7.1
4	IMPEDED	7.3 + 20.0 = 27.3	10.0	6.1
5		8.1 + 20.0 = 28.0	12.5	5.3
6		8.9 + 20.0 = 28.9	15.0	4.7
7		9.7 + 20.0 = 29.7 +?	17.5	(4.3)*
8	CONSTRAINED	10.6 + 20.0 = 30.6 +?	20.0	(3.9)
9		11.4 + 20.0 = 31.4 +?	22.5	(3.6)
10		12.2 + 20.0 = 32.2 +?	25.0	(3.3)
Crossing 34-ft roadway with 40 secs nongreen time per cycle				
0.5	OPEN	4.3 + 7.5 = 11.8	0.8	Adequate
1	UNIMPEDED	4.5 + 7.5 = 12.0	1.7	11.5
2		5.1 + 7.5 = 12.6	3.3	9.8
3		5.6 + 7.5 = 13.1	5.0	8.5
4	IMPEDED	6.2 + 7.6 = 13.8	6.7	7.5
5		6.7 + 7.9 = 14.6	8.3	6.7
6		7.3 + 8.3 = 15.6	10.0	6.1
7		7.8 + 8.7 = 16.5	11.7	5.6
8	CONSTRAINED	8.4 + 9.2 = 17.6	13.3	5.1
9		8.9 + 10.4 = 19.3	15.0	4.7
10		9.5 + 10.4 = 19.9 +?	16.7	(4.4)

Source: Developed from Oeding, *Verkehrsbelastung und Dimensionierung von Gehwegen.*
*Numbers in parentheses represent situations that probably do not exist.

trian viewpoint is, as Oeding puts it, "the side effect of short green phases or long signal cycles, namely the accumulation of standing pedestrians," for which the sidewalks were never designed and which causes considerable time loss to the pedestrians.

The primary objective of signalized intersection timing is to accommodate all the required flows with a minimum total delay. Usually, however, the emphasis is on minimizing delay to vehicles, in the hope that pedestrians will take care of themselves by seizing available opportunities whenever there are gaps in the traffic stream. Of course, pedestrians do this, traffic regulations notwithstanding, but a more explicit consideration of their needs is in order.[26] At issue may be, for example, the selection of a cycle length that is in rhythm with pedestrian speed so that opportunities for "being caught by a red light" are minimized. Some related aspects of the pedestrian-vehicular balance will be introduced in the next chapter. Other important subjects such as the effect of turning vehicles on pedestrian flow at intersections and the entire field of pedestrian accidents caused by vehicles, will have to remain outside our purview.

Notes for Chapter 3

1. Edward T. Hall, *The Hidden Dimension* (New York: Doubleday, 1966), pp. 107-122.

2. John J. Fruin, "Designing for Pedestrians; a Level of Service Concept" (Ph.D. dissertation, Polytechnic Institute of Brooklyn, 1970). For an abbreviated version, see also John J. Fruin, *Pedestrian Planning and Design,* Metropolitan Association of Urban Designers and Environmental Planners, Inc. (New York, 1971).

3. New York City Planning Commission, *Metropolitan Mobility* (New York, 1965), p. 9. Comfort standard of 48,000 persons per hour, or 160 per 60-ft car, with 50 seats and a 353 sq ft clear floor area leaves 3.2 sq ft per standee.

4. Detlef Oeding, "Verkehrsbelastung und Dimensionierung von Gehwegen und anderen Anlagen des Fussgaengerverkehrs" [Traffic Loads and Dimensions of Walkways and Other Pedestrian Circulation Facilities], in *Strassenbau und Strassenverkehrstechnik,* no. 22 (Bonn, 1963).

S. J. Older, "Movement of Pedestrians on Footways in Shopping Streets," in *Traffic Engineering and Control* (London, August 1968), pp. 160-163.

Francis P. D. Navin and R. J. Wheeler, "Pedestrian Flow Characteristics," in *Traffic Engineering* (Washington, D.C., June 1969), pp. 30-36.

Fruin, "Designing for Pedestrians."

5. B. D. Hankin and R. A. Wright, "Passenger Flow in Subways," *Operational Research Quarterly* 81, no. 2 (London, June 1958).

H. Kirsch, "Leistungsfaehigkeit und Dimensioneirung von Gehwegen" [Capacity and Dimensions of Walkways], in *Strassenverkehr and Strassenverkehrstechnik,* no. 33 (1964). Based on dissertation at Techische Hochschule Aachen.

M. P. Ness, J. F. Morall and B. G. Hutchinson, *An Analysis of Central Business District Circulation Patterns,* Highway Research Record no. 283 (Washington, D.C., 1969), see esp. p. 17.

Coleman A. O'Flaherty and M. H. Parkinson, "Movement on a City Centre Footway," *Traffic Engineering and Control* (London, February 1972), pp. 434-438.

6. *Highway Capacity Manual,* Highway Research Board Special Report 87, (Washington, D.C., 1965), pp. 58-70.

7. The linearity of the speed-density relationship has been questioned, among other sources, by the *Highway Capacity Manual,* p. 69. Indeed, there is some tendency for observations to depart from a constant slope both in the high- and low-density ranges, for both vehicles and pedestrians: at very high densities flow resists grinding to a complete halt and attempts to maintain some speed even with minimal allocations of space, while at very low densities speeds may not expand proportionately to rising space allocations because of imposed or inherent speed limits. However, a thorough statistical investigation of seven different hypotheses concerning the shape of the speed-density relationship indicated differences among most of them to be rather small; the single linear relationship (sometimes named after B. D. Greenshields, who developed it in 1935) had the second highest correlation coefficient and was the only one to predict theoretical maximum speed at free flow—a figure we are using in subsequent analysis. For further detail, see Joseph S. Drake, Joseph L. Schofer, and Adolf D. May, Jr., *A Statistical Analysis of Speed Density Hypotheses,* Highway Research Record no. 154 (Washington, D.C., 1967), pp. 53-87.

8. L. A. Hoel, "Pedestrian Travel Rates in Central Business Districts," *Traffic Engineering,* January 1968, pp. 10-13.

9. L. F. Henderson, "The Statistics of Crowd Fluids," *Nature* 229 (February 1971), pp. 381-383.

10. Michael Wolff, and Verena Hirsch, "The Behavior of Pedestrians on 42nd Street, New York City" (Work sheets for City University of New York, 1969); for a published summary, see Michael Wolff, "Notes on the Behavior of Pedestrians," in *People in Places: The Sociology of the Familiar,* Arnold Birenbaum, and Edward Sagarin, eds. (New York: Praeger, 1973).

11. J. Rock, L. Greenberg, P. Hill, and J. Meyers, "Aspects of Pedestrian Walkways," (Paper for New York University Graduate School of Public Administration, 1971).

12. John Baerwald, ed., *Traffic Engineering Handbook,* 3rd ed. (Washington, D.C.: Institute of Traffic Engineers, 1965), pp. 113-120.

13. O'Flaherty and Parkinson, "Movement on a City Centre Footway."

14. Rai Y. Okamoto and Robert J. Beck, "Preliminary Report on the Urban Density Study," Prepared at Regional Plan Association under a grant from the National Institutes of Mental Health (May 1970).

15. Baerwald, *Traffic Engineering Handbook,* p. 111.

16. J. H. Callender, ed., *Time Saver Standards; A Handbook of Architec-*

tural Design, 4th ed. (New York: McGraw-Hill, 1966).

17. John A. Templer and Paul J. Corcoran, "Energy Expenditure as a Factor in Staircase and Ramp Design," in *Man-Transportation Interface* (Washington, D.C.: American Society of Civil Engineers, June 1972), p. 67.

18. Peter Fausch, "Simulation Tools for Designing Pedestrian Movement Systems in Urban Transportation Facilities," Paper presented at Pedestrian/Bicycle Planning and Design Seminar (San Francisco, December, 1972). Based on Barton-Aschman Associates, Inc., "Functional Specifications for a Transit Station Simulation Model," for U.S. Urban Mass Transportation Administration.

19. Wilbur Smith and Associates, *Pedestrian Impact Study for the Proposed 175 Park Avenue Building* (New York, May 1968).

20. For a more detailed discussion of reverse flow as well as directional considerations in design of stairways, see Gary H. Winkel and Geoffrey D. Hayward, "Some Major Causes of Congestion in Subway Stations" (City University of New York Environmental Psychology Program, May 1971).

21. Escalators in North American practice come in 32 or 48 in. "nominal" widths (measured at the hip) which correspond to 24 and 40 in. tread widths. The outside dimensions are at least 28 in. wider. See George R. Strakosch, *Vertical Transportation* (New York: John Wiley & Sons, 1967.) In European practice, a 1-m, or 39.4-in., tread width is common.

22. Robert S. O'Neil, "Escalators in Rapid Transit Stations," *Transportation Engineering Journal, ASCE* 100, no. TE 1, Proceedings Paper 10333 (February 1974), pp. 1-12.

23. Aside from the extensive manufacturers' literature on moving walks, the following references provide a good overview:

John M. Tough and Coleman A. O'Flaherty, *Passenger Conveyors* (London: Ian Allan, 1971). (Includes an extensive bibliography and an inventory of 150 installations).

Rick Kuner, *The Boston Moving Walk Study* (Chicago: Barton-Aschman Associates, 1972).

Tri-State Regional Planning Commission, *High Speed, Continuous Flow Person Conveyors,* Interim Technical Report 4089-0600 (New York, 1968).

Kaiser Engineers, *Peoplemover Systems for Mid and Lower Manhattan* (New York, January 1973).

"Moving Way Transit" *Lea Transit Compendium,* 1, no. 2 (Huntsville, Alabama, 1974).

Richard A. Fennelly, "People Movers on the New York City Transit System" *The Municipal Engineers Journal,* 60 no. 3, 1974, pp. 77-107.

24. Tri-State Regional Planning Commission, "Preliminary Application-Demonstration Project-High Speed Moving Sidewalk," For submission to Urban Mass Transportation Administration, U. S. Department of Transportation, Metropolitan Transportation Authority, Sponsor (New York, 1974).

25. John Baerwald, *Traffic Engineering Handbook.*

26. For an alternate approach to the issue of pedestrian delay, see J. R. Allison, et al., "A Method of Analysis of the Pedestrian System of a Town Centre (Nottingham City)," *Journal of the Town Planning Institute* 56, no. 8 (London, Sept./Oct. 1970).

See also: Hans-Georg Retzko and Wolfgang Androsch, "Pedestrian Behavior at Signalized Intersections" *Traffic Engineering and Control,* August-September 1974.

Chapter 4

Implications for Design

If people trained as designers are to influence the shape of the city, they must be present when the critical design decisions are being made. Instead of handing over city designs as an ostensibly finished product . . . designers of cities should seek to write the rules for the significant choices that shape the city.

Jonathan Barnett,
Urban Design as Public Policy

Aggregate Measures of Travel Demand

Having investigated the dimensions of pedestrian travel demand and analyzed the pedestrian's needs for space, we can now synthesize these findings and develop guidelines for design. However, before we pinpoint the pedestrian space requirements of individual buildings and installations, it is useful to gain an understanding of aggregate travel demand by modes other than walking.

Trip Generation in Urban Centers

The high concentration of pedestrians in urban centers is possible because they arrive there by modes of travel other than walking and can thus be drawn from a wide tributary area. Hourly counts intercepting all persons entering and leaving by all modes of travel in the course of a day can provide us, for an entire central business district (CBD), the kind of data on peaking and maximum accumulation we collected earlier for individual buildings. Related to the total floor-space in a business center, these counts can yield approximate measures of trip generation and suggest how many people are around who can be expected to make trips on foot.

A summary of available data for the central business districts of sixteen large cities is shown in Table 4.1, to give the reader a rough sense of scale. The Central Business District of New York stands out as being comparable in size only to the central area of London. However, with respect to the density of floor space and hence the density of pedestrian destinations, the differences among the urban centers listed are not that great. From earlier data for Manhattan's central square mile we can see that its ratio of total floor space to total land area is 6.6, but for the Central Business District as a whole it is shown to be 3.1, similar to the Chicago Loop. For the other centers, the floor-space-to-land ratios descend to a low of 1.5 in the CBD of Baltimore.

It can be further calculated from Table 4.1 that in most of the centers *1,000 sq ft (93 m²) of floor space attract between 6 and 12 one-way trips by mechanical modes per day, including through trips,* and that between 14 and 25 percent of these occurs during the peak hour. Peak-hour entries are similar to office employment in magnitude. It is also evident that the proportion of people arriving by public transit, rather than by automobile, increases with center size and density.

Manhattan's attractiveness for trips crossing the Central Business District cordon appears to be lower than that of any of the other centers listed: only 4.3 daily inbound trips per 1,000 sq ft of floor space. In part this is due to its island geography and high density, which tend to reduce the amount of travel, particularly through trips. In part this is due to its large area, which contains a residential population that attracts few outside trips but creates internal movement not registered by a cordon count.

Though comprehensive data for Manhattan are rather elusive and figures available from different sources not easy to reconcile, we can try to subtract through trips from persons entering Manhattan, as shown in Table 4.1, add estimated internal trips within the Central Business District, and see if the result matches our earlier findings about residential and nonresidential trip generation rates. This is done in the top part of Table 4.2.

The residential rate of 1.4 trips by mechanical modes per day in Table 4.2 must be multiplied by 2 to be comparable to the two-way trip definition in Table 2.1 earlier. It can be reconciled assuming that at residential buildings in the CBD roughly 60 percent of all trips are walk-only trips and that mechanical trips at the upper-middle income buildings in Table 2.1 are higher than average.

The nonresidential rate of 6.0 trips by mechanical modes per day per 1,000 sq ft (93 m²) of floor space, when multiplied by 2 and expanded on the basis of our earlier finding that some 26 percent of all trips at office buildings are walk-only trips, yields a travel rate by all modes of 16.2, which is reasonably higher than the 14.1 average of three Manhattan office buildings in Table 2.2. This rate accounts for the sharply higher trip generation of a relatively small amount of retail floor space as well as for the below-average trip generation of a large amount of loft, warehousing, institutional, and other nonoffice floor space. The 6.0 nonresidential rate is no longer out of line with the other central business districts in Table 4.1 and is, just as the 1.4 residential rate, only slightly higher than figures based on Tri-State Region-

al Planning Commission's home-interview surveys.

Having thus tentatively reconciled (1) hub-bound travel statistics, based on traffic counts, (2) trip-generation rates for mechanized modes of travel, based on home interviews, and (3) our own counts reported earlier, we can make a rough estimate of total pedestrian trips in the Manhattan Central Business District, which appears in the right part of Table 4.2. The estimate is 10.2 million walks on an average weekday.

To verify the general consistency of a long chain of measures of pedestrian movement presented so far in this book, an independent and more elaborate method of calculating the total number of trips on foot is given in Table 4.3. Some of the measures, notably the peaking factor and the average trip length, are extremely volatile, and small changes in them can strongly affect the result. Nevertheless, as it stands, Table 4.3 arrives at a very similar result, 10.3 million walks.

The peak daytime 1971 population found in the Manhattan Central Business District (south of 60th Street) at 2:00 P.M. is about 2.1 million. Of these, about 0.5 million are residents, about 1.4 million are workers living outside the CBD, and some 0.2 million are other visitors. These people plus those who either leave before or arrive after 2:00 P.M. spend at least one million hours a day walking in the CBD, more than 20 min per person. However, of the 10 million walks they take, only about 3 million

appear to be "pure" walks; the other 7 million are to or from mechanical means of travel: about 3.7 million to or from subway stations, 0.34 million to and from Grand Central Terminal and Penn Station, 0.22 million to and from the Port Authority Bus Terminal, and the rest to and from local buses, autos, and other surface modes. *Walking in the CBD emerges primarily as ancillary to travel by mechanical modes, with the underground modes—subways and railroads— accounting for about 40 percent of all trips on foot.*

The historic pattern of travel to the Manhattan Central Business District by both the underground and the surface modes is shown graphically in Figure 4.1, based on hub-bound travel statistics used in the preceding discussion.[1] The number of people entering on an average day on four major types of facilities is compared with the physical width of these facilities. The space-consuming nature of local streets (Manhattan avenues, in this case) and, to a lesser degree, of expressways compared with railroads and especially with rapid transit is apparent. We have discussed this matter in Chapter 1 and will return to its implications for pedestrian movement shortly.

Another message to which we will also address ourselves is the chicken-or-egg relationship between travel demand and the supply of transportation facilities. Figure 4.1 shows that the number of railroad tracks leading into the Manhattan CBD remained constant during the half-century shown and that the number of people using them has remained

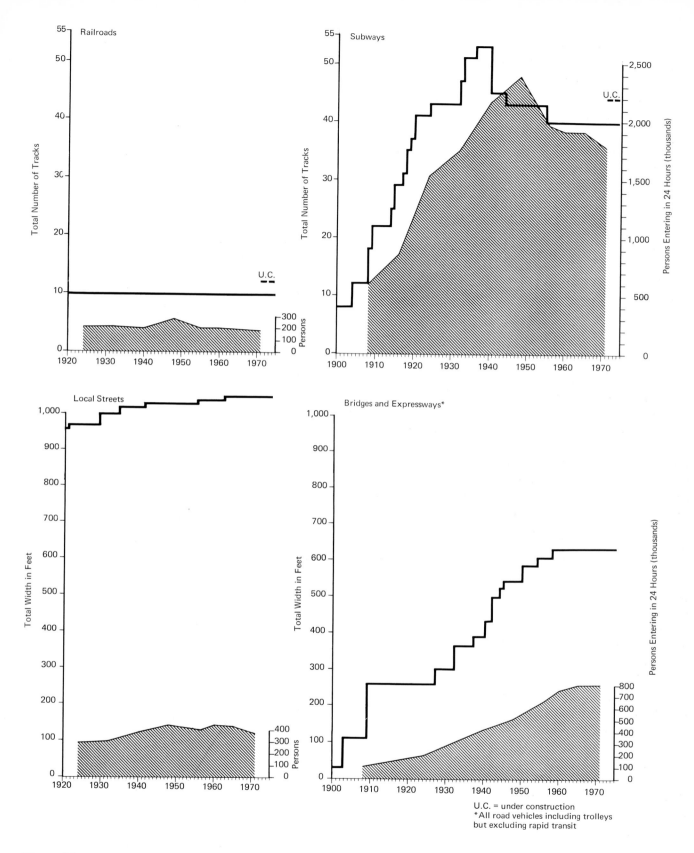

Figure 4.1
Trips entering the Manhattan CBD related to available capacity

Table 4.1
Travel and Floor Space in Selected Central Business Districts

| | Persons entering CBD during typical weekday | | | | total fl. space | office fl. space | Land area, | Total fl. space |
	persons (× 1,000)	% by transit	during peak hr (× 1,000)	Maximum net[†] accumulation (× 1,000)	(millions of sq ft)		(sq mi)	to land ratio
1. New York	3,167	71.1	805	1,538	739.8	245	8.6	3.1
2. London	(3,215)	76.4	722	n.d.	n.d.	125	10.0	n.d.
3. Chicago	864	59.0	206	282	92.3	(63)	1.1	3.0
4. Los Angeles	679	25.4	77	158	40.4	15.8	0.6	2.4
5. Philadelphia	900	52.7	155	210	124.2	(34)	1.9	2.3
6. Detroit	385	39.5	66	n.d.	50	(23)	1.1	1.6
7. San Francisco	672	52.9	(114)	165	n.d.	(26)	n.d.	n.d.
8. Boston	840	45.3	141	190	69.5	24.3	1.4	1.8
9. Pittsburgh	261	51.5	(52)	n.d.	32.3	15.8	0.5	2.3
10. St. Louis	348	26.5	62	89	39.2	11.3	0.9	1.6
11. Cleveland	273	43.0	(55)	92	46.8	15.3	1.0	1.7
12. Baltimore	385	30.8	54	118	33.0	(11)	0.8	1.5
13. Houston	324	22.6	55	55	n.d.	22	0.9	n.d.
14. Milwaukee	278	31.7	(47)	n.d.	31.2	14	n.d.	n.d.
15. Dallas	354	20.0	60	109	30.6	10.3	0.5	2.2
16. Seattle[‡]	100	32.0	n.d.	n.d.	27.0	5.0	0.3	3.2

Sources: Wilbur Smith and Associates, *Transportation and Parking for Tomorrow's Cities,* 1966, pp. 314-326; Manhattan floor space and travel (1971), Tri-State Regional Planning Commission.

Notes: n.d.-no data; numbers in parentheses are estimates.

Travel figures refer to various years between 1953 and 1971 and daily counts of persons entering are based variously on 24, 18, or 12 hrs.

*Railroad, subway, and bus; streetcar in some cities.

[†]Exclusive of persons living in CBD (518,000 in the case of Manhattan).

[‡]Excluding through trips and including 6 percent walk-only trips across the CBD cordon.

Table 4.2
Estimated Travel to and within the Manhattan Central Business District

	Person trips
Mechanical trips	
Inbound trips across CBD cordon	3,170,000
Through trips (double counted as inbound)	−600,000
Net inbound trips	2,570,000
Internal trips within CBD	+1,000,000
Total trips attracted by CBD floor space	3,570,000

	Residential	Nonresidential	Total
Trips	260,000	3,310,000	3,570,000
Floor space (sq ft)	186,000,000	554,000,000	740,000,000
One-way trips/1,000 sq ft of floor space	1.4	6.0	4.8

Table 4.3
Estimate of Pedestrian Travel in the Manhattan Central Business District Based on Aerial Photography of Midtown

Step 1: Calculate person-miles of travel on foot (PMT) in central 1.2 sq mi.

Total pedestrians at an instant between 1:30 and 2:00 P.M.	37,510
Pedestrians in walkways (sidewalks and plazas)	34,900 (93.0%)
Pedestrian pavement in walkways (from Table 2.17)	5,036,760 sq ft
Average walkway space per pedestrian	144 sq ft
Assumed speed including delays: 250 feet per minute, or per 30 minutes	7,500 ft/½ hr

Average flow, from equation (6) $\dfrac{7{,}500 \text{ ft}/½ \text{ hr}}{144 \text{ sq ft}/\text{ped}}$ = 52 peds/ft/½ hr

Total walkway width and length = $\sqrt{5{,}036{,}760}$	= 2,244 ft or 0.425 mi
Total flow = 2,244 ft × 52 peds/ft/½ hr	= 116,688 peds/½ hr
Person-miles of travel = 116,688 peds/½ hr × 0.425 mi	= 49,592 PMT/½ hr
Add 7 percent of travel not in walkways	53,321 PMT/½ hr
Flow 1:30 to 2:00 P.M. as a share of 24 hours (from Table 2.9 and 4.10)	5.56 percent
Expand PMT from ½ hour to 24 hours (÷ 5.56 × 100)	959,000 PMT/24 hrs

Step 2: Convert person-miles of travel into trips.

Average trip length (from Tables 2.12, 2.13 and 2.14 adjusting for high share of shorter trips to subway)	0.29 miles/trip
959,000 PMT/24 hours ÷ 0.29 miles/trip	**= 3,307,000 trips/24 hrs**

Step 3: Expand trip estimate for central area to entire CBD.

Subtract trips to and from subway stops in central area	− 1,496,000
Remaining trips assumed to depend on nonresidential space	1,811,000
Expand by ratio of nonresidential floorspace in central area to nonresidential floorspace in entire CBD (27.6 percent) or × 3.62	6,556,000
Add trips to and from subways in entire CBD (turnstile count × 2)	3,717,000

Estimate II: Total pedestrian trips in the Manhattan CBD	**10,273,000 trips/24 hours**

Source: Regional Plan Association.

Table 4.2 Continued	Person trips
Pedestrian trips	
Net inbound mechanical 2,570,000 × 2 (to include outbound trips)	5,140,000
Internal mechanical trips 1,000,000 × 2 (one walk at each end)	2,000,000
Walk-only trips assumed as 26 percent of all two-way nonresidential trips	2,326,000
Walk-only trips assumed as 60 percent of all two-way residential trips	750,000
Estimate 1: Total pedestrian trips per 24 hrs in the Manhattan CBD	10,216,000

Sources: Tri-State Regional Planning Commission, *Hub-Bound Travel; Trips Crossing the Manhattan Central Business District Cordon in 1971*, 1973. Also unpublished data from Regional Plan Association and Tri-State Regional Planning Commission.

surprisingly stable. Local street width was expanded somewhat by cutting back sidewalks, and the period of expansion coincides with expanded travel. The periods of dramatic expansion of capacity on subways and later on limited access highways are periods of dramatic growth in patronage. It is usually assumed without question that capacity is expanded in response to rising demand. However, it is useful to look at the other side of the coin, the rise in demand in response to available capacity. Between 1927 and 1957 highway width increased some 140 percent and the number of people carried on these highways, 190 percent. Between 1957 and 1971 no additional highways were built, and the people carried increased only 11 percent. The continuing decline in rapid transit patronage is, at least in some part, a response to a deficiency of capacity at an acceptable level of comfort. The cutbacks of 1940 and 1955 represent removal of elevated lines, and new construction to rectify the deficiency is shown in dashed lines.

Pedestrians and Rapid Transit
To make daily averages such as those shown in Figure 4.1 meaningful for design, peaking patterns have to be known. These are shown, in summary form, in Table 4.4 and illustrated graphically, hour by hour, in Figure 4.2. Commuter railroads have the sharpest peak (they carry some 46 percent of their inbound daily riders in one hour), followed in a regularly descending order by subways, buses, taxis, and private cars.

While autos and taxis are responsible for one-quarter of all travel to the CBD during the course of a day, their share of peak-hour travel is only 9 percent. By contrast, *some 80 percent of all peak-hour inbound travel occurs underground, by subway and rail.* In the daily total the share of the underground modes is smaller; still, they remain the largest source of pedestrians circulating in the Central Business District.

From the figures presented here, some criteria for the design of pedestrian approaches to the underground modes and for the land use around them can be derived. For example, if nonresidential space attracts 8 one-way trips per 1,000 sq ft in the course of a day, if 40 percent of these trips is by subway, and if almost 33 percent of subway travel in any one direction occurs during the peak hour, then *1,000 sq ft of nonresidential floor space attracts 3.2 subway trips in the course of a day and about 1 trip in the peak hour, on the average.* Of course, nonresidential destinations vary from hour to hour; trips to office jobs are heavily concentrated between 8:00 and 9:00 A.M., and the office building rate can be estimated at about *1.5 peak-hour subway trips per 1,000 sq ft of office floor space.* Our office building interviews described earlier suggest a somewhat lower figure because of what appears to be an unusually high proportion of bus and railroad trips at the buildings sampled.

It can be further shown that in the course of an average weekday residential buildings attract 0.5 subway trips per resident of Manhattan outside the CBD* and 0.3 trips per resident of other parts of the city with good sub-

way service. For *each 1,000 sq ft (93 m²) of residential floor space,* this corresponds to between 1.3 and 0.8 one-way daily trips by subway, or *0.40 to 0.25 peak hour trips.*

One 600-ft (183 m) long and 10-ft (3 m) wide subway train carries 1,500 passengers at a moderately comfortable service level ("constrained," rather than "congested," in Table 3.2) and *can thus serve, in the rush hour, one 1-million sq ft (93,000 m²) office building* at one end *and the equivalent of 4,000 to 6,000 dwelling units* at the other. One track with a 30-train hourly capacity can, accordingly, serve 30 million sq ft (2.8 million m²), of office floor space (the equivalent of three World Trade Centers) and a residential population in excess of 300,000.

Of course, these ratios are applicable only given the relative usage of travel modes characteristic of New York. Even there, caution should be exercised in applying them. The mistake is often made of applying such rates directly to estimate subway requirements of new office buildings. In reality, much new office construction in Manhattan (perhaps 60 percent) has occurred to replace obsolete space and to provide more space per worker, not to accommodate additional workers. Moreover, the increase in office workers in one area can be cancelled out by blue-collar job declines in other

---

*This includes incidental commercial and institutional uses in the residential area. It reflects a trip generation rate higher than in Table 4.2 for that reason, and also because mechanical trips within the CBD are fewer due to walking.

Table 4.4
Peaking Patterns of Persons Entering the
Manhattan CBD

	Percentage of each mode's inbound passengers carried during		Percentage of total inbound passengers carried by each mode during	
	Highest Hr	Highest 12 Hrs*	8-9 A.M.	24 Hrs
Railroad	45.6	93.1	9.7	5.4
Subway	31.0	89.7	70.0	56.5
Bus	22.4	86.5	8.1	8.1
Auto & taxi, truck	8.7	71.1	11.0	28.9
Ferry	26.6	91.0	1.2	1.1
All mechanical	**24.6**	**83.8**	**100.0**	**100.0**
Estimated pedestrians crossing cordon	11.9	91.1	+1.6	+5.4

Sources: Regional Plan Association, *CBD
Cordon Crossings Analysis 1965*, Tri-State
Regional Planning Commission, *Hub-Bound
Travel 1971*.
*The highest 12 hrs are 6:00 A.M.-6:00 P.M.
for rail and subway, 7:00 A.M.-7:00 P.M.
for the surface modes and 8:00 A.M.-8:00
P.M. for pedestrians.

Figure 4.2
Hourly distribution to trips entering
and leaving the Manhattan CBD

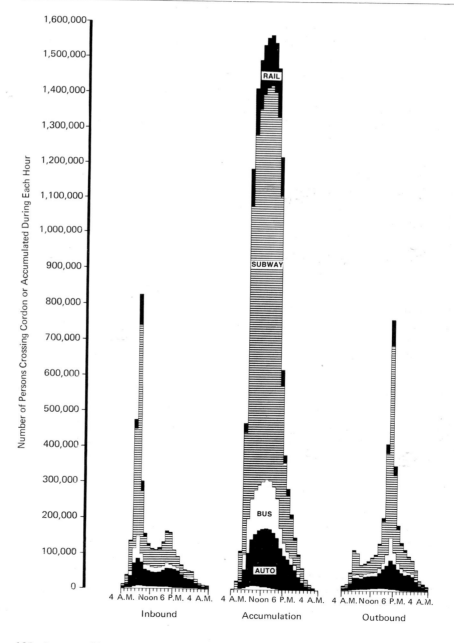

areas. Thus, during a period of intensive growth between 1959 and 1968, daily subway turnstile counts in Midtown Manhattan increased by 62,000 but declined by 36,000 in the rest of the Central Business District, leaving a net increment of only 26,000. Also, the location of residential areas in relation to the office destinations has to be considered. For example, the location of some 150,000 housing units along the waterfront of the Manhattan Central Business District, (assuming 2 residents per unit and 1 track for return trips) would obviate the need for one subway tunnel. Even without such spectacular development, continuing shifts in residential patterns affect transit travel demand both positively and negatively.

Another use of these figures is to calculate pedestrian space requirements at the interface between the subway system and the pedestrian circulation system, such as at the juncture between an office building and a subway station. Thus, should one-third of the "comfortable" trainload of 1,500 passengers decide to disembark at one station (a condition that is actually exceeded at some stations), then 125 feet (38 m) of exit width, equivalent to an exit more than half a block wide, would have to be provided at that station, if the passengers were to leave only at a moderately IMPEDED service level in platoons, as defined in Table 3.13.

This makes it clear that the impact of subways on pedestrian circulation design lies not only in the fact that they are the most

important mode of delivery to the Central Business District but also in the fact that they create the highest concentration of pedestrians at the point of delivery. The ten tracks of railroad and forty tracks of subway which cross the Central Business District cordon can be considered to have a combined width of 750 ft (229 m); at our standard of 2 pedestrians per foot per minute (6.5 per meter per minute), these tracks require 5,660 ft (1,725 m) of walkway width to adequately carry away the 680,000 passengers they bring in during the peak hour. By contrast, the 632 ft (193 m) of limited-access type roadway width plus the 1,050 ft (320 m) of width of other surface streets crossing the CBD cordon require only 1,040 ft (317 m) of walkway width to take care of the 125,000 pedestrians they bring in. Thus, under existing Manhattan conditions, the underground rail modes use space seven and one-half times more intensively than comfortable walkways, while, in the aggregate, the surface modes, even including bus travel, are less intensive space users than walkways.

Moreover, the subway and railroad modes are basically complementary to the pedestrian circulation system; at a cost, the 680,000 pedestrians they bring in during the peak hour can be provided with adequate space. The relationship between the surface modes and the pedestrian is complementary to some extent but also competitive; the 125,000 pedestrians brought in during the rush hour by the surface modes get in their own way while riding surface vehicles. They also get in the way of the rail users and the

"pure" pedestrians. The basic relationship of 80 percent of the people arriving in the CBD on 30 percent of transportation channel width underground and 20 percent arriving on 70 percent of channel width on the surface leads us to consider the trade off between pedestrian and vehicular surface use.

Pedestrians Versus Vehicles
Our analysis of the competition between pedestrians and vehicles for the use of the street and sidewalk surface will be confined to the central 1.2 sq mi of Midtown Manhattan, for which aerial photography provides data on vehicular as well as pedestrian densities and for which detailed characteristics of vehicular travel have been collected. In order to compare pedestrian and vehicular performance properly, we have to go briefly through the same exercise on capacity, flow, and speed-space relationships for vehicles as we did earlier for pedestrians.

The vehicular capacity of urban surface streets is limited by the discharge rate of intersections. An intersection of two traffic lanes cannot, at any one time, be occupied by more than one vehicle; thus, if vehicles on a free-flowing lane, once brought to a stop, can pass a point at a maximum rate of 1,500 an hour, the maximum flow rate of a 10-ft (3 m) wide intersection approach is about 700 cars per hour, if the green signal time is evenly split between the two perpendicular directions. This theoretical capacity is seldom achieved because of interference from trucks, turning vehicles, parked vehicles, and so on.

Adjustment factors exist to account for such conditions as well as for the character and size of the urban area.[2] Because the character and size are rather unusual in our case, a look at maximum flow rates actually observed in Manhattan's central square mile is appropriate.

Counts on Midtown avenues and streets by the New York City Department of Traffic were canvassed, and the 70 highest hourly observations were plotted against curb-to-curb pavement width. The resulting relationship is

(15) maximum flow (vehicles/hr)
= 50 × pavement width (ft)
− 800.

This can be interpreted to mean that, on the average, street or avenue pavement up to a width of 16 ft (4.9 m) does not contribute to vehicular flow, presumably because curb lanes are largely blocked by standing vehicles. For every foot (0.3 m) of pavement width in excess of 16 ft (and regardless of whether the green signal time is 33 or 55 percent of an hour), maximum flow increases by 50 vehicles per hour. Extreme observations indicate that on some streets with well-enforced no-standing regulations the blocked width in curb lanes is equivalent to only 10 ft (3 m); maximum flow remains at 50 vehicles per hour per foot (164 per meter) of moving lanes. That is occasionally exceeded on Park Avenue, where hourly flow rates can reach 60 to 75 per foot (197 to 246 per meter), largely because of the absence of heavy vehicles and a predominance of taxis.

Of course, these maxima are extremes that occur only in spots, and during one hour; over a wide area and for longer periods, Midtown traffic operates at substantially lower rates, as shown in Table 4.5. Only on northbound avenues in the evening is a flow of 45.3 vehicles per hour per foot (149 per meter) attained at a speed of 11.5 mph (18.5 km/hr). The southbound avenues attain a somewhat lower flow at a somewhat higher speed in the morning. The streets, which have a shorter green time and do not have the advantage of progressive signal timing, operate at lower average flow rates and much lower average speeds throughout the day. Though data on speed in Table 4.5 are incomplete, it can be seen that traffic in Midtown can generally move with comfort only before 8:00 A.M. or after 8:00 P.M.; the morning and evening rush periods are characterized by very heavy flow at rather slow speed; during midday, between 10:00 A.M. and 4:00 P.M., both speed and flow drop further, compared with the rush hours, and observations fall on the bottom half of the speed-flow curve, indicating a classic case of congestion, when more vehicles enter the area than its pavement can handle.

In fact, approximate speed-flow curves for vehicles, similar to those shown earlier for pedestrians, can be drawn on the basis of the data shown in Table 4.5, and flow-space curves can be derived from them. These are compared in Figure 4.3 with the flattest of the pedestrian curves; the vertical scale is changed to persons per *hour* per unit of walkway width for comparison

with vehicles per hour per unit of pavement width. A fourth curve, portraying vehicle performance on an expressway,[3] is added and so is an estimate of bicycle performance.

How do the space requirements of pedestrians and vehicles compare? We have previously found pedestrian standing room to be about 3 sq ft (0.28 m²). Motor vehicles are at a standstill, "bumper to bumper," with an average allocation of 500 to 650 sq ft (47 to 60 m²), according to Figure 4.3. The actual dimensions of motor vehicles range from 100 sq ft (9 m²) for a passenger car to 320 sq ft (30 m²) for a bus. Interestingly, vehicles parked on Midtown streets likewise take up about 500 sq ft (46 m²), as can be seen from Table 4.7.

As space per person increases above 3 sq ft (0.28 m²) to about 5 or 8 (0.46 to 0.74 m²), pedestrians begin to move and can pass a point with extreme crowding at a rate in excess of 1,200 persons per foot (3,900 per meter) of walkway width per hour.

Vehicles attain their maximum average, rather than their extreme flow rates (36, 47, and 166 vehicles per foot [118, 154 and 594 per m] of pavement width per hour on Manhattan streets, avenues, and on expressways, respectively), at a space allocation of somewhat more than 1,000 sq ft (93 m²) per vehicle. With that amount of space, they are moving at 7 to 11 mph (11.3 to 17.7 km/h) in Manhattan and at 35 mph (56 km/h) on expressways.

For comfortable movement, we have found that the pedestrian

Table 4.5
Flow, Speed, and Space use of Motor Vehicle Traffic in Midtown Manhattan by Time of Day

Time	5 Northbound avenues			6 Southbound avenues			21 Streets (both directions)		
	Flow	Speed	Space	Flow	Speed	Space	Flow	Speed	Space
4-6 A.M.	6.9			7.6			5.8		
6-8	15.1			20.0			15.0		
8-10	33.5	15.4	2,427	40.5	13.9	1,812	32.7	7.7	1,243
10-12	36.6	11.1	1,601	36.0	8.8	1,290	34.1	5.1	790
12-2 P.M.	36.8	10.7	1,535	35.1	11.2	1,684	31.0	5.0	852
2-4	39.5	9.2	1,230	34.8	10.4	1,578	33.6	6.7	1,053
4-6	45.3	11.5	1,340	36.2	11.0	1,604	35.6	7.3	1,083
6-8	39.6			33.3			31.4		
8-10	28.9			25.6			24.0		
10-12	27.0	21.2	4,145	23.1	20.3	4,640	22.0	10.7	2,568
12-2 A.M.	16.3			12.7			13.4		
2-4	8.6	27.0	16,577	6.8	27.0	20,965	7.0	15.0	11,314
24-hour flow (vehicles)	155,900			157,800			241,600		
Total width (ft, and m, excluding curb lanes)	233 (71 m)			253 (77 m)			423 (129 m)		

Sources and Notes: *Flow is vehicles per hour per foot of pavement width* subtracting 16 ft in curb lanes; based on 90 New York City Department of Traffic counts, (unadjusted for season or day of the week) taken in 1961-1965 and adjusted to 1970 conditions on avenues converted to one-way operation since 1965.
Speed is miles per hour, average overall speed (including delays), based on 185 speed-and-delay runs in October 1965 and November 1970 by Regional Plan Association.
Space is square feet of pavement in moving lanes per vehicle, ratio of speed to flow, as per equation (6).

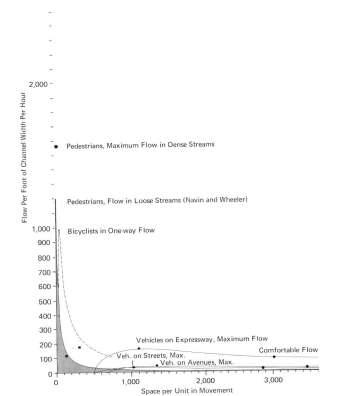

Figure 4.3
Flow-space relationships of pedestrians and vehicles compared

needs 130 sq ft (12 m²) of space, which represents a flow rate of over 120 people per foot (394 per meter) of walkway per hour. Vehicles require some 3,000 sq ft (280 m²) for comfortable movement. This represents a flow rate of 23, 30, and 100 vehicles per foot (75, 98, and 328 per m) per hour on Manhattan streets, avenues, and on expressways, respectively, at speeds of 12, 19, and 55 mph (19 to 31, and 88 km/h), respectively, as shown in Table 4.6. These relationships were briefly summarized earlier in Chapter 1 in connection with space requirements for movement.

We can see that *even at the comfortable space allocation of 130 sq feet (12 m²) per pedestrian, pedestrian flow is three times greater than maximum possible vehicular flow on an equally wide strip of pavement* of a street or an avenue. However, vehicular flow does begin to exceed pedestrian flow at space allocations between 700 and 800 sq ft (say, 70 m²), which may suggest one answer to the question of when pedestrian space allocation tends to become excessive. We can also see that expressways at 1,100 sq ft (102 m²) per vehicle can match the sidewalk at 130 sq ft (12 m²) per pedestrian, in terms of flow. In making these comparisons we are equating, for a moment, pedestrians and vehicles. As Table 4.9 will show shortly, the average combined auto and taxi occupancy in Manhattan is indeed close to 1 person per vehicle. Other conditions will call for appropriate adjustments.

With these general relationships in mind we can now look in detail at how the Midtown Manhattan street surface is used. An inventory of its use at an instant between 1:30 and 2:00 P.M. is available from aerial photography, from which the pedestrian counts were taken; the results are shown in Table 4.7, which indicates both the number of vehicles counted and the share of the pavement they occupy. Using equation (15) it is assumed that 8 ft (2.4 m) of pavement alongside each sidewalk curb is not used for movement; thus, 35 percent of the pavement is allocated to standing vehicles, of which 4,685 were counted in the area. The number moving on the remaining 65 percent of the pavement is not much greater—4,887 vehicles.

The average space per moving vehicle is thus 1,035 sq ft (96 m²), according to Table 4.7. Traffic flow and speed data, on which Table 4.5 is based, would suggest that at the time the aerial photography was taken the space should have been about 1,290 sq ft per moving vehicle, using the same allocation procedure. This discrepancy can be explained if one assumes that during the aerial count speeds were about 10 percent lower and flow about 10 percent higher than those indicated in Table 4.5, in part perhaps because of seasonal variation. Thus, one can assume that during the period of the aerial count average vehicular speed was 7.4 mph (11.9 km/h) and average flow was 37.75 vehicles per hour per foot (123.8 per meter) of pavement width in moving lanes. For the entire 1.2 sq mi (3.1 km²) study area, this represents

37,400 vehicle-miles of travel (VMT) (60,177 vehicle-kilometers) per hour and, if the hour during which the observations took place accounts for 5.63 percent of daily travel, 664,000 vehicle-miles (1,068,600 vehicle-kilometers) of travel per day.

This total volume of movement is not distributed among the various classes of vehicles in the same proportion as listed in Table 4.7 because different types of vehicles move at different speeds. In Table 4.8 a procedure is shown by which the proportions of vehicles photographed at an instant in time on the ground are converted into proportions of flow, the kinds of proportions usually reported by traffic counts. It is evident, for example, that trucks account for a smaller share of total flow than Table 4.7 would indicate, because they move slowly, whereas taxis account for an even greater proportion, because they move faster than the average. The proportions shown in the last column of Table 4.8 generally correspond to available traffic classification counts at midday.

It is quite clear that vehicular flow cannot be balanced against pedestrian flow with accuracy unless we know how many people occupy the vehicles and thus convert vehicle-miles of travel into person-miles of travel in vehicles. Moreover, for a proper comparison with pedestrians, one should distinguish between bona fide passengers in vehicles and persons who merely travel to serve a passenger; taxi drivers are most numerous in the latter category. Occupancy counts of persons per motor vehicle, appli-

Table 4.6
Pedestrian and Vehicular Space Requirements

	Pedestrians	Streets (Manhattan)	Avenues (Manhattan)	Expressways (general)
Zero flow				
Space sq ft (m²)	3 (0.28)	500 (47)	650 (60)	500 (47)
Maximum flow				
Space sq ft (m²)	5-8 (0.46-0.74)	1,026 (95)	1,236 (115)	1,100 (102)
Flow/ft/hr (flow/m/hr)	1,200-1,550 peds. (3,900-5,080)	36 veh. (118)	47 veh. (154)	166 veh. (544)
Speed mph (km/hr)	1.7-1.8 (2.7-2.9)	7 (11.3)	11 (17.7)	35 (56.3)
Comfortable flow				
Space square ft (m²)	130 (12)	2,750 (255)	3,340 (310)	2,900 (269)
Flow/ft/hr (flow/m/hr)	120-140 peds. (394-459)	23 veh. (75)	30 veh. (98)	100 veh.* (328)
Speed mph (km/hr)	3-3.5 (4.8-5.6)	12 (19)	19 (31)	55 (88)

Source: Regional Plan Association.
Note: Lane width assumed as 12 ft (3.66 m).
*Borderline between service levels "B" and "C" according to *Highway Capacity Manual.*

Table 4.7.
Composition of Motor Vehicles in Midtown Manhattan at Midday (May 1969, 1:30 to 2:00 P.M.)

	Avenues	Streets	Total	Percentage
Moving vehicles*				
Cars	521	902	1,423	**29.1**
Taxis	968	975	1,943	**39.8**
Buses	91	91	182	3.7
Trucks	514	825	1,339	27.4
Total, moving	2,094	2,793	**4,887**	**100.0**
Parked vehicles*				
Cars	943	1,180	2,123	45
Trucks	833	1,729	2,562	55
Total, parked at the curb	1,776	2,909	4,685	100
Parking spaces in garages and lots			19,201[†]	
Space per Moving Vehicle sq ft (m²)	1,322 (123)	820 (76)	**1,035** (**96**)	65
Space per parked vehicle sq ft (m²)	991[‡] (92)	488[‡] (45)	583 (54)	35
Linear feet of curb per parked vehicle (m²)	124[‡] (37.8)	61[‡] (18.6)	73 (22.3)	

Source: Regional Plan Association.
*Inventory covers area defined in Table 2.17, with 7,789,880 sq ft (725,680 m²) of public vehicular pavement, covering 39th to 60th streets and Second to Eighth avenues, inclusive.
[†]Based on inventory of off-street parking spaces in June 1968.
[‡]Based on assumption that each parked vehicle occupies an 8-ft wide strip, per equation (15).

130   Implications for Design

Table 4.8.
Composition of Motor Vehicle Flow in Midtown Manhattan at Midday (2:00 P.M.)

	Pavement width occupied		Assumed speed, mph	Assumed flow,[‡] veh./hr/ft	Estimated vehicle-miles of travel/hr	
	%[*]	ft			no.[§]	%
Cars	29.1	264	8	40.8	11,730	31
Taxis	29.8	362	8.6	43.9	17,400	47
Buses	3.7	39	4	20.4	760	2
Trucks	27.4	249	5.5	28.0	7,510	20
Total	100.0	909[†]	7.4	37.75	37,400	100

Source: Regional Plan Association.
[*]From Table 4.7.
[†]From Table 4.5.
[‡]Assumed speed (ft/hr)/1,035 sq ft (average space from Table 4.7).
[§] Flow per foot × pavement width occupied × 1.09 mi (average length of avenues and streets in study area)

Table 4.9.
Estimated Occupancy of Motor Vehicle Flow in Midtown Manhattan at Midday (2:00 P.M.)

	Vehicle-mi of travel per hr	All persons in vehicles		Passengers in vehicles	
		persons/veh.	person-mi of travel per hr	persons/veh.	person-mi of travel per hr
Cars	11,730	1.40	16,400	1.30	15,250
Taxis	17,400	1.88	32,700	0.88	15,310
Buses	760	26.00	19,760	25.00	19,000
Trucks	7,510	1.11	8,340	—	—
All vehicles	37,400	2.06	77,200	1.32	49,560
Cars and taxis	29,130	1.69	49,100	1.05	30,560

Source: Occupancy factors from Regional Plan Association, *CBD Cordon Crossings Analysis 1965*.

cable to Midtown conditions at midday, are available from data by the New York City Traffic Department, the New York City Transit Authority, as well as from field checks. These are summarized in Table 4.9 and applied to the vehicle-miles of travel from Table 4.8 to derive person-miles of travel by each vehicle type. Total person-miles of travel and person-miles of bona fide passenger travel are shown separately.

Referring back to Table 4.3 for a calculation of person-miles of travel on foot, we recall that such travel occured at an hourly rate of over 100,000 during the period of the aerial photography; this figure can now be legitimately compared with the hourly rates of 19,000 in buses and 30,000 in autos and taxis shown in Table 4.9. Person-miles of travel (PMT) per hour, which these figures represent, is an appropriate way to compare transportation performance; the figures have built into them both the dimension of time and the dimension of distance, essential for evaluating transportation service objectively. They cannot, of course, account for such subjective factors as the satisfaction derived from being in a car or the distress experienced because of walking under crowded conditions in an auto-dominated environment. Without balancing the qualitative considerations involved, we can simply say this: *during the midday period in Midtown Manhattan, more than two-thirds of all surface person-travel occurs on foot and less than one-third is carried by vehicles. The apportionment of circulation space in the area is almost the opposite:* from the space inventory in Chapter 2,

we may recall that only slightly more than one-third of the circulation space is devoted to pedestrians and the remainder, to motor vehicles.

Of course, midday represents an extreme situation. To get a full view of what happens during the entire day, estimates of person-miles of travel, by mode, should be constructed for each of the 24 hrs. With a few assumptions, this is done in Table 4.10. The table does show that in the course of 24 hrs, movement on foot accounts for barely more than half the total travel on the surface of Manhattan's central 1.2 sq mi. After midnight, especially, the auto is king and the few scattered pedestrians comprise a minor proportion of all travel. However, *for 11 hrs of the day, from 8:00 A.M. to 7:00 P.M., travel on foot exceeds travel by auto and taxi;* for 9 hrs of the day pedestrian travel is greater than travel by auto, taxi, *and* bus. The *3 critical hours of pedestrian congestion on sidewalks, 12:00 to 2:00 P.M. and 5:00 to 6:00 P.M., account for 35 percent of all pedestrian travel but only for 16 percent of all vehicle travel.* It becomes amply clear that for the entire daytime period, design for pedestrians should take precedence over design for vehicles in Midtown Manhattan merely on the grounds of transportation performance, which is what person-miles measure. If one uses other yardsticks, the contrast can be even more glaring. Thus, while the ratio of person-miles on foot to person-miles in autos and taxis during the three critical hours is about 7.2, the ratio of pedestrians to autos and taxis on the ground in our aerial

photography is 11:1, suggesting that at midday one motorist or taxi rider can be actually inconveniencing eleven pedestrians at any one moment. The data in Table 4.10 are shown graphically in Figure 4.4, and compared to the allocation of surface pavement in the bar at the right.

The issue of design for people on foot or people in vehicles is, to a large extent, one of apportioning scarce circulation space. While an accurate assignment of space to the different users does require a more sophisticated analysis, average values from Table 4.7 and the inventory from Table 2.17 can serve as an approximate yardstick. On that basis, we may take travel during the entire business day, from 8:00 A.M. to 8:00 P.M., and see how it relates to existing circulation (see Table 4.11).

Of course, the apportionment of circulation space among the different modes cannot be exactly proportional to their transportation productivity; however, it is not unreasonable to suggest that it be somewhat better related to the productivity of space in each use, that is, to the ability of a square foot or square meter in each use to produce person-miles or person-kilometers of travel. It is evident from Table 4.11 that *25 percent of all circulation space, or 40 percent of all vehicular pavement, has to be assigned to trucks and buses,* both moving and standing. While a reduction in the volume of truck movement may be feasible in the long run, this magnitude probably must be considered a given for the time being. The space devoted to goods movement is not wasted for the movement of people, if one puts buses in the same category as trucks; in fact, the moving lanes are then shown to have a productivity almost as high as walkways.

This cannot be said for the lanes assignable to autos and taxis. During the entire period between 8:00 A.M. and 8:00 P.M., *autos and taxis produce, on almost the same amount of space, less than half the person-miles of travel that pedestrians do.* Clearly, the pavement assignable to cars and taxis is the least intensively used. This is especially true of the lanes devoted to standing or parking at the curb. As evident from Table 4.7, the distances between standing vehicles are long (largely becuase of partial enforcement) and much of the space in curb lanes is used neither for movement nor for the storage of vehicles. If sidewalks were to be expanded at the expense of the vehicular pavement, the share of the curb lanes devoted to parked passenger cars would seem to represent a prime target, which would expand space by 25 percent while affecting vehicular movement only marginally, to the extent that some standing would occur in the moving lanes.

If one wished to expand pedestrian space further, one might consider curtailing auto and taxi travel to an extent that street capacity would be able to handle only the auto and taxi flow off peak, before 8:00 A.M. and after 8:00 P.M. This would expand walkway space by an additional 15 percent. About 5 percent of the person-miles of travel would be affected; the motorists and taxi riders involved would have

to seek alternative modes or forego travel. On the other hand, pedestrians would be in the possession of 54 percent of all circulation space, which comes close to the 57 percent of person-miles they log under present conditions.

Of course, more radical steps can be envisioned. The banning of all private cars from the Manhattan CBD has been frequently suggested, at least for daytime hours. This would give pedestrians 60 percent of all circulation space. However, the amount of person-travel to be diverted or eliminated would be significant—about 13 percent of the 12-hr flow. A ban on taxicabs would inconvenience roughly the same proportion of surface travel but would yield more space. These various options are summarized in Table 4.12.

In a real-life situation, none of the options listed in Table 4.12 would likely be applied across-the-board. In contrast to Lower Manhattan, which is essentially a cul-de-sac, inviting an opportunity to exclude most traffic but buses and local deliveries,[4] more arteries in Midtown have through-traffic functions, connecting different parts of the city. That traffic, too, can be curtailed by congestion pricing, bans on particular classes of vehicles, bans on taxi cruising, and so on, but in the context of this book we are not as concerned with the reduction of vehicular travel as we are with the provision of pedestrian space. So we will look at localized rationing of vehicular travel by means of space allocation.

Auto-Free Zones

The theory of rationing by space allocation should by now be apparent. The amount of motor vehicle travel in any area is, in part, dependent on the amount of available space. Given two business districts with equal amounts of floor space, the one with less space for travel will have less travel. Congestion never does, in fact, build up to a standstill; the average vehicular speed of about 8 mph (13 km/h) is quite characteristic of urban centers in general, ranging in size from Chicago to New Haven. It represents flow near maximum capacity. If congestion gets much worse, traffic either shies away or chooses alternative modes; but whatever street space there is, is filled up to a more or less tolerable level of flow. Thus, a gradual reduction of street space will not have the effect of creating a monumental jam but rather of gradually reducing the amount of vehicular travel.

This dynamic response of traffic to space, which we have alluded to earlier in this chapter, has been habitually overlooked by traffic engineers, who have assumed that if a street is closed, 100 percent of its vehicular traffic will be diverted to parallel streets. In fact, only part of the 100 percent will be diverted. The other part disappears or switches to other modes of travel.

Unfortunately, during the avenue-closing experiments in 1970 and 1971 in Manhattan, traffic counts were not made to document the magnitude of this reduction. Only speed-and-delay measurements were taken, which showed, quite plausibly, that

Table 4.10
Estimated Hourly Distribution of Person-Travel in Midtown Manhattan by Surface Modes

	% of daily vehicular flow*	% of daily pedestrian flow†	Estimated hourly PMT, auto & taxi pass.‡	Estimated hourly PMT, bus pass.§	Estimated hourly PMT, peds.	Pedestrian PMT as % of total
4-5 A.M.	1.10	(0.03)	4,900	496	(288)	"
5-6	1.06	(0.03)	4,700	1,333	(288)	"
6-7	1.77	0.45	9,200	4,216	4,320	24
7-8	3.56	1.85	20,400	15,097	17,760	33
8-9	5.50	7.61	32,100	31,744	73,056	53
9-10	6.01	6.45	32,600	21,607	61,920	53
10-11	5.80	4.60	31,400	14,818	44,160	49
11-12	5.75	5.98	30,900	16,647	57,408	55
12-1 P.M.	5.52	11.76	29,700	17,763	112,896	70
1-2	5.50	11.90	29,900	17,980	114,240	70
2-3	5.75	8.38	31,300	19,809	80,448	61
3-4	5.86	6.60	32,400	22,010	63,360	54
4-5	6.17	8.05	36,400	26,691	77,280	55
5-6	6.39	11.36	39,600	31,372	109,056	61
6-7	6.03	5.32	38,300	22,258	51,072	45
7-8	5.12	3.09	33,500	12,927	29,664	39
8-9	4.54	2.27	29,700	9,362	21,792	36
9-10	3.86	(1.42)	25,100	6,851	(13,632)	"
10-11	3.81	(1.02)	25,000	6,541	(9,792)	"
11-12	3.92	(0.90)	25,400	5,673	(8,640)	"
12-1 A.M.	2.71	(0.50)	15,900	2,573	(4,800)	"
1-2	1.86	(0.30)	9,800	992	(2,880)	"
2-3	1.35	(0.10)	6,800	775	(960)	"
3-4	1.06	(0.03)	5,000	465	(288)	"
24 hrs	100.00	100.00	580,000	310,000	960,000	1,850,000
Percent by each mode			31	17	52	100

Source: Regional Plan Association.
Note: Numbers in parentheses are estimates.
*Based on New York City Department of Traffic counts used in Table 4.5.
†Based on averages from Table 2.9, extrapolated for nighttime hours.
‡VMT reduced by percent trucks and buses by hour, multiplied by occupancy counts by hour adjusted following Table 4.9.
§PMT for period 1:00-3:00 P.M. expanded by hour in relation to peaking pattern of bus travel across 61st Street.
"No percentages listed because pedestrian estimates before 6:00 A.M. and after 9:00 P.M. are not reliable.

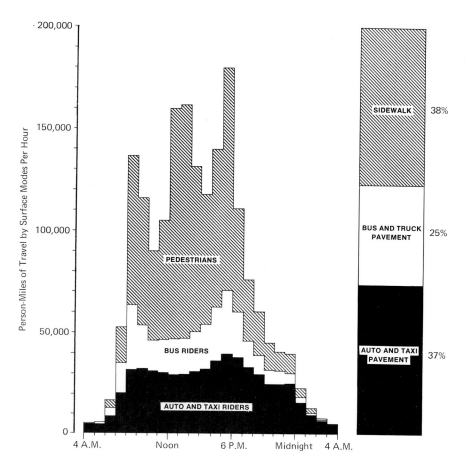

Figure 4.4
Estimated hourly distribution of person-travel in Midtown Manhattan by surface modes

Table 4.11.
Vehicular and Pedestrian Use of Public Circulation Space in Midtown Manhattan

	Circulation space (sq ft)	% of space	% of PMT 8 A.M.-8 P.M.	sq ft per PMT 8 A.M.-9 P.M.
Total public vehicular pavement	7,790,000			
Moving lanes assignable to trucks and buses	1,575,000			6.2 (— share of trucks)
Curb lanes assignable to trucks and buses	1,500,000			
Curb lanes assignable to bus stops	100,000			
Pavement assignable to trucks and buses	3,175,000	25	17 (+ trucks)	12.4 (—share of trucks)
Moving lanes assignable to cars and taxis	3,485,000			8.8
Curb lanes assignable to cars	1,130,000			
Pavement assignable to cars and taxis	4,615,000	37	26	11.6
Public walkway pavement	4,762,000	38	57	5.7
Walkway plus vehicular pavement	12,552,000	100	100	8.3

Source: Regional Plan Association.

Table 4.12.
The Effect of Alternative Restrictions of Vehicular Travel on the Expansion of Pedestrian Space

| Policy | Walkway pavement | | | |
	sq ft added (× 1,000)	Resulting % of total circulation space	PMT on foot as % of total	Share of 12-hr PMT diverted by restriction of autos and taxis
1. Existing conditions	4,762*	38	57	none
2. Eliminate share of curb lanes devoted to parked cars	+1,130	49	57	negligible
3. Eliminate vehicular capacity in excess of off-peak demand†	+697	54	60‡	5%
4. Ban all private cars†	+1,464	60	64‡	13%
5. Ban all taxicabs†	+2,021	65	64‡	13%

Source: Regional Plan Association.
*Plus 498,000 sq ft in plazas.
†In addition to the elimination of curb lanes, as in policy 2.
‡Assuming that diverted auto and taxi travel evenly divided between walking and bus.

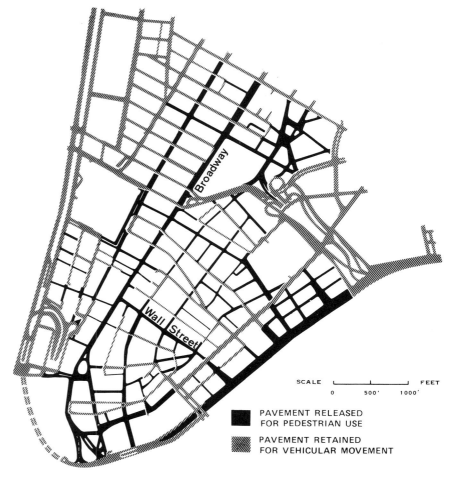

PAVEMENT RELEASED FOR PEDESTRIAN USE

PAVEMENT RETAINED FOR VEHICULAR MOVEMENT

Many narrow streets in Lower Manhattan, sparsely used by vehicles, are spontaneously taken over by pedestrians. Some offer inviting opportunities for pedestrian malls at the surface, others could be more effectively used for below-ground walkways to transit stations, open to light and air.

"Perhaps in the decades ahead the crudity and cruelty of motor cars bearing down on and intimidating pedestrians will be reflected upon by historians as a barbarism of the past." *Auto-free Zones in CBD's and an Example for Lower Manhattan,* by Tri-State Regional Planning Commission.

The map is intended "to graphically illustrate the upper limit to which an auto-free zone may be stretched" in Lower Manhattan.

pedestrianized street. If exact figures are often difficult to come by because of the reticence of the merchants, the general pattern is quite clear[10] and is confirmed by the fact that in no case has storekeeper opposition to a street closing continued after the street was in fact closed, except from stores that were not on the mall and felt that the competition from stores on the mall put them at a disadvantage. Of course, not all mall users come there to shop. In an analysis of the noncirculation areas of the Sacramento Mall, Becker[11] found middle-class shoppers to be in a minority and working-class people who use the sitting and standing areas of the mall for watching other people or for socializing to be the largest single group. He also found that alcoholics comprise 3 percent of the mall users, reflecting the residential composition of the surrounding downtown neighborhood; he points out that merchants and middle-class shoppers "would simply prefer people unlike themselves not to exist."

The German experience, by contrast, suggests that the atmosphere of exclusively pedestrian environments induces changes in the behavior of the middle class itself. "The tendency is everywhere for leisure activity to increase . . . seventeen cities report an increase in promenading, an activity which seemed restricted in the past to Mediterranean countries . . . perhaps people feel more relaxed and have time to look at each other again as they do in countries with fewer cars . . . people in pedestrian areas are said to be more considerate of their fellows."[12] It was also

found in Germany that people preferred large, open walkway areas, uncluttered by design paraphernalia, such as display cases. The resentment seems similar to that voiced in Sacramento against large, sculptured, concrete forms that dominate the mall. William H. Whyte voices a similar concern when he states that people, rather than physical objects, are the key attraction of a pedestrian space.

In summary, the weight of the evidence is that the expansion of downtown pedestrian space at the expense of vehicles causes only modest increases in vehicular traffic on parallel streets, that it does reduce noise and air pollution very significantly, at least in the areas immediately affected, that in relation to the rest of the downtown area it increases the sales by retail establishments fronting the improvement marginally to moderately, and that it increases outdoor leisure activities of the population most accessible to the improvement a great deal. In the Midtown Manhattan case, this population is, of course, overwhelmingly composed of office workers. So it behooves us now to look at space allocation from the viewpoint of the pedestrian and see how much additional space he actually needs.

Sidewalk Widths and Standards

In the preceding chapter we characterized the quality of pedestrian movement at different levels of spaciousness. Recapitulating Table 3.8 briefly, we can summarize the first four service levels as follows:

1. An OPEN FLOW prevails at average rates of less than 0.5 persons per minute per foot (1.6 per meter) of walkway width, when platoons do not form and pedestrians are quite independent of each other. With the large space allocations characteristic of that range, autos on downtown streets are more efficient users of space than pedestrians, if judged solely in terms of flow.

2. An UNIMPEDED average flow rate of 0.5 to 2 persons per minute per foot (1.6 to 6.5 per meter) of width results in an IMPEDED flow in platoons, with between 60 and 40 sq ft (5.6 to 3.7 m^2) per person. Psychological interaction with other pedestrians is inevitable, but it does not lead to significant physical constraints on the speed or direction of movement. Travel on foot in this and all the following ranges is more space-efficient than auto movement.

3. An IMPEDED average flow rate of 2 to 6 persons per minute per foot (6.5 to 20 per meter) will result in a CONSTRAINED flow in platoons, with between 40 and 24 sq ft (3.7 to 2.2 m^2) per person. With that kind of space allocation, flow in platoons, where most people walk, is characterized by some physical restrictions on speed, some interference with passing maneuvers, and a probability of contorted evasive action:

This huge lunch-time turnout on the
first day of the Madison Avenue
closing experiment on April 19, 1971
illustrates the latent demand for
vehicle-free space. At the end of the
second week of the experiment pedestrian flow on Madison Avenue was still
somewhat more than twice the normal
level, and no losses of pedestrian traffic from parallel avenues could be
observed.

vehicular speeds on parallel avenues were somewhat slower because of some diversion from the avenue that was closed. However, after the West Side Highway collapsed in 1973 it became clearer that at most 80 percent of the cars which used this freeway to enter the Manhattan CBD showed up on parallel routes; the other 20 percent disappeared. Similarly, one year after the pedestrianization of the Stroget in Copenhagen in 1963, only 76 percent of the former auto traffic on it appeared on parallel streets on an average day and only 38 percent during rush hours.[5]

Of course, the reduction in vehicular movement which occurs in response to the reduction in pavement can mean a net loss in accessibility and hence in the people-potential and the business-potential of a central area. However, this situation applies mainly to smaller places that are heavily dependent on the auto for access and where the provision of complementary parking near a mall is essential. In an area overwhelmingly dependent on public transportation, such as Midtown Manhattan, such effects can only be marginal and can be largely compensated, for example, by greater ease of bus travel on an avenue from which autos and taxis are excluded.

It is clear from Table 4.5 that even small reductions in volume can lead to large increases in speed in a central business district; buses on exclusive bus streets can be the prime beneficiaries of increased speed and can take over most of the taxi

travel, which, as Table 4.8 has shown, accounts for 47 percent of the vehicular travel in Midtown Manhattan at midday. As for the 31 percent that is private auto travel, one should bear in mind that fully 39 percent of the auto trips destined for Manhattan originate in Manhattan and represent strictly local use that responds to the opportunity of the pavement being in place. These auto trips can in no way be considered essential, since alternative modes of travel are easily available. Only 26 percent of the vehicular trips in Manhattan come from suburban areas outside New York City, where public transportation access may, in fact, be inconvenient.[6] The only truly irreducible claimants to surface street space in core areas of Manhattan and other major business districts are buses and trucks. They, in the case shown in Table 4.11, need only about 40 percent of the existing vehicular pavement, or 25 percent of total street space.

Policies for excluding the auto and the taxicab from the densest parts of urban centers have gained momentum since the late sixties, not only on the grounds of reducing the congestion that results from their large requirements for space, but also very strongly on environmental grounds. A major public opinion survey by Regional Plan Association in spring 1973 found 72 percent of the respondents in the tri-state Region favoring the conversion of selected streets into pedestrian malls (with only 15 percent against and the rest undecided) and 58 percent favoring the exclusion of the auto from entire pedestrian

precincts in cities (with 33 percent against).[7]

Among the environmental benefits of such street closings are dramatic reductions in air pollution and noise. The New York City Department of Air Resources has estimated that 79 percent of the carbon monoxide, 51 percent of the hydrocarbons, and 43 percent of the oxides of nitrogen in Midtown Manhattan are traceable to autos and taxis. The experimental midday closing of Madison Avenue in April 1971 resulted in a local drop of carbon monoxide concentration in the air from 21 to 8 parts per million. Similar figures reported for Tokyo indicate a decline from up to 14 parts per million before to just under 4 after.[8]

The noise level on Madison Avenue during the 1971 experiment dropped from about 75 dB(A) with mixed traffic to only 65 dB(A) with just pedestrians and buses, meaning that perceived noise was cut in half. Virtually identical figures are reported for downtown Copenhagen streets with vehicles as compared with the pedestrianized Stroget.[9] Added to these environmental improvements must be an increase in pedestrian safety and enhanced opportunities for landscaping and greenery.

In response to the increased provision of pedestrian amenities and space, there is invariably an increase in pedestrian movement, which takes place at improved levels of comfort. And increased pedestrian movement is consistently translated into increases from 1 or 2 to 35 percent in retail sales in stores fronting a it is broken-gait walking. At signalized intersections, the necessary waiting space becomes as wide as the sidewalk, necessitating overflow into the street; space in crosswalks can reach the JAMMED level of 5 sq ft (0.5 m²) per person. Voluntary groups can no longer easily walk together.

4. A CONSTRAINED average flow rate of 6 to 10 persons per minute per foot (20 to 33 per meter) of walkway width results in CROWDING in platoons, with only 24 to 16 sq ft (2.2 to 1.5 m²) per person. Flow in platoons with that kind of space allocation has a significantly depressed average speed, restricted choice of direction, and passing maneuvers that are rarely possible without touching the other person. On a sidewalk, this is obstacle-course walking. In a crosswalk, the crossing time begins to exceed the green time actually available, the waiting space is deeper than existing sidewalk width, and the space available while crossing the street would, if people were to follow the crosswalk, shrink to standing-room levels. As a rule, this is the highest degree of crowding encountered on downtown walkways.

Average flow rates in excess of 10 people per foot per minute, or 600 per hour (33 or 2,000, respectively, per meter) are generally not found on outdoor walkways and cannot be handled by signalized intersections.

With these criteria as a guide, we can now look at how Midtown Manhattan sidewalks actually perform.

Evaluating Walkway Service

The pedestrian counts from the aerial photography at midday and in the evening can be converted, with the help of equation (9), into flow rates, shown earlier in figures 2.11 and 2.12. Now we can relate the flow rates to the width of the walkway on which they occur and classify them according to the quality of flow in the platoons that they produce. Using the procedure shown by Figure 3.6 and equation (11), this was done to prepare figures 4.5 and 4.6, with adjustments to reflect the full peak periods between 12:30 and 1:30 P.M. and between 5:00 and 5:30 P.M.

CROWDING in platoons at midday occurs, according to Figure 4.5—
on both sides of Fifth Avenue from 39th to 57th streets,
on both sides of Madison Avenue from 44th to 54th streets and intermittently to the north and south,
on Lexington Avenue from 42nd to 60th streets, with a few gaps,
in scattered locations on Third, Sixth, and Seventh avenues,
in four blocks on 42nd Street, and in scattered locations on side streets, such as 45th, 47th, and 50th.

CONSTRAINED flow in platoons is characteristic of a much wider area, surrounding these congested locations and extending from Eighth Avenue in the Garment District, to Third Avenue near Grand Central Terminal, to the shopping area on Lexington Avenue near 60th Street. The map shows CONSTRAINED flow to be concentrated largely on avenues, but each of the side streets in the study area has at

least two and often several blocks that experience this degree of crowding, especially in the Rockefeller Center area.

IMPEDED flow in platoons, a service level that is generally deemed acceptable, covers most of the remainder of Figure 4.5, which is left white. Some of the white area along the periphery of Midtown, notably in residential blocks off Second Avenue and on side streets near Columbus Circle, actually operates at rates below 30 persons per foot of walkway per hour, when platoons do not form and OPEN FLOW prevails; this service level is not differentiated on the map.

CROWDING in platoons in the evening occurs, according to Figure 4.6—
on Madison Avenue from 42nd to 60th streets,
on Lexington Avenue from 42nd to 60th streets, with some breaks,
on 42nd Street and its approaches,
on the approaches to the Port Authority Bus Terminal, for four blocks along Eighth Avenue, and along 40th and 41st streets,
on Park Avenue approaching Grand Central Station, and
on Third Avenue near 53rd Street.

CONSTRAINED flow in platoons in the evening shows a pattern somewhat different from midday; it shifts away from Fifth Avenue, the focus of midday CROWDING, toward commuter destinations—the Port Authority Bus Terminal and Grand Central Station. Also prominent is the CONSTRAINED flow on side streets leading to subway stops—notably in the Times Square area, along Eighth and Sixth avenues, and along 53rd and 59th streets. The Garment District streets south of 42nd Street, which had mostly an adequate service level at midday, all experience constrained flow; the Rockefeller Center area stays at the same level as in midday, while most of Fifth Avenue improves.

IMPEDED flow in platoons in the evening covers generally the same peripheral area of comparatively low floor space density as in midday.

These different degrees of crowding on sidewalks are also reflected in intersection performance. Though the operation of intersections was not studied on the ground, the criteria developed in Chapter 3 can be applied to the flow rates derived from aerial photography and to known intersection dimensions and signal phases. In this manner, estimated intersection characteristics for the midday period were arrived at and are shown in figures 4.7 and 4.8.

Estimated reservoir space at intersections was calculated by assuming that sidewalk flow is evenly split by direction (a reasonable assumption for midday), that the approach flow at midblock equals the crossing flow (turning movements generally balance each other out), that accumulation in the reservoir space occurs for the duration of the nongreen phases, and that half the area of a sidewalk corner is used for waiting. In real life, some pedestrian flow occurs against an amber or even a red light and some of the green time

may be blocked by vehicles; much of the waiting takes place in the roadway, rather than on the sidewalk. Nevertheless, the reservoir space as calculated represents a valid index of how good or bad service at an intersection is. Figure 4.7 shows the service level for the more poorly served of the two flows at each corner.

One can see that intersection reservoir space is adequate only along the periphery of the Midtown area. The area of inadequate service at midday extends from Third Avenue to Broadway in a pattern very similar to CROWDING and CONSTRAINED flow in platoons, shown on Figure 4.5. Fifth, Madison, and Lexington avenues are especially bad, with some 30 intersections that have, theoretically, less than 3 sq ft (0.3 m²) of reservoir space per pedestrian; this indicates that waiting *must* occur in the roadway.

The same story is told, in still another way, by the pattern of crosswalk service levels at midday in Figure 4.8. This indicates how many square feet per person there are, theoretically, in the middle of the roadway the moment the two platoons that are crossing the roadway start interpenetrating each other. Again, the assumption that people confine themselves to the two white lines painted across the roadway or that this area is fully available to pedestrians and not blocked by vehicles is unrealistic; nevertheless, the calculated areas per person represent another index of service. Intersections along the periphery, once more, have adequate space.

Most intersections operate with 5 to 10 sq ft (0.5 to 0.9 m²) per person in crosswalks. However, twenty-eight intersections are shown to have less than 5 sq ft (0.5 m²) per person in crosswalks. These are located along Fifth, Madison, and Lexington avenues.

Sidewalk Widths for Heavy Flow
In figures 4.5 through 4.8 we have defined the areas of pedestrian crowding in Midtown. What these maps do not show is the range of pedestrian flows encountered. That is illustrated in Figure 4.9, which depicts flow on the northern sidewalks of 34th and 48th streets between First and Ninth avenues—two profiles of Midtown Manhattan.

At the eastern end of 34th Street, in a residential area, the midday pedestrian stream is very sparse— not much more than 100 people per hour, well within OPEN FLOW. Four blocks to the west the stream swells up to 1,000 people per hour, very comfortably within the UNIMPEDED range on the 23.5 ft (7.2 m) wide sidewalk. However, west of Madison Avenue, alongside Altman's department store, flow rises threefold into the IMPEDED range, and west of Fifth Avenue it rises threefold again, exceeding roughly 11,000 per hour. This is the upper range of CONSTRAINED walking, with CROWDING in platoons, bordering on CONGESTION. Within a short distance of six blocks (0.75 mi, or 1.2 km) there is a one-hundred-fold increase in pedestrian flow. Farther west, alongside Macy's department store, flow drops to the IMPEDED level (most pedestrians

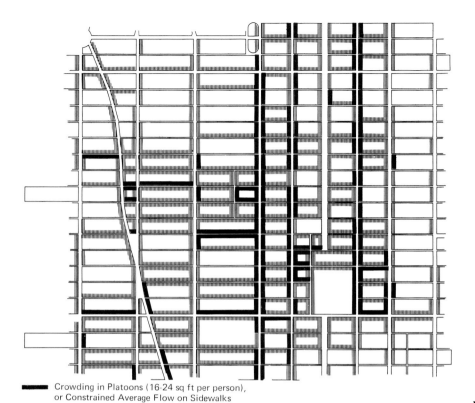

■■■■ Crowding in Platoons (16-24 sq ft per person),
or Constrained Average Flow on Sidewalks

⊞⊞⊞⊞ Constrained Flow in Platoons (24-40 sq ft per person),
or Impeded Average Flow on Sidewalks

Figure 4.5
Midday pedestrian service levels in
Midtown Manhattan

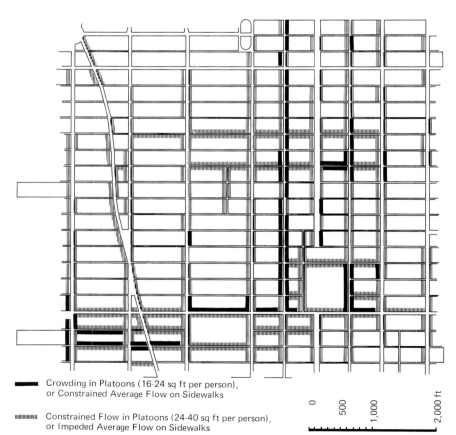

■■■■ Crowding in Platoons (16-24 sq ft per person),
or Constrained Average Flow on Sidewalks

⊞⊞⊞⊞ Constrained Flow in Platoons (24-40 sq ft per person),
or Impeded Average Flow on Sidewalks

0   500   1,000   2,000 ft

Figure 4.6
Evening pedestrian service levels in
Midtown Manhattan

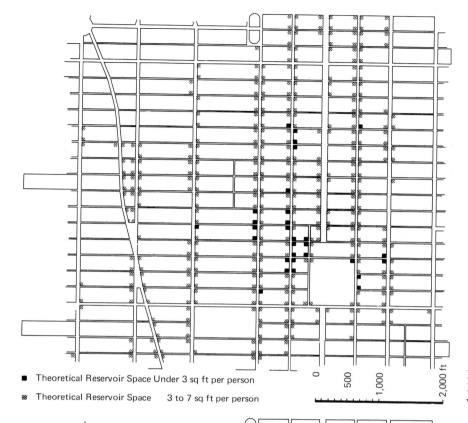

■ Theoretical Reservoir Space Under 3 sq ft per person

▨ Theoretical Reservoir Space   3 to 7 sq ft per person

0   500   1,000   2,000 ft

Figure 4.7
Estimated midday intersection reservoir space in Midtown Manhattan

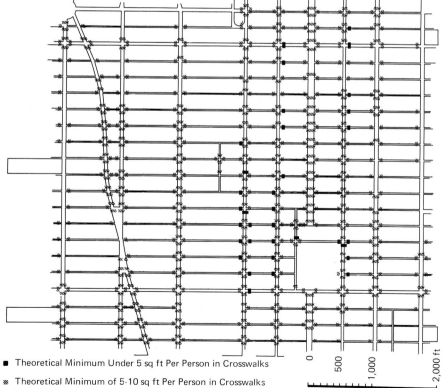

■ Theoretical Minimum Under 5 sq ft Per Person in Crosswalks

▨ Theoretical Minimum of 5-10 sq ft Per Person in Crosswalks

0   500   1,000   2,000 ft

Figure 4.8
Estimated midday intersection crosswalk space in Midtown Manhattan

143   Sidewalk Widths and Standards

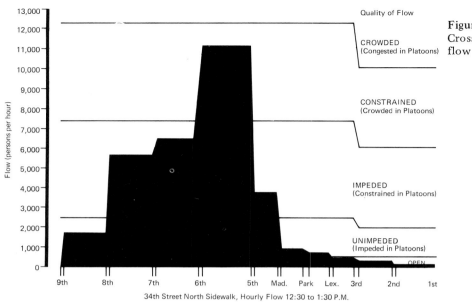

Figure 4.9
Cross-town profiles of pedestrian
flow

Quality of Flow

CROWDED
(Congested in Platoons)

CONSTRAINED
(Crowded in Platoons)

IMPEDED
(Constrained in Platoons)

UNIMPEDED
(Impeded in Platoons)

OPEN

34th Street North Sidewalk, Hourly Flow 12:30 to 1:30 P.M.

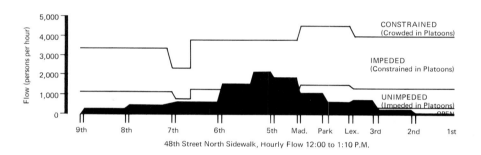

CONSTRAINED
(Crowded in Platoons)

IMPEDED
(Constrained in Platoons)

UNIMPEDED
(Impeded in Platoons)

OPEN

48th Street North Sidewalk, Hourly Flow 12:00 to 1:10 P.M.

The upper limit of UNIMPEDED FLOW—2 persons per min per ft (6.5 per m) of walkway width—is recommended as a design standard for moderately heavy pedestrian streams in downtown areas. It is illustrated here by Market Street in San Francisco.

The PARTIALLY IMPEDED FLOW of 4 persons per min per ft (13 per m) of walkway width is recommended as a design standard for very heavy pedestrian streams in downtown areas. It is illustrated here by the Sears Crescent in Boston.

are inside the store), and west of Eighth Avenue it becomes UN-IMPEDED again.

Because 48th Street does not have the heavy concentration of shopping that 34th Street has, variation in flow is less dramatic. Still, there is roughly a twenty-fold increase within seven blocks, and walking is IMPEDED between Madison and Sixth avenues as hourly flow reaches 2,000 on a 13-ft (4 m) wide walk.

If we tried to dimension sidewalks strictly on the basis of the upper limit of UNIMPEDED average flow, 2 people per minute per foot (6.5 per meter) of unobstructed walkway width, 34th Street would present us with two paradoxes. First, at its eastern end, the sidewalk would have to be less than 1 ft (0.3 m) wide. Second, in its central section, considering that the south sidewalk carries 7,000 people in addition to the 11,000 on the north side, total sidewalk width would have to be 150 ft (46 m), which is 50 ft (15 m) more than the width of the street, building line to building line. Even if it were decided to close 34th Street to all vehicular traffic and rebuild it with 25-ft setbacks, a 150-ft wide promenade could not be effectively used by pedestrians because they would tend to hug the shopping windows and leave the central area empty. Rather than applying one standard across the board, *we need a set of standards which would expand pedestrian space as flow increases, but not in direct arithmetic proportion to flow.* With what we have learned, three tentative guidelines can be set.

1. The density-based upper limit of UNIMPEDED flow, or 2 people per minute per foot (6.5 per meter) of walkway width, *cannot be used as a design standard for pedestrian streams smaller than about 1,500 per hour.* Walkway width needed for these lighter streams should be primarily a function of desired opportunities for passing pedestrians who walk in voluntary groups, as we will describe shortly.

2. The upper limit of UNIMPEDED flow *can be a legitimate design standard for pedestrian streams in the 1,500 to 6,000 per hour range.* For such streams, this standard suggests unobstructed walkways of 12.5 to 50 ft (roughly 4 to 15 meters) in width. This covers pedestrian flows encountered on the most heavily used streets in major North American cities, including most situations in Manhattan, and can provide a rationale for large-scale downtown sidewalk widening and pedestrianization. For example, the sidewalk expansion on Market Street in San Francisco is generally in scale with this standard: per foot of gross sidewalk width at midday, it handles a flow of about 1.5 persons per minute; per foot of unobstructed width (except at subway entrances), it handles a flow of about 2.5 persons per minute. For another West Coast example, the circulation areas (that is, not counting the sitting and ornamental area) of the Third Street pedestrian mall in Santa Monica operate in the 1.7 to 2.0 range at midday.

3. The upper limit of UNIM-PEDED flow is generally *inapplicable to pedestrian streams in excess of 6,000 per hour and may*

be waived for somewhat smaller streams in favor of a PARTIALLY IMPEDED standard of 4 pedestrians per minute per foot (13 per meter) of walkway width.

The introduction of this new PARTIALLY IMPEDED standard requires explanation. It represents the midpoint of the IMPEDED range, as defined earlier in Table 3.8. According to equation (11), it would correspond to a space allocation of 30 sq ft (2.8 m^2) in platoons, considered "tolerable" by Oeding and the midpoint of Fruin's "service level B," recommended for heavily used pedestrian facilities. However, platooning does appear to be attenuated on wide walkways, and equation (11) may not apply for clear walkway widths in excess of about 25 ft (7.6 meters).

If platoon flow on wide walkways at the PARTIALLY IM-PEDED rate is not 8 pedestrians per minute per foot (26 per meter) but closer to 6 (20 per meter), as a small number of observations on wide walkways, shown in Figure 3.6, suggest, the space allocation in platoons at that rate of flow may be not much different than at the UNIMPEDED rate on narrow walkways.

Pragmatically, the PARTIALLY IMPEDED standard is more in scale with the physical conditions of Midtown Manhattan than the UNIMPEDED standard, when heavy pedestrian streams are involved. For example, toward the end of the Madison Mall experiment in 1971, when the avenue was closed at midday to all but pedestrians and buses, pedestrian flow over its total 80-ft width averaged about 19,300 per hour, meaning just about 4 per minute per foot (13 per meter). This did not appear objectionable to the users, about half of whom represented voluntary traffic induced by the added space for walking.

In Table 4.13 existing sidewalk widths and flows on critical sections of Midtown Manhattan avenues and streets are compared with what would be required to attain UNIMPEDED and PARTIALLY IMPEDED walking. It is evident from the fourth column that to attain average UNIMPEDED flow would require closing Lexington, Madison and, Fifth avenues to all vehicular traffic and also closing portions of Eighth Avenue and of 42nd, 41st, 40th, and 34th streets. The building-to-building widths of Fifth Avenue, of 40th Street (near the bus terminal), and of 34th Street would be insufficient to satisfy this standard.

An auto-free zone of this scale in Midtown Manhattan would have to leave some pavement for busways, as in the Madison Mall proposal of 1971. These could not be provided with UNIMPEDED walking on the streets or avenues marked C or CC in the table.

By contrast, attaining the PARTIALLY IMPEDED standard is physically possible in all cases, as the fifth column shows. On Fifth Avenue it would require adding only 14 ft (4.3 m) to each sidewalk, which would still leave 27 ft (8.2 m) for a bus roadway and a buffer strip. On Lexington and Madison avenues the walk-

ways would be widened by roughly 8 ft—nearly doubling their unobstructed width. Given a minimum 22-ft wide bus roadway, that would leave 18 ft (5.5 m) on Lexington Avenue and 21 ft (6.4 m) on Madison for a noncirculation buffer strip to accommodate street furniture, benches with sitting areas, and trees.

Gross walkway widths (including 2.5 ft, or 0.75 m, for obstructions) suggested by the PARTIALLY IMPEDED standard range from a high of 36.5 ft (11.1 m) for pedestrian streams on the order of 8,000 per hour on Fifth Avenue down to only about 17 ft (5.2 m) for pedestrian streams on the order of 3,300 per hour, such as on Park and Third avenues. The latter is barely wider than the existing sidewalks. It is doubtful that the marginal widenings of 2 or 3 ft (less than 1 m) in this lower range of flows would be very meaningful. By eliminating the curb lane at least partially (perhaps leaving bays for vehicles loading and unloading), widenings of 5 to 12 ft (1.5 to 3.6 m) could be achieved in many places. Thus, for the range of pedestrian streams between, say, 2,700 and 5,200 per hour, a *compromise* between the UNIMPEDED and PARTIALLY IMPEDED standards might simply be a sidewalk 25-ft (7.6 m) wide, including a 2.5-ft (0.75 m) buffer strip for obstructions. This is shown in the last column of Table 4.13 and in Figure 4.11.

A theoretical reason for some additional width provided in this manner is the phenomenon of induced traffic, not considered

so far in this discussion. If added walkway space in an area such as Midtown Manhattan indeed induces 3 pedestrians per 1,000 sq ft (93 m²) of walkway area, as the correlation equations in Chapter 2 suggest, then at the PARTIALLY IMPEDED standard some 20 percent and at the UNIMPEDED standard some 40 percent of the walkway width added are preempted by flow induced by the added width.

Referring back to figures 4.5 and 4.6, application of the PARTIALLY IMPEDED standard would eliminate virtually all the black areas, where CROWDING in platoons occurs. By definition, it would not do much to reduce the large area with CONSTRAINED flow in platoons; that could be cut back by selective application of the UNIMPEDED standard, or the 25-ft sidewalk compromise.

An illustrative diagram of sidewalk widening needs in Midtown, using the three yardsticks as appropriate, is shown in Figure 4.10. Traffic management measures, to make the remaining vehicular pavement work would have to be separately determined and are not shown on the map. They would likely require street closings beyond the area indicated.

Sidewalk Widths for Light Flow
Outside the business core of any city, pedestrian streams become so light that the standards just discussed lose their relevance. Considerations of spatial composition gain in importance and so do the noncirculation areas of the pedestrian environment: areas for sitting, standing, and

Table 4.13
Sidewalk Widening Needs in Midtown Manhattan

Avenue or Street	From to	Estimated hourly peak flow av. per sidewalk*	Existing sidewalk width without obstructions† ft	Av. additional sidewalk width needed to attain:‡		
				UNIMPEDED FLOW 2/ft/min ft	PARTIALLY IMPEDED 4/ft/min ft	Compromise 25-width§ ft
Second Ave.	40-57th	1,300 M	12.5	0	0	0
Third Ave.	40-60th	3,300 M	12.5	15	2	10
Lex. Ave.	40-60th	4,100 M	9.5	25 C	8	13
Park Ave.	46-51st	3,300 M	12.5	15	2	10
Mad. Ave.	38-60th	4,400 M	10.5	26 C	8	12
Fifth Ave.	38-57th	8,100 M 4,900 E	20.0	48 CC	14	14
East Side Sixth Ave.	42-57th	4,200 M	14.5	21	4	8
West Side Sixth Ave.	46-52nd	4,300 M	22.5	13	0	0
Seventh Ave. and	38-43rd 47-53rd	3,600 M	17.5	13	0	5
B'way (incl. Times Sq.)	38-50th	3,900 M	17.5	15	0	5
Eighth Ave.	38-44th	2,600 M 5,200 E	12.5	9 31 C	0 9	9 9
42nd St.	3rd-8th	4,150 M 5,900 E	20.0	15 29 C	0 5	3 5
Av. 11 Sts. (43-53d)	Park-6th	2,300 M	11.0	8	0	8
41st St.	6th-8th	3,000 E	10.5	15 C	2	12
40th St.	6th-8th	4,300 M	10.5	25 CC	8	12
34th St.	5th-8th	7,800 M 5,800 E	21.0	44 CC 13.5	12 3	12

Source: Regional Plan Association.
Note:
M = midday
E = evening
C = closing all vehicular pavement required
CC = more width than available in the vehicular pavement required.
*Averaged over the area indicated in the first column, does not represent highest flow on a particular block.
†Actual sidewalk width minus 2.5 ft.
‡Rounded to the nearest foot; does not take into account traffic induced by the sidewalk widening.
§For hourly streams between 2,700 and 5,200.

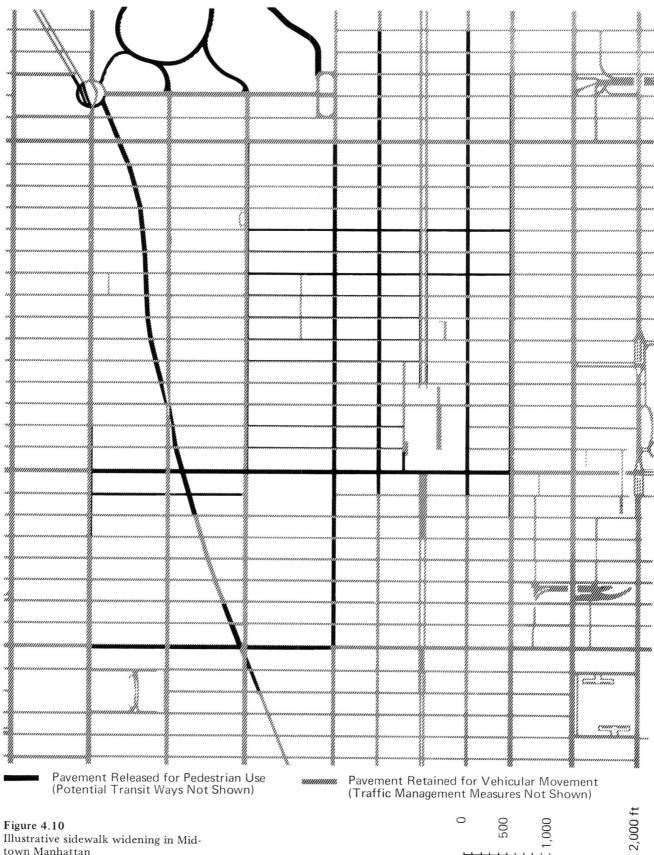

━━━━ Pavement Released for Pedestrian Use
(Potential Transit Ways Not Shown)

⫶⫶⫶⫶ Pavement Retained for Vehicular Movement
(Traffic Management Measures Not Shown)

Figure 4.10
Illustrative sidewalk widening in Midtown Manhattan

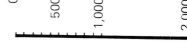

playing, areas reserved for trees and landscaping. The sidewalk is an important reservoir of outdoor residential space, adding to the distance between buildings and establishing the ambiance of a neighborhood. On occasion, a neighborhood appears to have excessive density simply because its sidewalks are not wide enough. If significant vehicular traffic is present, the pedestrian's needs for security and territoriality must be recognized by proper buffer zones and adequate room on the walkway. He should feel sheltered from vehicular traffic and know that he is in a space that belongs to him. All these multiple physical and psychological uses of residential sidewalks must be considered in establishing their dimensions.

With respect to the width of the walking path proper, the ability for pedestrians to form voluntary groups and to pass each other becomes a controlling factor when flow is light. The manuals on subdivision layout[13] typically say that the minimum walkway width is 4 ft (1.2 m), and, in fact, most of the concrete walkways in American suburbia are 4- to 5-ft wide. This provides enough room for two adults either to walk abreast or to pass each other, if there is unobstructed lateral space on either side of the walk. With grass strips reserved for trees and utilities, the total curb-to-property-line width becomes 10 to 15 ft (3 to 4.6 m), adequate for low-density settlement, where perhaps 1 to 10 pedestrians may pass a point in an hour.

In areas of greater density, the requirement of group walking

alone dictates an unobstructed path wider than 5 ft (1.5 m). Okamoto and Beck, in their previously cited study, found that as many as 45 to 55 percent of people in a downtown area at lunchtime walked in voluntary groups of two, three, and four; the proportion was smaller in the evening and still smaller in the morning. Somewhat surprisingly, spot checks in a residential neighborhood of Manhattan (with pedestrian streams on the order of 100 to 200 people per hour) revealed a very similar pattern at midday on a Saturday: about 2 percent of the people walked in groups of four, about 8 percent in groups of three, and 37 percent in groups of two. Close to half of the people counted were in groups. Clearly, walking in groups is an important social function. As far as possible, such groups should not be disturbed by pedestrians walking in the opposite direction or by physical sidewalk obstructions.

As we established earlier, a group of three needs about 6.5 ft (2 m) of walkway width. For an individual to pass a couple, closer to 7.5 ft (2.3 m) are desirable. The latter figure is a reasonable minimum for the pathway of a lightly used urban sidewalk. Adding 1 ft for unused space near the property line and at least 4.5 ft for a tree cut and the curb, the nonwalking part becomes 5.5 ft (1.7 meters) wide and the entire sidewalk, 13 ft (4 m) wide. This happens to be a fairly common dimension, but the important thing is to realize what kind of behavior it enables: with a row of trees, it enables a group of three to walk together or an individual to pass a couple.

With pedestrian streams on the order of 100 per hour or less, this can be a reasonable arrangement, though a few extra feet of width would not hurt and trees on both sides of the sidewalk are better than on one side only. However, when flow rises to roughly 200 people per hour on a 7.5-ft (2.3 m) path, it begins to reach the limit of what we have previously termed OPEN FLOW. With an individual or a voluntary group passing a point about every 24 secs, the probability of encounters and evasive maneuvers becomes high. Moreover, with the higher flow, groups of four are likely to show up, who will need about 8.6 ft (2.6 m) of width. One way to deal with this increased activity is to adopt OPEN FLOW as a design standard and widen the pathway proportionately.

However, OPEN FLOW is an extremely spacious standard and would, if applied to streams much in excess of 375 per hour, result in unnecessarily wide, sparsely used walkways. If we keep the 12.5-ft (3.8 m) unobstructed walkway width needed to maintain OPEN FLOW in a stream of 375 per hour for heavier streams, as well, we can maintain flow at the UNIMPEDED level for up to 1,500 pedestrians per hour. That width will allow groups of three and two to pass each each other freely and groups of three and three to pass each other with only minor maneuvering. Keeping the noncirculation space the same, our sidewalk is 18 ft (5.5 m) wide. This, again, should be viewed as a minimum, and a few extra feet will not hurt.

The UNIMPEDED and PARTIALLY IMPEDED space standards are not applicable to light pedestrian streams. For streams of less than about 1,500 persons per hour, walkway width is governed by the ability of voluntary groups to pass each other.

Top view shows a residential sidewalk in Midtown Manhattan with a total width of 7.5 ft (2.3 m). Pavement wear suggests that 1 ft (0.3 m) alongside the fence on the right, and 1.5 ft (0.5 m) along the curb are not used, leaving a 5-ft (1.5 m) wide traveled path. This is enough for 2 people to walk comfortably abreast, but a third person could not pass without disturbing them.

Middle view shows a residential sidewalk in Midtown Manhattan with a total width of 15 ft (4.6 m). The distance from the left curb to the tree is 11.5 ft (3.5 m); about 1 ft (0.3 m) along the former and 1.5 ft (0.5 m) near the latter are not used, leaving a 9-ft (2.7 m) wide traveled path. Three people are passing each other with room to spare, but the space could be somewhat tight for four.

Lower view shows a 12-ft (3.7 m) wide walkway on a pedestrian mall in Santa Monica. Two groups of two are passing each other with room to spare, but the fifth person is engaged in a slight evasive maneuver.

In Figure 4.11 the two light flow conditions just described are charted, together with the heavy flow conditions described before. Obviously, there is an infinite variety of sidewalk dimensions and densities at which pedestrian streams ranging from 100 to over 10,000 can be satisfied. Under different conditions, relationships other than the stepped function shown in Figure 4.11 may be appropriate. One alternative is suggested by a continuous curve, extrapolated from the relationship shown later in Table 4.17. The important point in Figure 4.11 is that there be *some* relationship and that the same sidewalk width not be considered adequate for both 40 and 4,000 pedestrians per hour, as is now frequently the case.

An example of this traditional practice is the 1963 New York City Highways Department formula, which set sidewalk width at 10 percent of the right-of-way plus 5 ft. On a 60-ft (18.3 m) wide street, that automatically meant 11-ft (3.4 m) sidewalks; on a 100-ft (30.5 m) wide avenue, 15-ft (4.6 m) sidewalks were granted. Both of these represent outside dimensions, not the width actually available for walking. Clear width has subsequently been specified as follows: on a 60-ft right-of-way, a clear sidewalk width of 8.5 ft (2.6 m) is required for newstands, vegetable stands, and similar obstructions; on a 100-ft right-of-way, the requirement was increased to 12.5 ft (3.8 m)[14] Again, there was no reference to pedestrian flow or to the surrounding land development, which generates this flow.

The Design of Walkway Space

Our reference to unobstructed sidewalk width leads us now to consider those parts of a sidewalk which are obstructed and generally not available for walking. Table 4.14 enumerates forty-seven different obstructions encountered by pedestrians on a sidewalk. Straightforward policies can be formulated toward most of these.

With respect to *street furniture,* efforts have been underway for some time to develop well-designed street fixtures that would combine a luminaire, signs, a wastebasket, and a parking meter in one element and reduce the cluttering of sidewalk space. However, even with careful design and placement, such fixtures, just as the traditional light poles, project at least 2.5 ft (0.8 m) inward from the curb. If they occur with any frequency, their effect on sidewalk flow must be considered.

The most frequent element of *public underground access* is ventilation gratings for subways and transformer vaults. These are not direct obstacles but are consciously avoided not only by women who may wear thin heels but by pedestrians in general. A more serious condition is created by subway stairways, which can easily preempt half the sidewalk width and thus create congestion in the spot where sidewalk flow is most intensive. Whenever new buildings are erected adjacent to subway stations, subway entrances must be located off sidewalk. However, skylights to give underground stations and passageways more amenity can become competitive with the pedestrian

for walkway space. Though not yet in use in New York, they have been successfully introduced in Boston, Oakland, and Berkeley. More on these subjects will be said in connection with subway station design.

Landscaping provides amenity but can also interfere with pedestrian flow; as indicated in Table 4.14, 3 to 5 ft (0.9 to 1.5 m) must be subtracted from the sidewalk width to accommodate trees or planting boxes.

Commercial uses may also provide amenity but can severely interfere with pedestrian flow. The worst offenders are newsstands near subway stairwells, which are often located parallel to the stairway, rather than behind it, and reduce usable sidewalk width to only a few feet. These should be moved to adjacent locations where they do not interfere with the traffic stream. Sidewalk cafes are best located on plazas or on wide sidewalks with light flow and should not obstruct heavily travelled walkways.

Buildings represent an impediment to pedestrian flow by their very nearness to the walkway. The lateral displacement of vehicles due to the proximity of roadside objects is well known to highway designers and is one reason why highway structures are being set back farther and farther from the roadway. Similarly, pedestrians do not like to brush a wall with their shoulder, so they stay away from it; this means that a strip of walkway immediately adjacent to a building wall remains unused. Also, if store windows are facing the sidewalk, an allowance must be

Table 4.14
Sidewalk Obstructions to Pedestrian Flow

	Approximate walkway width preempted (curb to edge of object or building face to edge of object)	
	ft	m
1. Street Furniture		
Light poles	2.5-3.5	0.8-1.0
Traffic signal poles and boxes	3.0-4.0	0.9-1.2
Fire alarm boxes	2.5-3.5	0.8-1.0
Fire hydrants	2.5-3.0	0.8-0.9
Traffic signs	2.0-2.5	0.6-0.8
Parking meters	2.0	0.6
Mail boxes	3.2-3.7 (1.7 × 1.7 dimensions)	1.0-1.1
Telephone booths	4.0 (2.7 × 2.7 dimensions)	1.2
Waste baskets	3.0 (1.8 diameter)	0.9
Benches	5.0	1.5
2. Public Underground Access		
Subway stairways	5.5-7.0	1.6-2.1
Subway ventilation gratings	6.0 +	1.8
Transformer vault ventilation gratings	6.0 +	1.8
Skylights for subway stations	(presently not used in New York)	
3. Landscaping		
Trees	3.0-4.0 (5.0-6.0 pavement cut)	0.9-1.2
Planting boxes	5.0 (3.7 diameter)	1.5
4. Commercial Uses		
Newsstands	4.0-13.0	1.2-4.0
Vending stands (fruit, vegetable, etc).	variable	
Advertising displays	variable	
Store displays	variable	
Sidewalk cafes	variable, say 7.0 (two rows of tables)	2.1
5. Building Protrusions		
Columns	2.5 × 2.5 to 3.0 × 3.0 dimensions	0.8-0.9
Stoops	2.0-6.0	0.6-1.8
Cellar doors	5.0-7.0	1.5-2.1
Standpipe connections	1.0	0.3
Awning poles	2.5	0.8
Trucking docks	(trucks protruding)	
Garage entrances	(cars entering and exiting)	
Driveways	(cars entering and exiting)	
6. Temporary Obstructions		
Excavations		
Stored materials or rubbish		
Construction equipment		
Scaffolding		
Ice		
Snow		
Puddles		
7. Moving Obstacles		
Vehicles (crossing walkway, see above)		
Queues (at movie theaters, bus stops)		
Window shoppers		
Crowds (in front of shows, window displays, hawkers)		
Loiterers		
Wheelchairs, baby carriages, etc.		

Source: Regional Plan Association.

Figure 4.11
Walkway width related to pedestrian flow

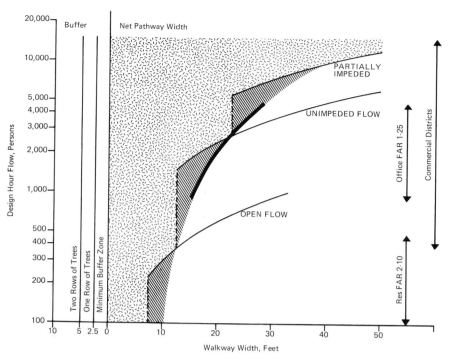

Obstacles to pedestrian flow.
Top, a total sidewalk width of 16.5 ft (5 m) would suggest that the pedestrians seen in the view have about 50 sq ft (4.6 m²) of space per person. In reality, a 6-ft (1.8 m) wide strip obstructed by the subway grating, by light poles and the mailbox is not used; actual space available for walking is closer to 30 sq ft (2.8 m²) resulting in visibly CONSTRAINED movement (conflict near mailbox).

Bottom, Planting boxes, intended as an amenity, take roughly 5 ft (1.5 m) from a 23-ft (7 m) wide sidewalk. It is evident that the space between them is only sporadically used for walking.

Newspaper kiosks, cellar doors, awning poles, goods stored for delivery, trucks protruding from loading docks, advertising signs and queues of people are some of the 47 sidewalk obstructions listed in Table 4.14.

153 Sidewalk Widths and Standards

made for window shoppers. *Columns* can be an important obstruction in building plazas and arcades; people avoid them at some distance, so that a column has a much greater effect on pedestrian flow than its dimensions would suggest; added to that is the psychological reluctance to go behind columns. Wherever possible, columns should be dispensed with in favor of a *cantilever*. The other building obstructions listed in Table 4.14 are generally not a problem in new buildings, with the exception of garage driveways and loading docks, which should be located away from the major pedestrian streams.

The exact effect of the various obstacles on pedestrian capacity and flow is a good subject for further study; paths could be traced with time-lapse photography. The effect is less than the widths listed in Table 4.15 because the obstacles are generally not continuous but substantially greater than the physical area they occupy, since each obstacle leaves an unused sidewalk area in its "wake" in the pedestrian stream.

Based on informal observation of pedestrians in Midtown Manhattan and on the factors calculated by Oeding, we have, so far in this chapter, assumed an unused width of 2.5 ft (0.75 m), which was used across the board to calculate the service levels in figures 4.5 and 4.6 as well as the widths in Table 4.13. However, if planting is to be provided on new sidewalks, greater widths are necessary, as indicated in the left margin of Figure 4.11.

Different pavement textures are a logical expression of the distinction between the pedestrian *traveled way* and the underused *shoulders*. Not only can cuts be made for trees but an entire strip about 5-ft (1.5 m) wide can be paved with cobblestones or another material pervious to water, which would help the trees to grow and accommodate the various items of street furniture or even subway skylights, while keeping pathway pavement clearly differentiated. The maintenance of an appropriate standard of flow on the unobstructed portion of the sidewalk should also be the first criterion for permitting the various sidewalk encroachments.

A differentiated shoulder can be developed into a buffer zone between pedestrians and vehicular traffic. It can take the shape of a landscaped mall, a continuous planting box, or, if the space is scarce, even a structural barrier. Simon Breines[15] has pointed out that existing landscaped malls, such as the median dividers on upper Broadway and on Park Avenue, would be of much greater use to pedestrians if they were located adjacent to a sidewalk, rather than in the middle of traffic. Such buffer parklets could be 20 to 30 ft (6 to 9 m) in width on the extra-wide avenues. On narrower rights-of-way, continuous planting boxes 5 to 6 ft (say, 1.6 m) wide can be erected, with skylights for subway stations incorporated into the same structure. Such barriers will shield pedestrians from vehicles, protect vehicles from jaywalkers, and discourage vehicles from illegally standing in the curb lane since the sidewalk

would be inaccessible to the exiting driver or passenger. Present vehicular curb lanes and sometimes surplus walkway space could be used for such landscaped barriers. In general, a detailed investigation of the intensity of use of existing pavement, both pedestrian and vehicular, in the light of criteria developed in this study, would reveal many opportunities for converting pavement into landscaped areas.[16]

A well-designed sidewalk would thus consist of a *pathway* dimensioned in relation to the flow standards we have proposed. Where appropriate, it would have shoulders, or *buffer zones,* developed into a positive amenity. Third, it would have *auxiliary spaces* for standing and sitting. As William H. Whyte has shown, pedestrians will stop to chat anywhere on the sidewalk, even in the middle of the busiest flow. But, aside from such spontaneous standing, there are important areas of more predictable standing: at display windows and other commercial attractions, at bus stops, and at intersections. Each of these should have its own reservoir space, dimensioned as indicated in the previous chapter. Added space at intersections is by far the most important of these. If curtailment of vehicular intersection capacity is acceptable or desirable, such added walkway space can take the form of sidewalk widening at intersections at the expense of the roadway. If not, at least the crosswalk should be widened to dimensions that exceed the width of the sidewalk, enabling pedestrians to wait and to walk across the street in a wider front. The

Right; landscaped buffer separates the walkway from vehicular traffic in Leningrad. Below; a modest effort to do a similar thing on Third Avenue in Manhattan. The trees are where they belong; in the former sidewalk, which has natural earth beneath the pavement. The plaza space to the right, which has a cellar beneath the pavement, is better suited for walking. Where vehicular traffic is to be retained, continuous buffers should be developed between the people and the cars. They can incorporate trees, sitting areas, as well as underground ventilation gratings and some of the other obstructions shown earlier. Bottom photograph by Anthony Callender.

A 10.5-ft (3.2 m) wide cantilevered overhang protects a good portion of the 25-ft (7.6 m) walkway from inclement weather. A much wider employment of this design device should be encouraged through zoning.

A formerly solid building corner remodelled as a rounded open corner for a new bank entrance. It provides space where it is needed most and offers an improved sight distance. In new construction, this condition, too, can be handled with a cantilever, avoiding the bulky column.

Fulton Street arcade plan in Brooklyn provides some widening at intersections as well as a weather-protection canopy supported from the buffer zone of the pedestrian mall.[17]

In the design of all these facilities, the geometry of a pedestrian's movement should be given greater attention than heretofore. While the details of a pedestrian's navigation must remain outside our scope here, a few points should be emphasized. Unlike railroad trains, pedestrians do not move along totally straight lines but rather along very mildly undulating paths, even when there are no obstructions. Therefore, slight changes in the direction of the pathway are not against the nature of pedestrian movement. However, within this mode of walking, pedestrians highly value economizing on walking distance, as evidenced by our analysis of the cost of walking. Any obvious detour that the designer introduces for esthetic or engineering reasons is an insult to the pedestrian. Conversely, any shortcut is viewed as a valuable gain.

Any building corner represents a detour for those pedestrians who are making a turn. Though it seems difficult to visualize a city without corners, from the viewpoint of the pedestrian any move in that direction should be encouraged, for at least four reasons. First, a corner that is cut provides the psychological satisfaction of reduced walking distance, even though the actual gain is small. Second, pedestrians do not turn at right angles but rather in curves that have radii of 6 to 10 ft (1.8 to 3.0 m). These

turning radii, like any others, vary with the square of the speed. Any rounded corner is more in the nature of pedestrian movement than a square corner. Third, collisions between pedestrians at corners on heavily used downtown streets are quite frequent because of lack of sight distance. A corner that is cut back provides the necessary sight distance. Fourth, sidewalk space at corners is more heavily used than elsewhere because it not only carries two intersecting pedestrian streams but also provides crosswalk reservoir space. Thus, cutting back a corner provides added walkway space where it is needed most.

Finally, a point on guiding pedestrian flow. *Pedestrians totally disregard any color patterns on the walkway,* be they different shades of brick or concrete, or painted lines. Very often patterns like that are annoying to the eye precisely because they are totally unrelated to pedestrian movement. However, *pedestrians respect physical barriers* and strong changes in texture. Earlier we mentioned the avoidance of ventilation gratings. Very rough cobblestone pavement will also be avoided if paralleled by a smooth surface. Mounting a curb is avoided if a curb cut is available. Thus, the small curb cuts introduced as part of the campaign against architectural barriers, to help the handicapped, are heavily used by pedestrians in general. With these design considerations in mind, we can now turn to the provision of walkway space at specific buildings.

Walkway Space for Buildings

While sidewalk widening at the expense of vehicular space can provide room for pedestrians retroactively, in new construction adequate room should be provided on the building site. Pedestrian flows vary a great deal from block to block, depending on building density and use, so that a uniform sidewalk width over a long distance, required by design for motor vehicles, cannot be easily fitted to them. More generally, it is desirable to reduce the external costs imposed by a building on its neighbors and on the public.

Walkway Space and Building Bulk

As a result of the comprehensive approach taken in the beginning of this book, we can now relate walkway width not only to the magnitude of the pedestrian stream but also to building density. Completing the series of steps outlined in Figure 1.2, we will take the procedures applied earlier in this chapter to the Manhattan Central Business District as a whole and apply them to one building. We will start with what we have called conventional travel analysis.

Table 4.2 and subsequent discussion suggested that 1,000 sq ft (93 m^2) of Manhattan's nonresidential floor space generate an average of 16.2 in and out trips during the day. Referring to tables 2.9 and 4.10, we can find how much of that travel occurs during a peak period selected for design. Since we are dealing with flow on sidewalks, it is appropriate to use the outdoor peaking, not the much sharper peaking at

building entrances. Having determined the flow during an average minute of the design period, we can apply to it a chosen service level, such as UNIMPEDED, which with 2 people per foot (6.5 per meter) of walkway width per minute, requires 0.5 ft (0.15 m) of walkway width per person. Multiplying the design flow rate by this walkway width per person, we find how much total walkway width is needed to serve the unit of floor space. Multiplying the width by average trip length, we get walkway area required. The procedure is as follows: Assumed daily number of two-way pedestrian trips per 1,000 sq ft of nonresidential floor space 16.2
Percent of daily travel during design period, 12:00 to 2:00 P.M. 23.7
Average minute flow during design period 16.2 × 0.237 ÷ 120 = 0.0319
Walkway width per pedestrian per minute at UNIMPEDED service 0.5 ft
Average trip length (from Table 2.12) 1,720 ft
0.0319 × 0.5 × 1,720 = *27.3 sq ft of walkway per 1,000 sq ft floor space*

At this point we might recall that in Chapter 2 we found empirically that in the Midtown study area there are, in the average, 27 units of walkway space for every 1,000 units of floor space and that each pedestrian has an average of 136 sq ft (12.6 m²) of walkway space. Though the floor space in that instance included a small residential component, in a general way the calculation confirms once more the consistency of the trip generation, peaking, and trip length factors

but does not tell us how these vary by density and building use. To find out, we have to turn to direct estimation of pedestrian density.

Before using equations (1) and (2), which exemplify the direct estimation approach, we will, for comparability with the calculation just made, make three adjustments to them. First, to represent the entire period of 12:00 to 2:00 P.M., rather than the aerial photography half-hour period between 1:30 and 2:00 P.M., we multiply the equations by 1.064. Second, we combine them into one, applicable to an average half-block in Midtown Manhattan, rather than to the block sectors used earlier. Third, we combine the floor space areas and deal with a mix of nonresidential floor space that has 80 percent offices, 5 percent retail, 1.8 percent restaurants, and 13.2 percent miscellaneous uses. The resulting simplified equation takes the form

(16) pedestrians = 3.2 walkway + 0.075 nonresidential floor space + 22,

where pedestrians are those to be found at an average instant at midday on roughly half a city block in Midtown Manhattan and where both walkway and floor space are measured in thousands of square feet. The equation tells us that—
1,000 square feet of walkway induces 3.2 pedestrians,
1,000 square feet of nonresidential floor space adds 0.075 pedestrians, and
22 pedestrians are on the half-block regardless of the above.

At UNIMPEDED service with 130 sq ft (12 m²) per person, 1,000 sq ft (93 m²) of walkway accommodate 7.7 pedestrians; however, 3.2 of these places are preempted by induced traffic, leaving 4.5 places to serve pedestrians added by building floor space. If 1,000 units of floor space add 0.075 pedestrians and 1 unit of walkway serves 0.0045 pedestrians, then *each additional 1,000 units of floor space require 0.075 ÷ 0.0045, or about 17, additional units of walkway space* on top of the base of 2,860 sq ft (264 m²) that is required to accommodate the 22 "floating" pedestrians.

The application of this increment for the hypothetical average half-block with the average mix of floor space is illustrated in Table 4.15. The half-block measures 200 × 300 ft (61 × 91 m) and has 14-ft (4.3 m) sidewalks on streets and 17-ft (5.2 m) sidewalks on the avenues, meaning that it is supplied with 12,270 sq ft (1,140 m²) of public sidewalk space. The first column lists the floor space density and the second column the resulting amount of floor space on the site. Walkway space is left constant up to a floor space density of 7.5, at which point the amounts provided with 17 additional units of walkway per 1,000 units of floor space are added to it in the third column. The number of pedestrians on the half-block at an instant during the two-hour midday period, calculated from equation (16), is shown in the fourth column. The resulting space per pedestrian—the ratio of the preceding two columns—is given next. The sixth column indicates what portion of the lot is not needed for pedestrian circulation and is thus available either to be covered by the building or to be, in part, devoted to noncirculation amenities, such as sitting and planting areas. The last column is the ratio of the third to the second columns. From this exercise we can draw a number of conclusions.

First, the average of 27 units of walkway space per 1,000 units of floor space calculated by the conventional method is, as the last column shows, a case characteristic of the middle range of densities. Buildings with lower densities do require a relatively greater supply of walkway space to maintain UNIMPEDED movement, because of the "overflow" phenomenon. In reality, they may have more than enough to satisfy that service level.

Second, the existing supply of space on public sidewalks in Manhattan can generally accommodate building densities up to roughly an FAR of 7.5 at the UNIMPEDED standard of flow if the buildings in question have an average nonresidential mix of uses. This happens to match very closely Thomas Adams' estimate of 1931, mentioned in Chapter 1, which called floor-area ratios higher than 8 "excessive."

Third, these so-called "excessive" densities can be accommodated, while maintaining UNIMPEDED flow, with relatively small encroachments on private property, at the rate of about 17 units of added walkway space for every 1,000 units of floor space.

Fourth, even densities twice as high as those presently allowed can maintain UNIMPEDED pedestrian circulation with no more

than half the lot devoted to walkway areas. On this latter point, it could be argued that relationships such as that represented by equation (16) should not be extended beyond the range of actual observations into floor space densities that do not exist. Indeed, the likelihood is that the walkway requirements for the extra-high densities in Table 4.15 would in reality be smaller, because there would be less retailing, more trips would be internalized, and the UNIMPEDED standard would be excessively spacious on the very wide walkways.

Our exercise with Table 4.15 should be viewed primarily as an illustration. It shows that smaller buildings actually do require relatively more walkway space because they take the overflow from big buildings and that big buildings with densities much greater than those currently allowed can provide for comfortable walking with relatively modest setbacks from the building line.

Walkway Space and Building Use
To calculate the setbacks actually required, it is preferable to use the original equations (1) through (4), for two reasons. First adjustments can be made to serve specific uses, not an average mix of use. Second, the equations have known standard errors. If the design objective is not to provide for UNIMPEDED flow on the average but rather to make sure with a stated probability that PARTIALLY IMPEDED flow is not exceeded, use of the standard errors is essential.

Use of the equations to evaluate proposed designs is generally as

follows. First, one assumes a proposed walkway area and determines its capacity for pedestrians at an instant at a chosen level of service, such as IMPEDED (130 sq ft, or 12 m², per pedestrian) or PARTIALLY IMPEDED (65 sq ft, or 6 m², per pedestrian). Then that walkway area is inserted into the equation, as are the values for the pertinent amounts of building floor space in different uses, and the equation is solved. The result is compared with the capacity previously determined, if an average flow condition is the design objective. If the design objective is to not exceed a particular flow condition with a stated probability, then one standard error (for a 68 percent probability) or two times the standard error (for a 95 percent probability) from Table 2.19 is added to the result, and this larger number is compared to the capacity of the walkway. If it is found insufficient, more walkway space is added and the process repeated until balance is achieved. An important procedural point is that the sites tested should be generally in scale with those on which the equations were calibrated, that is, averaging 24,000 to 30,000 sq ft (2,223 to 2,785 m²) and not exceeding 60,000 (5,570 m²). Larger sites should be divided into sectors.

For low floor space densities, there is always a base walkway space requirement, determined by the pedestrians induced by the walkway initially in place, by the floating pedestrians, and, very strongly, by the standard error. The effect of the latter is analogous to the effect of platooning. It is very large for small flows and light densities and is

Table 4.15
Variation of Walkway Space Requirements with Floor Space Density (on a hypothetical half-block in Midtown Manhattan)

Average
nonresidential
floor space

Density (FAR)	Total sq ft	Walkway, sq ft	Av. Peds. at midday	Av. walkway per ped., sq ft	Bldg. coverage %	Sq ft walkway per 1,000 sq ft of fl. space
1	60,000	12,270	66	186	100	205
4	240,000	12,270	79	155	100	51
5	300,000	12,270	84	146	100	41
7.5	450,000	12,270	95	129	100	27
10	600,000	14,820	115	129	96	25
12	720,000	16,880	130	130	92	23
15	900,000	19,930	153	130	87	22
18	1,080,000	22,980	177	130	82	21
20	1,200,000	25,020	192	130	79	21
25	1,500,000	30,120	231	131	70	20
30	1,800,000	35,220	270	131	62	20
35	2,100,000	40,320	309	131	53	19
40	2,400,000	45,420	347	131	45	19

Source: Regional Plan Association.

Table 4.16
Walkway Space for Increments of Floor Space, by Use

Building use	Additional walkway space needed for additional 1,000 units of fl. space, assuming UN-IMPEDED walking on the average (130 sq ft, or 12 m²) per pedestrian, 12:00 to 2:00 P.M.	
	On avenues	On streets
Office buildings	11	13
Retail	79	28
Restaurants	276	172
"Average" floor space	17	

Source: Table 2.18, adjusted by 1,064 to reflect full midday period; average floor space from equation (16).

Table 4.17
Setbacks from the Property Line for Office Buildings

Floor-area Ratio	Setbacks required to satisfy PARTIALLY IMPEDED standard (65 sq ft, or 6 m²) per ped. at midday with a 95% probability				% of Av. half-block Area Devoted to Setback under the standard
	On avenues, assuming 17 ft (5.2 m) existing gross width		On streets, assuming 14 ft (4.3 m) existing gross width		
	ft	(m)	ft	(m)	
1	9	(2.7)	4	(1.2)	7.1
5	10	(3.0)	6	(1.8)	10.1
10	11	(3.6)	8	(2.4)	11.7
15	12	(3.7)	9	(2.7)	13.0
20	13	(4.0)	11	(3.6)	15.3
25	14	(4.3)	13	(4.0)	17.5

Source: Tables 2.18 and 2.19.
Note: Table assumes that 40 percent of ground floor use consists of retailing and 20 percent of restaurants, regardless of building density.

progressively attenuated as these get higher.

Beyond the base condition, increments of walkway have to be provided for each increment in floor space. They are shown in Table 4.16 for four building uses. It is evident that to satisfy midday flow conditions, the increment for retail use has to be over four times that for offices and that for restaurants, about eighteen times greater, keeping the same space per pedestrian. While restaurant space comes in relatively small amounts and should be fully taken into account, in large concentrations of retailing, pedestrian space must be reduced to less than 130 sq ft (12 m^2) so as not to result in unreasonably wide setbacks. The last line in the table shows the increment for average floor space, referred to earlier in Table 4.15, for comparison.

Since the dominant use in downtown areas is offices, we have calculated an illustrative series of setbacks from the building line for office buildings of different floor space density, and this is shown in Table 4.17. The table incorporates the assumption that regardless of building density, 40 percent of the ground floor area will be devoted to retailing and 20 percent to restaurants. Also, it does not use the criterion of UNIMPEDED walking as a standard but rather the criterion of not exceeding PARTIALLY IMPEDED walking with a 95 percent probability. The effect of the change in assumptions—compared with Table 4.15—is to reduce the share of the lot devoted to walkway space at densities above an

FAR of 15 and to increase it in the lower density range. It can be seen that the requirement of not exceeding the PARTIALLY IMPEDED level with a 95 percent probability requires more room than the UNIMPEDED standard in the lower density range. In the case of Manhattan, this requirement demands a minimum walkway width (existing sidewalk plus setback) of at least 26 ft (7.9 m) on avenues and 18 ft (5.5 m) on streets, irrespective of density. By contrast, the increases in walkway width with rising density which it requires are rather modest, about one-fifth to one-third of a foot (say, 0.18 m) per 1 FAR of office space. The increments shown in Table 4.17 are not always even because of rounding to the nearest foot. The flows that will occur on the walkways under average conditions (rather than the extreme 5 percent probable condition), shown in Table 4.17, are related to walkway width by the solid part of the continuous curve in Figure 4.11. Because the standard used is very liberal in the low density range, the 2.5-ft buffer zone is not subtracted in this instance.

Together with the sidewalks already in place, the office building setbacks shown in Table 4.17 offer reasonable dimensions for what we might call *mandatory circulation space* in a dense urban center, specifically Midtown Manhattan. If the sidewalks in place are narrower than indicated, the setbacks should be proportionately wider. If they are wider, the setbacks should not be reduced so that room is left open for noncirculation amenities. Before we turn to

these, several additional points about walkway dimensions related to building density and use are in order.

1. Sidewalks greater than 30 ft (9 m) in width may not always be the best way to provide needed pedestrian space. On long blocks, part of the width requirement can be advantageously satisfied with through-block walkways, underground passageways, and other off-sidewalk circulation spaces. Such *passageways* have their own minimum width requirements—in no case should they be narrower than 15 ft (4.6 m)—and are likely to increase pedestrian space beyond the ratios shown in Table 4.17. Unless they are part of a continuous network, their use is likely to be lighter than that of sidewalks. In practice, the newer through-block walkways in Midtown Manhattan attract between 10 and 20 percent of the total flow in one direction on a block. If they are to have lively movement, they are most appropriate for office densities above an FAR of 15 or for intensive concentrations of retailing.

2. Additional circulation space should be provided near *transit station entrances*. In Manhattan, the situation is particularly critical on side streets leading to stations. Some of them would be most profitably closed to vehicles to provide adequate pedestrian space. In new construction, equation (4) would suggest about 2,000 sq ft (610 m^2) of walkway space on sites adjacent to a transit entrance, in addition to the space shown in Table 4.17. This would ensure, with a high probability, that PARTIALLY IMPEDED service is not exceeded

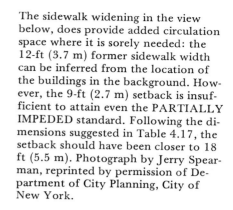

The sidewalk widening in the view below, does provide added circulation space where it is sorely needed: the 12-ft (3.7 m) former sidewalk width can be inferred from the location of the buildings in the background. However, the 9-ft (2.7 m) setback is insufficient to attain even the PARTIALLY IMPEDED standard. Following the dimensions suggested in Table 4.17, the setback should have been closer to 18 ft (5.5 m). Photograph by Jerry Spearman, reprinted by permission of Department of City Planning, City of New York.

Application of the plaza principles without concern for the magnitude of pedestrian movement often results in too much or too little space for circulation. Setbacks such as the one in the top view frequently occur on side streets, where they are excessive. Elevated plazas, such as the one in the lower view, often fail to provide additional circulation space where it is needed most. The heavy pedestrian flow in the picture is caused by the proximity of a subway station.

On long blocks, part of the requirement for circulation space can be satisfied by mid-block walkways. Unless they are continuous, however, their use will be substantially lighter than that of parallel sidewalks, a factor that is important for calculating the prospective use of walkway space around a building.

on the walkway near the transit entrance, in the range of densities covered by that table. Of course, this says nothing about conditions in the transit entrance proper, a subject to which we will come shortly.

3. *Theaters* and other establishments that generate queues should provide for them off the sidewalk. Since 1971, the New York City Zoning ordinance has required 4 sq ft (0.4 m^2) of queuing area per seat. The 8 sq ft (0.7 m^2) of standing room, characterized in Table 3.2 as "comfortable for standing without being affected by others" (with no walking between standees), is thus provided for half the seats in the house.

4. Heavy concentrations of *retailing* in a downtown area pose a special design problem. Table 4.16 illustrates the magnitude of walking space requirements for retailing if spacious walking conditions are to be met. If UNIMPEDED walking is to be maintained, Manhattan sidewalks as they exist could support only a floor-area ratio of 1 for retail use. If PARTIALLY IMPEDED walking is to be tolerated on the average, which is the standard we allowed for the widened walkways of Fifth, Madison, and Lexington avenues, rather than only with a low probability, then the FAR for retail space could go as high as 6. Department stores with higher floor-area ratios should provide setbacks at a rate of roughly 25 units of walkway for each additional 1,000 units of floor space (the average of the two figures in the second line of Table 4.16 divided in half). If above-average concentrations of

pedestrians are already present in an area, lower floor space density or greater setbacks are definitely called for, to be determined by a detailed analysis of the site.

5. *Residential floor space* generates, relatively speaking, so few trips that sidewalk-space-to-building-space relationships have little meaning, and considerations spelled out in our discussion of sidewalks for light flow are governing. To relate the pedestrian streams discussed there at least very roughly to building density, we might estimate that a residential FAR of 1 produces a pedestrian stream of on the order of 50 per peak hour on one sidewalk and an FAR of 5 produces a stream of 250, given Manhattan walking habits and building occupancies. The controlling demand on residential walkways will be imposed by neighborhood retail stores.

Space for Amenities
The concern with off-street parking for automobiles has dominated downtown thinking of cities for a long time; curiously, it has not been matched by an analogous concern: how to provide off-sidewalk resting areas for people. Until the early nineteen sixties, benches and other places to sit in the business areas of Manhattan were conspicuously absent. When the plaza bonus began to provide off-sidewalk pedestrian spaces near new office buildings, many building managements—rather incredibly—tried to discourage their use by people. As late as 1970, the management of a new building that had up to fifty people sitting on the edge of the planting box in its plaza at any one time during midday

installed a spiked metal railing to deliberately prevent people from sitting. Nor did the original wording of the 1961 zoning ordinances do much to encourage pedestrian use of plazas. Permitted obstructions in plazas included steps, railings, flag poles, fountains, statuary, canopies, and planting boxes, among other things. Not listed among permitted uses were either benches or outdoor cafes, and an adequate inducement was not provided for large trees. A departure from this policy began in the Special Greenwich Street Development District,[18] where the provision of pedestrian decks called for "pedestrian facilities including, but not limited to benches, outdoor cafes and kiosks," and in 1975 a more comprehensive revision of plaza regulations was promulgated. Still, edges of fountains, planting boxes, and tops of retaining walls represent the basic outdoor "seating capacity" of Manhattan.

Given these rather hard choices, it is instructive to see how pedestrians behave in the plaza spaces. Several examples are shown in tables 4.18 and 4.19. The first table suggests that as long as the plaza is flush with the sidewalk, 30 to 60 percent of the pedestrians entering the block will walk through it and avail themselves of the expanded space. The higher percentages apply to wider plazas and those that help to cut a corner. The lower ones apply to the narrower plazas and those that have physical obstructions. Interestingly, even a short sidewalk widening in the middle of the block (case 8 of table 4.18) will cause a significant number of pedestrians to detour and use the expanded space as long as there

Table 4.18
Use of Selected Plazas in Midtown

Type of use: building and type of plazas	Time of day	% of peds. entering block who walk through or stay in plaza	% of plaza users who are *not* using the building
1. Lever House (wide arcaded plaza, flush with sidewalk with obstructions)	Rush hours	39	76
	Midday	28	60
2. Equitable (wide plaza, flush with sidewalk partially arcaded, full block)	Midday	46	58
3. Burroughs (very wide plaza, flush with sidewalk with short arcade, full block)	Midday	53	52
4. Time-Life (open plaza, flush with sidewalk, at corner)	Rush hours	47	49
	Midday	46	34
5. 1411 B'way on 7th Ave. (wide plaza, flush, obstructed by planting boxes, full block)	Early rush hour	32	36
6. GM Bldg. at Mad. Ave. (widened sidewalk, flush, full block)	Midday	48	32
7. Random House (sidewalk widening at corner, part of block)	Midday	66	33
8. 633 3rd Ave. (half-block long, widening at mid-block)	Midday	33	28
9. CBS Bldg. (plaza somewhat below sidewalk, separated by barrier)	Rush hours	24	3
	Midday	18	4

Duration of stay (1:00 to 3:30 P.M.), Plaza	% of users not destined for the building staying:		
	less than 1 min (walk through)	1 to 5 min (linger)	more than 5 min (sit down)
1. Lever House	58	13	29
2. Time-Life	24	35	41
3. CBS Building	20	28	52

Sources: Items 1, 4, and 9, Regional Plan Association. Other items, Louis Mascola; "A Study of Reduced Congestion in Sidewalks," Unpublished paper for New York University Graduate School of Public Administration, 1971.
Note: Based on manual counts in summer 1969 and spring 1971; first column refers to total flow entering block on one side; second column based on through traffic in plaza plus persons entering and leaving building regardless of direction: its total is thus unrelated to the total of the first column.

Table 4.19
Pedestrian Occupancy of Selected Parks and Plazas in Midtown

Location (plaza, unless noted otherwise)	No. of peds.	% sitting	Space per ped. sq ft	(m²)	Notes
1. Paley Park	180	95	23	(2.1)	Vestpocket park with chairs, food, fountain, and greenery
2. Greenacre Park	260	95	24	(2.3)	Vestpocket park with chairs, food, fountain, and lush greenery
3. 1 Dag Hammerskjold Plaza	109	90	96	(8.9)	Plaza designed like vestpocket park with seats, fountain, and potted trees
4. Time-Life	144	72	104	(9.7)	Expanded sidewalk with fountains and substantial sitting areas
5. 437 Madison Ave.	30	30	120	(11.1)	Raised plaza with steps and seats
6. 1740 Broadway	14	0	181	(16.8)	Expanded sidewalk
7. Duffy Square	14	50	190	(17.7)	Traffic island with a bench
8. Seagram	77	78	234	(21.7)	Gently raised with substantial sitting, fountains and trees
9. **Average, all Midtown Plazas**	**1,620**	n.d.	**307**	**(28.5)**	497,700 sq ft of plazas
10. **Average, Midtown Parks**	**690**	n.d.	**323**	**(30.0)**	Pedestrian pavement in Bryant Park and along south rim of Central Park
11. Equitable	34	0	353	(32.8)	Expanded sidewalk
12. CBS	12	100	417	(38.7)	Depressed plaza with barrier and potted trees
13. 1700 Broadway	16	31	449	(41.7)	Expanded sidewalk with planting box
14. 245 Park Ave.	8	25	450	(41.8)	Raised plaza with barrier
15. Union Carbide	18	0	544	(50.5)	Expanded sidewalk
16. FDR Post Office	12	0	667	(62.0)	Expanded sidewalk

Source: Regional Plan Association.
Note: Items 1-3 based on manual counts in May 1974 and represent maximum midday occupancy. Items 4-16 based on aerial photography in May 1969 and represent midday occupancy on a random weekday. Item 9 excludes Paley and Greenacre parks and may be undercounted due to the difficulty of distinguishing pedestrians under trees; space for this item refers to pedestrian pavement only; including green areas in two parks, space per pedestrian is 1,244 sq ft (115.6 m²).
n.d. — no data.

are no obstructions. On the other hand, even isolated barriers (planting pots in case 5) will depress through movement, and a continuous barrier (case 9) will limit it to virtually only the building occupants. Nonoccupants range from a high of 76 percent of the plaza users to a low of 3 percent. The width, the continuity of the plaza, and the absence of a strong barrier seem to influence this number. Two of the plazas for which midday and rush hour comparisons are shown appear, in fact, to be more important as rush-hour facilities than as places for midday walking. We should note that the plazas acting as a sidewalk widening serve not only their users: those who remain in the sidewalk also benefit from the expanded space.

Conversely, the plazas with strong barriers not only serve very few users but also provide little benefit to people in the sidewalk, whose visual space may be expanded but whose physical space is no better than if the plaza did not exist.

The lower part of Table 4.18 further suggests that it is the plazas that do not act as thoroughfares which cause the people who come there to stay the longest. Of the three plazas listed, Lever House courtyard invites the smallest proportion of pedestrians to sit down. The Time-Life plaza attracts many more sitters and the largest proportion of those who linger—perhaps to watch the fountains. Of the few people who enter the CBS plaza, most come to sit down. We can say that the functions of a plaza as a circulation facility and as an

amenity are, if not incompatible, then at least clearly distinct.

William H. Whyte[19] found that under relaxed conditions, with plenty of space around, people will sit on a ledge, a bench, or a similar element about 6 to 8 ft (1.8 to 2.4 m) apart, suggesting a comfortable seating space of 36 to 64 sq ft (3.3 to 6 m^2) per person. This is one-half to one-quarter of the space we have found necessary for comfortable walking. Thus, sitting areas can attain a higher instantaneous density than areas that must be reserved for circulation.

This is confirmed by the examples shown in Table 4.19, comparing the densities of occupancy in several plazas and parks. On the average, the density of plaza use is similar to the density of park use in Midtown Manhattan if pedestrian pavement alone is used for comparison. However, some parks and plazas attract above-average numbers of pedestrians: these are generally the ones that provide sitting space. Greenacre and Paley parks particularly stand out with above-average densities of occupancy and a space per person as low as about 30 sq ft (2.8 m^2) Aside from their exceptionally pleasant design and the exclusion of all through movement, these occupancies are in part due to the presence of snack bars, which give these parks, to a mild degree, trip-generation characteristics of restaurants. Without the food service and the close seating made possible by chairs, space per pedestrians becomes three to eight times greater, depending on the degree of through movement. But 30 to 80 percent of

the users are still sitting, even though the sitting space itself typically occupies less than 10 percent of the plaza.

The plazas that get below-average use are generally characterized by the absence of sitting areas, by significant differences in elevation—up or down—and by architectural barriers. The sitting in the three plazas that have below-average densities, illustrated in Table 4.19, occurs on planting boxes and retaining walls. As for the four plazas with no seats, their occupancy by walkers depends on their size and on the magnitude of walking streams in the surrounding area. They all operate at the UNIMPEDED level, sometimes bordering on OPEN FLOW.

In a high-density office district, the latter can be considered excessive, suggesting that part of the plaza space could have been profitably used for noncirculation amenities, such as sitting or greenery.

The provision of greenery—grass, shrubs, and trees—is rather difficult to justify by statistics on pedestrian density because areas devoted to vegetation cannot support any but the very lightest pedestrian use. The problem, nevertheless, is an acute one. Central business districts in America, with the exception of Washington, are notorious for their lack of greenery. We have previously shown that in all of the central 1.2 sq mi (3.1 km^2) of Midtown Manhattan, there are, outside of Bryant Park and the south rim of Central Park, only a little more than 4 acres (1.4 ha) of private and public ornamental

The usefulness of plazas for pedestrian circulation depends on their continuity and the absence of barriers. In the top view, at 1411 Broadway (item 5 in Table 4.18) most pedestrians confine themselves to the former sidewalk on the left. Compared to other plazas, use of the expanded space closer to the building is significantly depressed because the planting boxes act as psychological barriers. In the right view, the Lever House plaza (item 1 in Table 4.18) by Gordon Bunshaft of Skidmore, Owings and Merrill is used as a major thoroughfare because it affords the opportunity to cut a corner on the way to a subway station.

Pedestrian amenities, such as sitting space, have been traditionally in short supply in the centers of American cities. The left scene in front of the Empire State Building has been much more typical than the right one near an entrance to Central Park. Right photograph by Paul Cardell.

Sitting space and amenities—such as water and trees—is what attracts people into plazas, to the extent they are not used for circulation. Right view is in the Time-Life plaza by Harrison and Abramovitz (item 4 in Table 4.19). Lower view is in the Seagram Plaza by Mies van der Rohe and Philip Johnson (item 8 in Table 4.19). Both plazas display above-average pedestrian occupancies, largely because of the sitting space they offer. Photographs by Paul Cardell.

Wasted plaza space, with about 2,000 sq ft (184 m^2) per person in the upper view, and one lonely derelict on 7,000 sq ft (644 m^2) left. Part of the space should have been used for sidewalk widening. Another part could have been used to create a more intimate sitting space. A third part should have been left unpaved, with no construction underneath, to allow the growth of large trees, in lieu of the maintenance-prone potten specimens shown.

Eating, talking, playing, sleeping are among the things pedestrians would like to do in plazas. However, formal seating arrangements make group activities difficult. By contrast, the flexible seating of the type provided in Greenacre Park, shown on this page, offers a choice of socializing or seclusion. Photographs by Paul Cardell.

Outdoor cafes are an outstanding urban amenity, but not when they cut narrow sidewalk space in half and become a pedestrian obstruction. The place for outdoor cafes is in plazas and on widened sidewalks, where those who sit and those who walk have room enough to watch each other with pleasure.

space, which includes landscaping and fountains. Occasional street trees, not included in this figure, are persistently replanted but die just as persistently. Among other things, trees need a certain minimum depth of earth—at least 4 ft (1.2 m)—for their roots to hold; the surface around them, preferably in a radius as large as their crown, should be pervious to water and should not be poisoned by salt or other chemicals. If these conditions are satisfied, hardy specimens can grow in Manhattan to large size, as exemplified by the relatively small but contiguous patches of greenery in Madison Square or Union Square.

Thus, rather than dissipating planting in small planting boxes with half-alive bushes, which become receptacles for garbage, planting space in plazas should be concentrated in patches of at least 1,000 sq ft (13 m^2), a minimum depth of earth should be provided, and the patches should be equipped with automatic watering devices and protected by a curb of sufficient height to prevent salt from snow removal operations from getting to the roots. A major reason why greenery is generally lacking in existing plazas is that basement space for garages and other rental uses is underneath them rather than undisturbed earth. There are three remedies to that. First, the plaza can be made wide enough to accommodate all walking, and the former sidewalk space outside the building line can be converted into an area for greenery, doubling as a buffer zone between pedestrians and vehicular traffic. Second, zoning incentives can be devised to en-courage underground setbacks, to allow space for vegetation. Third, tubs of adequate dimensions can be imbedded into the plaza. The latter solution, representing somewhat of a trend, is probably least desirable.

In summary, three basic uses of plaza space are as (1) circulation areas, required to provide adequate space for walking; (2) sitting areas, needed to provide room for pedestrians to relax; and (3) vegetation areas, desirable to provide greenery. Table 4.20 indicates that there is enough room for all three. With the suggested mandatory setbacks given in Table 4.17, to be used strictly for circulation, all the plazas illustrated in Table 4.20 except one would have more than half their area available for sitting areas, greenery or fountains. This includes the typical plaza in Manhattan stimulated by zoning, which leaves 30 percent of the site open. The area of amenities could be increased beyond about half the plaza space, or 15 percent of the site, if part of the mandatory walkway space were provided under cantilevers or arcades or, in the case of large buildings, if the coverage were further reduced by bonuses. The major change from current practice would not be in the amount of space but in the use of space: the circulation area should be an extension of the sidewalk and should not be obstructed in any way. The sitting area should be separate from the walking path but visually oriented toward it. The planting area should be large enough to support natural tree growth.

Grade Separation and Transit Access

Grade-separated, multilevel walkways in an urban center offer at least four advantages: they provide added room for pedestrian movement, eliminate pedestrian conflicts with motor vehicles, offer opportunities for visual drama and diversity, and offer opportunities for increased interaction, which is the purpose of an urban center. On the latter point, we noted in passing in Chapter 2 that there is considerable segregation between uses in Midtown Manhattan: where the office buildings are, the restaurants and retail stores are not. Also, we found zero relationship between building bulk and proximity to transit stations.

The segregation results, in large part, from the competition for scarce ground floor area. Multilevel walkways, which in effect create two ground floors, enable a richer mixture of uses in a multipurpose environment. They make it possible to rent what would otherwise be less desirable basement or second-floor space at retail store rents. Clustering building bulk around transit stations affords the opportunity to build such multilevel walkways, to improve dramatically the subway station environment, to reduce office encroachment on older buildings and the amenities they offer, and to reduce walking distances. These points were developed architecturally by Rai Okamoto and Frank Williams in the "access tree" principle[20] and subsequently elaborated by Raquel Ramati and Ada Karmi-Melamede in their Second Avenue studies.[21]

Table 4.20
Selected Building Plazas Related to Requirements for Walking Space

Building	Building density, FAR	Actual share of site in plaza, %	Required share of site for circulation (Table 4.17), %	Remaining share of site available for amenities in plaza, %
Seagram	11.6*	38.4	12.4	26.0
Lever House	12.5*	59.2†	12.7	46.5
CBS	17.5*	56.0	14.5	41.5
Time-Life	18.8*	22.3	15.0	7.3
Union Carbide	19.4*	42.4†	15.2	27.2
1411 Broadway	19.6*	33.7	15.2	18.5
FAR 10 Districts	12.0	33.0	12.5	20.5
FAR 15 Districts	18.0	30.0	14.7	15.3

Source: Regional Plan Association.
*According to the accounting of this study, lower by zoning definition.
†Includes extensive arcaded space.

The second pedestrian level. Top view, an extensive network of elevated pedestrian walkways at the edge of the San Francisco business district is rather lightly used, because the density of building floor space in the area is insufficient to fill both the ground level and the second level with pedestrians. Lower view, a pedestrian underpass receives a rare 100 percent usage in Leningrad. The entire sidewalk ramps down gently into the underpass, making it the only reasonable path to follow.

The difficulties of the second pedestrian level. Top view, a sunken court whose only function is to provide some daylight to private basement space. The court leads nowhere and is not used. It takes away valuable circulation space from the surface, which remains the dominant pedestrian level.

Lower view, four sunken courts in the Place Ville Marie in Montreal provide vital daylight and orientation to the extensive underground network of shopping concourses. The lower level is the dominant pedestrian level, and the surface plaza is sparsely used, except during occasional outdoor performances, such as the one in the photograph. Photograph courtesy of Canadian National.

In the first case, the court could have been dispensed with so as not to constrain surface movement. In the second case, the courts could have been much larger, to provide a meaningful open air concourse at the level where most people walk.

Multilevel walkways, however, do not lend themselves to ubiquitous application. If provided in the lower range of densities they will remain sparsely used. Following the methodology outlined earlier we can estimate about how sparsely. It certainly makes no sense to provide two pedestrian levels in a purely residential area, when pedestrian streams on one level rarely exceed OPEN FLOW. Some justification might arise in office areas. An office building with a floor-area density of 10, with only incidental retail, as assumed in Table 4.17, and with a minimal 15-ft (4.6 m) wide second level sufficiently accessible to attract its proportionate share of pedestrians on what we have called the avenue side of the building, would attain a flow at about the midpoint of the UNIMPEDED range on that second level—say 1.2 pedestrians per foot (3.9 per meter) per minute. That is slightly more than the average we found in ground level plazas.

Generally, it takes either an extra level of retailing, or transit access, or exceptional trip generators such as theaters or office densities much in excess of an FAR of 10 to fill a second level with people. The Barbican scheme in London, sometimes mistakenly hailed as a successful design for pedestrians, remains an empty architectural exercise simply because there are not enough people in the development to fill the numerous elevated walks, and the few that there are are dispersed in too many directions.

The Second Level: Over or Under?
The success of a second level, or how many people can be attracted

to it, also relates to the issue of "over" versus "under." The traditional arguments[22] for "under" are: people need less headroom than vehicles (about 8 ft versus 17 ft, or 2.4 versus 5.2 m), and therefore an "under" solution requires (1) less of a grade differential and (2) less horizontal space on approaches. Also, it (3) presents less of an obstruction and (4) offers weather protection. The arguments for "over" are: (1) capital cost is much lower (particularly if utility relocation is involved) and (2) visibility is greater, both from the passageway and of the people on it. However, overhead walkways can be enclosed and climate controlled and underground walkways can be opened to light and air by means of sunken courts and light wells. So, the basic trade off is between capital cost and the benefits of a minimum grade differential, which accrue because of the pedestrians' reluctance to climb stairs.

With what we have learned, we can make a rough estimate of pedestrian diversion to an isolated grade separation approached by stairs. Let us assume a red signal phase or maximum waiting time of 55 secs and a time loss from climbing up and down steps of 18 secs. From Figure 3.7 we can see that a wait up to 10 secs does not seem to encourage the use of stairs. So only pedestrians having to wait more than 28 secs are candidates for the grade separation, and they will distribute themselves in a curve similar to the ones in Figure 3.7, suggesting that less than 10 percent of those crossing the intersection will be voluntarily attracted to the grade separation; the rest will prefer to wait for the light to change.

The example is oversimplified in some ways, but it makes the point that an isolated grade separation approached by stairs will generally not work—unless aided by barriers that preclude alternate paths or assisted by escalators. *For a grade separation to work, it must be an extension of a major continuous level on which the pedestrians find themselves in the course of their natural itinerary and which involves no obvious vertical or horizontal detours.*

Topographical differences in grade provide excellent opportunities for grade separation. Lacking these, *the level at which the dominant number of pedestrians are discharged by mechanical means of travel should also be the second pedestrian level.* Thus, the downtowns of Los Angeles[23] and Minneapolis, which receive large numbers of pedestrians from parking garages, opted for the "over" solution. In the case of Minneapolis, an inducement to use the elevated skyways is that they are enclosed. Under severe winter conditions, one of the first passageways had a peak-hour flow in excess of 2,000 people, which dropped to just over 800 in summer.[24] By contrast, Montreal, with perhaps the world's most distinguished grade-separated pedestrian system, totalling over 3 mi (4.8 km) in length, and serving more than 8,000 pedestrian peak-hour trips,[25] is largely dependent on subway access and opted for the "under" solution integrated with subway stations. Dallas,[26] dependent on garages but contemplating rapid transit, is developing a mixed approach. Downtown Brooklyn, which has the beginnings of a below-grade level in subway stations and adjacent department store basements, is seeking to open it to light and air through the provisions of a special zoning district[27] and also to provide supplementary elevated walkways where underground connections are structurally difficult.[28] A similar mixed approach, with emphasis on an elevated promenade, was earlier adopted by the Special Greenwich Street Development District in Lower Manhattan, justified by coordinated upper levels in adjacent development. To what extent this upper level becomes successful remains to be seen.

In the Manhattan Central Business District as a whole, 40 percent of all pedestrian trips made during the day originate or terminate underground, as we found earlier. During the peak hour, 80 percent of all trips crossing the CBD cordon arrives underground. Thus, emphasis should be unquestionably on the expansion of the underground level as the second pedestrian level. The addition of a third, elevated level poses the danger of dissipating pedestrian streams and making this third level rather anemic.

The existing underground pedestrian level in Midtown Manhattan is extensive. Not counting isolated subway stations, there are, in the four major interconnected corridor systems of Penn Station-Herald Square, Grand Central Station, Rockefeller Center, and Times Square, shown in Figure 4.12, more than 4 mi (6.5 km) of major pedestrian routes. The fact that some of the underground tentacles come temptingly

close together without linking up is not, however, reason enough to connect them, as planners would often like to do. When two parallel subway stations serve the same origins and destinations, they will not develop much traffic between themselves. The partially constructed underground corridor between parallel IND and IRT stations on West 50th Street is an example of such an unnecessary connection.

The pressing needs are for a dramatic expansion of underground pedestrian capacity in the major travel corridors and for better connectivity among the major nodes and directions of travel. These involve access from the two commuter terminals on the West Side to the East Side, from Grand Central Station to points north and west, and between intersecting subway lines, notably in the 53rd Street area. The Bryant Park underpass opened in 1971 to link perpendicular IND and IRT lines is an example of such a successful pedestrian interconnection; it now serves a rush-hour flow of some 3,000 pedestrians.

The major deficiencies in connectivity are shown schematically by arrows in Figure 4.13. The goal is to make the transit grid of the CBD function as a grid, with the possibility of omnidirectional movement, not as a series of isolated lines serving only selected origin-destination pairs. The goal could be satisfied by a combination of greatly enlarged underground walkways and some pedestrian-assistance devices, such as accelerating moving walks. The detailing of any such system

is the domain of transit planning and outside our scope here. Our focus will be on the kinds and amounts of space needed and the methods of providing it.

Room for Stairwells
The greatest barrier to the use of below-ground walkways by pedestrians is the ground level itself. In the scramble for every foot of ground which characterized Manhattan's growth between about 1860 and 1935, subway entrances lost out to vehicular pavement, to sidewalk pavement, and to ground-floor building coverage: there was simply no room for them. The street membrane was regarded as sacrosanct, and only the narrowest possible slots were allowed for pedestrians to squeeze through from the underground world to the world of daylight.

Conditions have changed since then. Some plazas provide walkways 30 to 60 ft (9 to 18 m) wide—much more than we recommended in Table 4.17 as necessary. But, incongruously, these ample walkways, leading to luxurious building lobbies, have on occasion embedded in their concrete, dingy, narrow 4.5 to 6-ft (1.4 to 1.8 m) subway stairs, built up to three-quarters of a century ago. The incongruity becomes intolerable when one realizes that dark mazes of subway corridors were excavated around and carefully protected during construction of the new buildings and that the ample plazas conceal several floors of basement space, which could have been made accessible to people thereby expanding the subway entrances, opening the underground to light and air, and providing higher rent spaces for the owner. Instead, the basement space was used to make an untenable situation permanent for another seventy-five years or so.

Subway entrances deserve the same high standards set out for surface walkways if the design objective is to make space proportionate to the pedestrian flow. In terms of amenity, subway entrances deserve compensatory treatment, to rectify the neglect of past decades. If surface travel by mechanical modes is to be curtailed for the sake of environmental quality at the ground level, the substitute offered underground cannot be so drastically inferior.

The existing station entrance arrangements discourage transit use and obstruct pedestrian circulation on the surface in six major ways.
1.
Stairways to the sidewalk are bottlenecks, mostly for transit users exiting during rush hours but especially for those trying to enter against the tide.
2.
The steps themselves are too steep, which makes them difficult to climb, especially for the elderly, and retards pedestrian flow.
3.
Access to stairways is indirect, thereby obstructing orientation, light, and air and causing security and nuisance problems.
4.
The stairways block sidewalks precisely in those areas where pedestrian demand for surface space is greatest.
5.
Nearby plazas usually remain underutilized because of lack of coordination with subway entries.
6.
Vehicular entries into buildings (loading docks, garages) are frequently in the way of heavy pedestrian flow toward stairway entrances.

All these deficiencies can be attributed to lack of space within the sidewalks. They can be eliminated if subway entrances are located off the sidewalk, either on private property, where the design of new buildings is coordinated with the subway stations or, if that is not possible, in the vehicular roadway, by taking over the curb lane for the needs of the station entrance or, where necessary, by even closing an entire street. More specifically, six rules should be followed.
1. To make below-ground space and the use of rapid transit inviting, *stairs should be wide.* The absolute minimum stairway width, regardless of the magnitude of pedestrian flow, should be 7.5 ft (2.3 m), based on the requirement that three people be able to pass each other without touching. If the addition of escalators can be expected, as with stations on new lines, 6 ft (1.8 m) must be added to the width of the opening, making it at least 13.5 ft (4.1 m). Obviously, wherever there is room, wider stairs are desirable.

2. The *steps themselves must be comfortable.* Instead of the 64 percent incline that a 7 X 11 in. step represents, the "minimum effort" 6 X 12 in. step, or a 50 percent incline, should be used. The incline can, if desired, be reduced to 44 percent. To key the stairway to the 58 percent

grade of an escalator is not sufficient, particularly if landings have to take up some of the horizontal distance. In some cases, it will even be desirable to ramp down entire sidewalks to achieve an imperceptible change between sidewalk space and underground space. This would be particularly appropriate where a subway mezzanine doubles as a grade separation for pedestrians underpassing an avenue that remains in vehicular use. Of course, this is possible only where about four to five times the horizontal distance needed by a stairway is available and where the ramp can be direct, without reverse turns.

3. For purposes of security as well as orientation, *subway entries should be direct and unobstructed,* so that the entire length of the stairway is visible at once both from the sidewalk level and from the mezzanine level.

4. The surface *sidewalk should in no way be reduced in width in the vicinity of a subway stairway.* On the contrary, in new construction an additional setback or plaza space should be provided near an entrance in the amount of about 2,000 sq ft (186 m²), as described earlier.

5. Any *new building adjacent to a transit entrance should be coordinated with it* not only by providing the necessary setback to accommodate an off-sidewalk stairwell but also *by providing amenities,* such as a canopy or cantilever over the stairwell to protect it from weather; building entrances, windows, or shops leading into the stairwell, treating it as a regular part of the street; and sunken courtyards and plazas, as subsequently discussed.

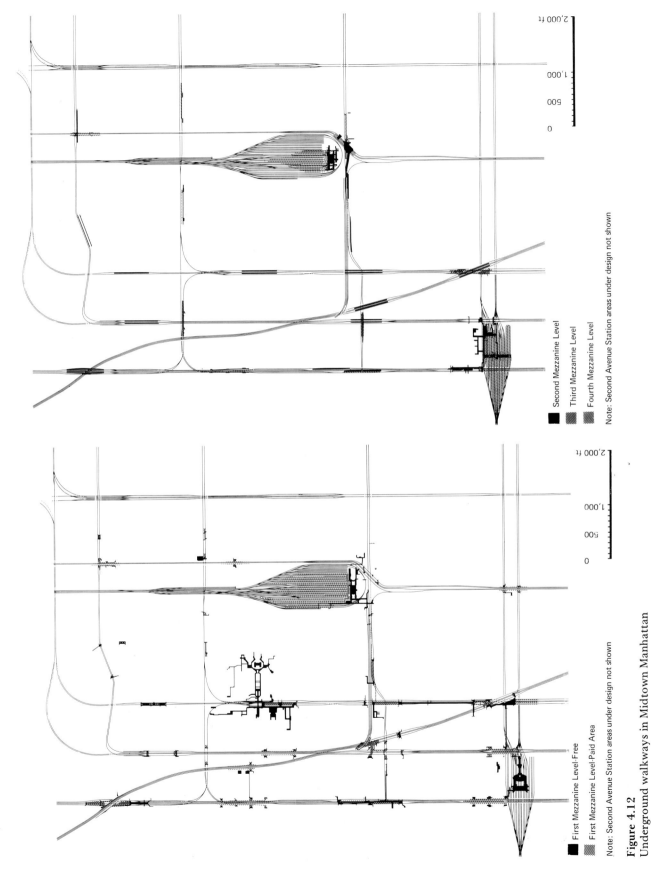

Second Mezzanine Level

Third Mezzanine Level

Fourth Mezzanine Level

Note: Second Avenue Station areas under design not shown

First Mezzanine Level-Free

First Mezzanine Level-Paid Area

Note: Second Avenue Station areas under design not shown

Figure 4.12
Underground walkways in Midtown Manhattan

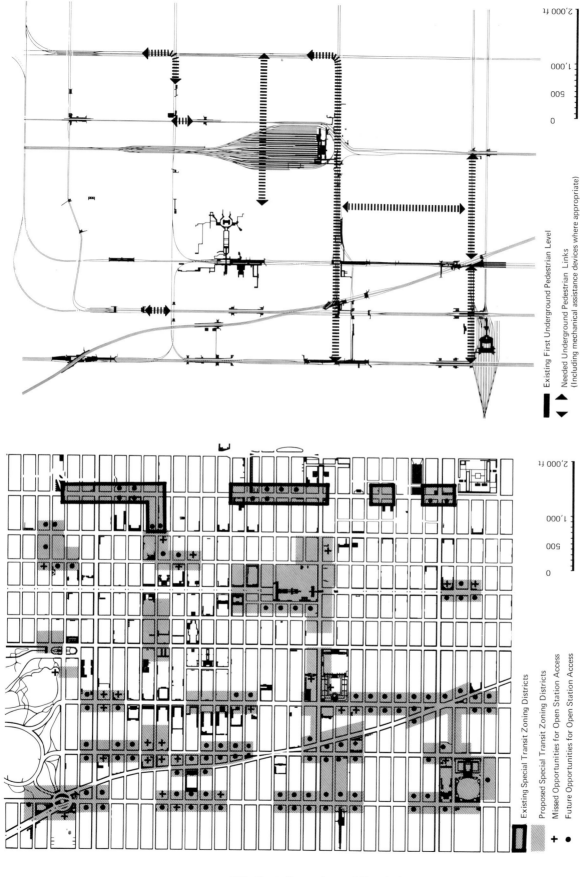

Existing First Underground Pedestrian Level

Needed Underground Pedestrian Links
(Including mechanical assistance devices where appropriate)

Existing Special Transit Zoning Districts

Proposed Special Transit Zoning Districts

Missed Opportunities for Open Station Access

Future Opportunities for Open Station Access

Figure 4.13
Illustrative transit zoning districts in Midtown Manhattan

6. *Driveways and loading docks* or any other vehicular crossings of the sidewalk *within 200 ft of any subway entrance* should be *prohibited.*

With respect to the number of stairways to be provided at a station and their aggregate width, the rule could be that the standard of flow adopted for the sidewalk in the area should also apply to the stairways leading from it. The aim would be to provide a smooth transition between the below-ground environment, necessarily more confined, and the ground-level environment. Thus, if UNIMPEDED is the governing standard for the sidewalk, the stairways should also operate at no more than 2 people per foot of width (6.5 per m) per minute, averaged on an hourly basis. Our observations in tables 3.10 and 3.12 confirm that this would indeed provide movement with no interference at all on the stairways. Table 4.12 shows that only two existing Midtown Manhattan stations operate at that level at present; fifteen stations would require extensive reconstruction, with up to 177 ft (54 m) of additional stairway width needed at Grand Central—double the existing width.

While this is a desirable long-run goal—three new 60-ft stairways would give proper physical expression to the importance of the Grand Central subway station as a people-moving facility—its attainment is obviously not imminent. We could try to scale down our demand to the PARTIALLY IMPEDED level, which

is acceptable for wide sidewalks on intensively used avenues. However, platooning on stairways is much sharper than on wide sidewalks. Our analysis of stairways in tables 3.10 through 3.13 suggests that while a flow at that level, namely, 4 people per minute per foot (13 per meter) of width averaged over the peak hour, generally avoids queues, it creates considerable reverse-flow friction.

Therefore, the PARTIALLY IMPEDED level at subway stairways in Table 4.21 is indicated as 3 people per foot per minute. That standard would mandate modest stairway additions at three stations in Midtown Manhattan and major additions at six stations. At each of two of the new stations on Second Avenue, this conservative standard would require only four stairwells 13.5-ft (4.1 m) wide, but at the United Nations station (between 42nd and 48th streets), it would mandate the equivalent of ten such stairways.

It should be realized that the figures in Table 4.21 represent estimates averaging one-way flow over all stairways at a station; this underrepresents the use of particular, heavily used stairways. For example, while the total capacity into the 42nd Street Eighth Avenue station appears adequate, that of the intersecting passageway of 41st Street is heavily deficient. Thus, the table gives only a very general picture of needs; detailed design will require detailed measures at particular stairways.

Sunlight Underground
The dimensioning of below-

ground pedestrian spaces relates to complex considerations of station design, alluded to earlier, and must remain largely outside our scope here. Limited observations in the Bryant Park pedestrian underpass suggest that the upper limit of PARTIALLY IMPEDED flow of 4 people per minute per foot (13 per meter) of width produces acceptable conditions in that particular 13-ft (4 m) wide corridor, with maximum flow of 7 people per minute per foot (23 per meter)—at the edge of discomfort—lasting only for 5 peak minutes. However, peaking and platooning patterns in stations are so varied that average flow has little meaning and the magnitude of these "micro peaks" has to be scaled in each particular case. In our view, CONSTRAINED flow in platoons, that is, 6 to 10 people per minute per foot (20 to 33 per meter), or Fruin's "service level B," is tolerable only under exceptional, restricted conditions and should in no way be exceeded.

This statement has far-reaching repercussions for any future program of station reconstruction, which pertain not only to subways but to the pedestrian spaces of the major commuter terminals as well. For example, in Penn Station in Manhattan, it would mean widening several corridors far beyond extant proposals.[29] Generally, other cities have been more lavish in the use of underground space than New York. Thus, Paris has a 56-ft (17 m) wide center platform on its express subway station under Defense and San Francisco has 35-ft (10.7 m) center platforms under Market Street, compared

Where existing buildings prevent the immediate expansion of subway entrances on private property, stairways should take over a part of the vehicular roadway. The example here shows a modest attempt to do that, by taking 2 ft (0.6 m) from the curb lane. This still allows only a 4.5-ft (1.4 m) wide subway entrance, and leaves only 10.5 ft (3.2 m) for the sidewalk. Had the city fathers dared to take the entire 8-ft (2.4 m) curb lane away from the automobiles, a somewhat more adequate 7.5-ft (2.3 m) stairway and 13.5-ft (4.1 m) walkway would have been the result. Photograph by Paul Cardell.

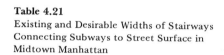

Subway entrances in the sidewalk are an obstruction to pedestrians at the surface. Because of their steep and narrow dimensions, they are also a barrier to greater use of underground transit by the public. To give enough room to both, subway entrances must be located off-sidewalk.

Table 4.21
Existing and Desirable Widths of Stairways Connecting Subways to Street Surface in Midtown Manhattan

Station	Main direction, estimated av. flow, pers./min/ft	Total present stair width ft	Additional stair width needed at:	
			UNIMPEDED service 2 pers./ft/min	PARTIALLY IMPEDED 3 pers./ft/min
1. Grand Central	3.9	186	177	56
2. Rockefeller Center	2.7	166*	58	none
3. Times Square	3.6	119	95	24
4. 42nd & 6th	4.2	89†	98	36
5. 53rd & 5th	13.4	22	125	76
6. Columbus Circle	2.8	72	29	none
7. 59th & Lexington	2.3	80*	12	none
8. 51st & Lexington	6.1	30	62	31
9. 42nd & 8th	2.1	82	4	none
10. 53rd & 3rd	3.9	33	31	10
11. 42nd & 5th	2.2	49	5	none
12. 57th & 7th	3.7	25	21	6
13. 60th & 5th	2.8	32	13	none
14. 49th & 7th	3.7	18	15	4
15. 50th & Broadway	1.7	38	none	none
16. 53rd & 7th	3.9	15	14	5
17. 50th & 8th	0.5	49	none	none
18. United Nations	‡	none	208	139
19. Kips Bay	‡	none	84	56
20. East Midtown	‡	none	67	44

Source: Regional Plan Association.
*Includes reconstruction as of 1974.
†Includes reconstruction, as above, but excludes sparsely used corridor to Herald Square.
‡Based on projected design hour volume.

with 25-ft (7.6 m) wide proposed platforms on the Second Avenue subway and a 20- to 22-ft (about 6 m) minimum on the new lines in New York in general. The national organization of the rapid transit industry has made no effort to raise pedestrian space standards above the barest possible minimum.[30]

Apart from sheer lack of space, the use of the below-ground environment has suffered from its dreary, cluttered, and disorganized image. Starting in the mid-sixties, a number of station design and reconstruction programs have aimed at correcting these deficiencies. The pioneering one was undertaken in Boston.[31] In New York, the Port Authority Trans-Hudson Corporation undertook a study aimed at stripping some of the visual clutter and improving the organization of underground space on its facilities.[32] In 1974 the New York City Transit Authority completed a pilot reconstruction of the 49th Street BMT station, providing bright color, a vastly simplified visual organization, and effective acoustical treatment. However, any fundamental improvement of the below-ground environment must go beyond brick veneer, acoustical treatment, and well-designed graphics. It must include basic structural changes.

Underground spaces are essentially of two types: true tunnels, carved out of earth or rock while leaving the surface undisturbed, or cut-and-cover constructions, that is, ditches that are later covered up to simulate undisturbed surfaces. The deeper tunnels tend to be the true tunnels,

architectonically characterized by clear vaults which carry their own weight. The shallower ones are cut-and-cover, where the man-made cover is usually supported by a profusion of columns. Beams are expensive, and so the more columns, the less costly the cut-and-cover construction. The Washington Metro decided to fight this relationship on a grand scale by providing clear, unencumbered vaults at all underground stations—simulating, as it were, true tunnels throughout the system, regardless of the type of construction. This is one way to gain a coherent image and continuity of space.

In the reconstruction of existing stations, that option does not exist. The remaining option is to connect the ditch visually to what it is in reality a part of—the space above ground. That means breaking the artificial street membrane and opening the underground to light and air.

Hardly anything on the Broadway IRT compares with the pleasure of sunlight penetrating the gratings in the median strip of Broadway. Occasionally, sunlight also brightens stairwells on other lines in New York, immediately identifying them as connections to the outside world and providing orientation as well as delight. But aside from these rare glimpses, the world below ground is sealed from the world above ground with uncanny consistency. Nor is the transit agency necessarily at fault. The New York City Parks Department vetoed an opening to light and air in Bryant Park, which was intended to provide amenity to the pedestrian passageway linking

two subway stations under that park. Likewise, an opening into Central Park from the BMT Fifth Avenue station, which displayed trees and the duck pond to pedestrians in the station mezzanine for a few months while platform lengthening was in progress, was walled up at the insistence of the Parks Department.

Private buildings have also pursued the policy of isolating themselves from the below-ground pedestrian level. Some twenty-five major buildings completed in Midtown Manhattan between 1950 and 1975 have done nothing at all to expand adjacent subway spaces. Perhaps ten buildings, mostly in the Rockefeller Center area, have provided some entrance expansion. Only four buildings have created sunken courts connecting to the below-ground level. Unfortunately, the arrangement of walls in these sunken plazas is such that daylight and openness are not provided to the subway stations themselves. Even New York's first sunken court, in Rockefeller Center, famous for its skating rink and outdoor cafe, was not developed to its full potential: it provides no daylight and no visibility to the extensive system of below-ground passages that converge upon it. In general, if below-ground space is in disrepute and if its rentals are depressed, the answer is not to close it up even more but rather to open it.

Properly designed sunken plazas and subway entrance courts have at least ten public purposes to fulfill, many beneficial to the private owner as well.
1.
Let sunlight penetrate at least to

Both private builders and public agencies have pursued a policy of isolating themselves from subway entrances, as if they were a plague. This is suicidal for any city that overwhelmingly depends on transit access, and merely reinforces the kind of antisocial behavior that is being feared.

Top view shows ample plazas in front of new buildings on 53rd Street in Midtown Manhattan, which did absolutely nothing to expand the old subway entrances.

Lower view shows a rare glimpse of Central Park from a Subway station undergoing reconstruction. Instead of making the opening a permanent feature, it is being walled up to Parks Department specifications.

181 Grade Separation and Transit Access

An open well, complete with escalators, is the central lobby feature of a new building. Alas, the well leads nowhere, other than to the building's basement.

A virtually identical building by the same architect stands astride a major subway station. It could have used a well like the first to provide an inviting and dignified access to the underground. Instead of making the subway entrance the focal point of the building, however, the architect walled it up and provided a twisting, long corridor leading to the black hole in the lower right-hand corner of the picture. As evident from the view, the dysfunctional arrangement is being kept closed to prevent vandalism.

the mezzanine pedestrian level and, where possible, to deeper levels.

2.
Provide natural ventilation for the below-ground space—unless it is air-conditioned—helping to eliminate some of the odors that plague the below-ground environment.

3.
Enhance security by providing a view of below-ground spaces from the street surface and minimizing the extent of hidden, unsupervised areas.

4.
Facilitate orientation by letting people disembarking from a train see where they are before they reach the surface.

5.
Provide identity to buildings and public spaces near station entrances by clearly singling them out as being different from the usual street frontage.

6.
Provide added space for retail stores in places of highest pedestrian accessibility.

7.
Provide added space for pedestrian amenities, such as sitting areas and fountains, in places where they can be enjoyed by most people.

8.
Relieve psychological feelings of confinement which many people experience underground.

9.
Provide a smooth transition from above-ground space to below-ground space, so that one merges imperceptibly with the other and invites people to use it.

10.
Expand pedestrian circulation space in places where it is needed most—at the junction of the two pedestrian levels.

Among these goals, the importance of sunlight has been often stressed.[33] Where full-scale sunken courts or plazas are inappropriate, lightwells and skylights can be provided, either on private property or within the buffer zone of a sidewalk. These can wash the walls of a station with daylight and provide a greatly expanded feeling of spaciousness. They can also serve the purpose of ventilation shafts, replacing the present system of gratings in the pavement.

Studies for the Market Street subway in San Francisco[34] have emphasized the point that for below-ground space to be attractive, it should not be essentially different from above-ground space, and that the visibility of vegetation is important. In numerous places where subway stations abut parks on top, the park space near the subway entrance can be reshaped to allow a smooth and commodious transition, bringing the amenity of the park to the lower circulation level. Ideally, every station near a park would be so arranged that trees could be seen at least from its mezzanine.

Finally, wherever feasible, an important purpose of structural changes in the rebuilding of existing stations should be greater ceiling height,[35] even if only in localized areas. Cut-and-cover construction results in backfilling with earth after a ceiling is built. While a minimum blanket of earth is necessary for pipes and conduits, some of the backfill depth could be profitably used to provide more space in areas

used by people. After the new subway lines currently under construction in New York are completed, a far-reaching program of basic reconstruction of the old system along the lines outlined here will have to move to the top of the public agenda.[36] The issue is equally important in Philadelphia, Chicago, and Boston.

Tall ceilings (above, in Montreal) and wide platforms (right, in San Francisco) make for a pleasant pedestrian environment underground.

Pedestrian passageway under Bryant Park, linking two subway stations was New York's first venture into dignified design of the underground environment; the enameled photomurals and tasteful finishes have gained the acclaim of critics. The ceiling height rises from 8 ft (2.4 m) in the foreground to a more adequate 11 to 12 ft (3.4 to 3.7 m) in the background. A proposed opening to sunlight was vetoed by the Parks Department. During peak hours, flow in the 13-ft (4.0 m) wide corridor is in the IMPEDED range, acceptable for facilities of this type, and reaches the undesirable CONSTRAINED level of 7 people per ft per min (23 per m) only for 5 min. The photo is taken off-peak.

A more typical underground condition in New York, the Flushing line corridor to Eighth Avenue, JAMMED in rainy weather, when significant diversion from the surface occurs. A suggestion of the huge unmet needs for expanded underground space.

Sunlight underground. Left, proposal for a new subway in downtown Buffalo. The principle is applicable to the reconstruction of existing subways with cut-and-cover tunnels close to the surface. Openings of this type could provide sunlight to the Broadway subway stations in New York, where room is available in the median strip of the roadway. At other locations, such as on 42nd Street, the openings could be features in the middle of a pedestrian mall. Below, a more modest type of skylight, designed by Cambridge Seven Associates for the new North Station on the Orange line in Boston. The skylight structures can be incorporated into the "buffer zone" of a sidewalk, separating pedestrians from vehicular traffic.

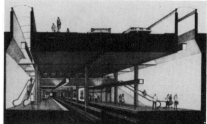

Sidewalk widening and landscaping at the expense of unused vehicular pavement. Before (left) and after (right), a proposal for Sixth Avenue near Broome Street in Manhattan made by Barry Benepe in the *Traffic Quarterly* in 1965. Four open space expansions of this kind, developed by the Urban Design Section, New York City Department of Highways, were implemented in 1974 as a part of the reconstruction of lower Sixth Avenue.

 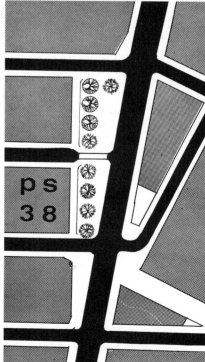

Aspects of Implementation

The use of urban space by people on foot is in some ways a subject so all inclusive that it involves the totality of human institutions. In other ways it is so specialized that it falls between the chairs of existing agencies with narrowly defined functional tasks.

The parks agency is concerned with people in parks; in its mind, allowing people in a subway station to enjoy the park would be antithetical to its purposes. The transit agency is concerned with moving people in trains; it wants to clear the platform before the next train arrives, but as long as it does not delay the next train, letting people stand in a long line for an escalator is quite all right: "You should teach the people to have more patience," a former chief engineer of a large transit agency said. The traffic agency is concerned with moving people in vehicles; in a downtown area, pedestrians are quite a nuisance: they delay vehicular flow and on occasion get killed. So the traffic agency has to deal with people on foot, but only insofar as they conflict with people in vehicles. Abstaining from a discourse on the general difficulty of designing institutions to fit the needs of people, we will focus instead on a few selected areas of change.

Pedestrian Affairs

Sidewalk widths on public streets are usually the domain of administrative rules established by the agency responsible for street construction—in the case of New York City, the Transportation Administration. Prior to 1963

the making of these rules was vested directly in the Board of Estimate, but, regardless of authority, the standard of minimum sidewalk width was shrinking: from 15 ft (4.6 m) in 1912, to 13 ft (4.0 m) in 1925, 10 ft 10 11 ft (3.4 m) in 1963.

Clearly, a public mood and political will are needed to initiate a reassessment of the priorities in the use of downtown space. This involves planning for environmental protection, for transportation, and for land use on a broad and unified front. When the City of New York tried to invoke its administrative powers of setting sidewalk widths to implement the Madison Avenue Mall, the court ruled that "to change the long-existing, intrinsic character and nature of a major thoroughfare . . . requires the exercise of powers over the City's streets that greatly exceed the power to plan the dimensions or other physical aspects of the streets".[37] The matter was judged to be one requiring legislative action by the Board of Estimate, which remained unconvinced of the benefits of reducing vehicular travel, particularly taxi travel, on that scale.

Accordingly, the emphasis on further pedestrianization was shifted to areas where the reduction of vehicular mobility would be smaller. Closing several blocks of Broadway in the Times Square and Herald Square areas would not reduce vehicular capacity at all (and might even improve the performance of intersections) because of the peculiar street geometry of Broadway. Closing the very narrow Nassau Street in Lower Manhattan would affect a

negligible number of vehicles; and Fulton Street in Brooklyn, another successful mall candidate, would improve its performance as a bus street if other vehicles were excluded.

However, beyond the implementation of specific pedestrian mall projects, there is a need for broad-scale administrative initiative and coordination in matters pertaining to pedestrian movement. This results from the multiplicity of agencies that have some jurisdiction over pedestrian space and the absence of any body that represents the interests of the pedestrian directly. Currently, most of the responsibility in New York City rests with two arms of the Transportation Administration, namely, the Department of Highways, which builds streets and grants permits for the placement of obstructions, and the Department of Traffic, which is responsible for traffic operation, including the installation of traffic signs and signal timing. Agencies less directly involved with sidewalk affairs are those dealing with planning and zoning, with housing and urban renewal, with parks (street trees), consumer affairs (licenses to vendors, sidewalk cafes, newsstands), franchises (private use of public property), buildings (standards for canopies and awnings and for temporary obstructions during construction), sanitation (wastebaskets and refuse collection), transit (bus stops and subway entrances), as well as the postal service (mail boxes) and the telephone company (phone booths). Building owners are responsible for keeping the sidewalk clear of snow, ice, and refuse, as well as for paving it to specified dimensions in the first place.

To attain more consideration of pedestrian needs within the Transportation Administration and better coordination with other agencies, an office of Deputy Administrator for Pedestrian Affairs[38] could be established. It would (1) maintain and publish statistics on pedestrian movement; (2) oversee the placement of sidewalk obstructions, making sure that they cause minimum disruption of pedestrian flow; (3) represent the interests of pedestrians before the Traffic and Highways departments, as well as before outside agencies, particularly with respect to street closings, sidewalk widths, and the timing of traffic signals; and (4) initiate design proposals for pedestrian improvements jointly with planning and development agencies. To fulfill these functions, it should have its own traffic engineers on the staff, as well as designers, psychologists, and environmentalists.

Zoning for Surface Space
Obtaining public space on private property is the domain of zoning regulations. With very few exceptions, pedestrian-oriented features in American cities are sought through incentive, rather than through mandatory zoning.[39] Only Atlanta provides for mandatory setbacks on portions of specified streets; Honolulu provides for mandatory setbacks that are applicable more widely but offers a floor space bonus to the developer in return.

With exceptions of this type, incentive zoning dominates the field, perhaps because generally recognized standards of what constitutes a necessary amount of pedestrian space have not been available. The provisions stipulate that a developer can exceed the generally permissible building density in a zoning district by specified amounts if he provides certain pedestrian features. There appears to be a general lack of variety in the features sought, and a clear distinction is not drawn between space needed for pedestrian circulation and space needed for amenity. The major feature sought is simply added ground space on the property—either as a ground-level setback, a plaza, or an arcade. There are few requirements as to how this space should be used or what obstructions are allowed and where they may be placed. Generally, the bonus given for 1 unit of area of sidewalk widening, plaza, or arcade ranges from 3 to 10 units of added floor area. Bonuses for functional features, such as proximity to transit stations, grade-separated connections to subway stations or parking garages, multiple building entrances, or "shortening the walking distance" are rather rare, confined mostly to San Francisco and, to a lesser extent, Minneapolis. Only the latter gives a bonus for weather protection in the form of canopies, although arcades, including enclosed arcades favored by Denver, can be counted in this category.

The initial provisions of the New York City zoning ordinance of 1961 did not depart far from this relative lack of imagination. In essence, they offered bonuses only for "plazas" and "arcades." The former are areas on private property "accessible to the pub-

lic at all times" and open to the sky; the latter have floors above and are partially obstructed by columns. Because of the powerful incentive—10 units of building floor space for each unit of plaza space in the highest density districts—plazas have been used extensively. The inducement for arcades—3 units of floor space for each unit of space under an arcade—was much weaker, and few arcades have been built.

The first decade of experience with these provisions led to much greater legal differentiation of pedestrian spaces in subsequent amendments to the Zoning ordinance. The Special Greenwich Street Development District in Lower Manhattan offered bonuses for a wide variety of pedestrian improvements, including an elevated shopping way, pedestrian bridges and decks over streets, loggias, underground pedestrian tunnels, "the penetration of daylight into subway stations and concourses", and trees. Several of these provisions became a model for other Special Districts.

Outside the Special Districts, post-1970 amendments introduced higher bonuses for arcades that penetrated through the block, for high arcades, and for covered pedestrian spaces, such as galleries. A 1975 revision of the regulations on bonusable open space in the highest density commercial districts introduced the differentiation among plazas, sidewalk widenings, small urban parks, and sunken open air concourses near transit stations.

In *plazas,* the new specifications encouraged the provision of sitting space, trees, and light commercial uses that attract pedestrians. They reduced permissible differences in grade, specified the area that may be occupied by permitted obstructions, and regulated the horizontal proportions and the location of plazas to make the spaces created by them visually more meaningful and to encourage southern exposure.

The *sidewalk widening* provisions, though not quite up to the standards recommended in this book, at long last recognized the need for unobstructed circulation space on private property in high density districts, a space quite different in function from the amenity space of the plaza.

The *urban park* provisions made it possible for developers to build parks such as Paley and Greenacre as a part of the regular development process, not as a matter of private philanthropy. They allowed the transfer of development rights from sites within 500 ft (152 m) of a building to that building if a mini-park of at least 4,000 sq ft (372 m²) is developed on the site. A bonus of 18 units of floor area for each unit of park area was granted, as long as the total bulk of the building does not exceed an FAR of 21.6, and as long as a specified minimum of pedestrian space is provided on the building site. Detailed standards of sitting space (1 linear unit for each 20 square units), shade trees (1 for every 500 sq ft or 46 m²), the presence of water, the absence of sharp differences in grade, and a number of other design features were specified.

The *open air concourse* provisions established the access of natural light and air to underground subway spaces as a separate and distinct function of urban open space, and in effect limited deep sunken plazas to subway entrances only.

All these revisions went a long way to remedy two basic deficiencies of the inital 1961 regulations: they reduced the likelihood that useless open space will be provided, and they encouraged beneficial uses that were previously discouraged. Still, the provisions are limited only to the highest density districts, and they remain optional, applicable only to builders who elect to provide open space in order to obtain a bonus. The provision of adequate circulation space for pedestrians is by no means guaranteed. As we have shown, added pedestrian space on a lot can be justified with floor-area ratios as low as 1 and is certainly required for those in excess of 7.5.

Following the logic of this book, any future comprehensive zoning revision would incorporate a number of additional features and a structure more explicitly based on pedestrian needs. It would start by making a clear distinction between *mandatory* and *optional* pedestrian features at the surface. The first category includes circulation space. The second includes space for sitting, landscaping, and other amenities.

Mandatory circulation space should be required in amounts similar to those specified by tables 4.16 and 4.17. The continuity of a walkway should be ensured through mandatory

ground-level setbacks from the property line, geared to permitted density and use in each zoning district and specified for each street or each category of streets. The setbacks would apply not only to the building proper but, very importantly, to any other obstructions on the site, such as retaining walls of plazas. They should ensure a level, uninterrupted walkway.

In the higher range of densities and for buildings covering a large site, the area required for circulation should be greater than that provided by the setback. This surplus can be used by the builder at his own discretion to provide more space near the building entrance, to provide cut or rounded corners, through-block walkways, and other off-sidewalk circulation spaces.

The mandatory circulation space does not have to be fully open to the sky but can, and, in fact, should, be partially covered to ensure the greater reliability of the walkway system in inclement weather, which we discussed in Chapter 2. This suggests that the regulations and incentives should favor covered circulation space over open circulation space, up to a certain point. The nature of this cover requires elaboration.

The current New York City zoning ordinance calls for a totally inadequate 10-ft (3 m) minimum arcade width from the outside column edge. Subtracting the width of the columns and the unused space alongside the columns and the wall, this leaves a walkway that is effectively perhaps 5 ft (1.5 m) wide. A more adequate 15-ft (4.6 m) minimum width has been established in the Special Greenwich Street Development District, and widths up to 20 or 25 ft (6 to 7.6 m) are desirable. Comparing these dimensions with the needed walkway widths shown in Table 4.17, it becomes apparent that while they can adequately serve avenue frontage in high-density areas, they would either provide too much space on street walkways or cut them up with columns. To avoid this, strong inducements should be offered for cantilevered overhangs covering part of the mandatory walkway without obstructing flow. Overhangs of 5 to 15 ft (1.5 to 4.6 m) would not call for major changes in present construction practices; in fact, the outside wall is sometimes built as a cantilever anyway, and false columns are introduced on the ground floor for appearance and to accommodate pipes.

In theory, the provision of mandatory pedestrian space to satisfy the circulation needs of a building with a given bulk and use should not require any bonuses. In practice, to maintain continuity with the wording of existing ordinances, an automatic bonus can be provided. For example, in an FAR 15 district, the allowable FAR would automatically be about 16.4 when the mandatory walkway provisions for that density, as suggested in Table 4.17, are satisfied.

This is about equivalent to the present plaza bonus, which would thus be extended to partially covered walkways as well. With equal inducements, the provision of partially covered walkway space is obviously more

lucrative to the developer, since he can build floors on top. The control over the extent of these floors on top is in the realm of provisions for light and air setbacks and tower coverage, which we will not go into here; suffice it to say that these provisions will place a limit on how much of the walkway is actually covered by floors above.

From the viewpoint of pedestrian space, an important consideration is to maintain a minimum clear height—perhaps 15 ft (4.6 m) in residential areas and 20 ft (6 m) in office districts—and to discourage column obstructions. The latter can be attained by excluding from the computation of mandatory walkway space a strip of walkway obstructed by columns or the space sterilized by each column. The latter may be as much as 100 sq ft (9.3 m²) of walkway for a 3 × 3 ft (0.9 by 0.9 m) column. A minimum clear width of 15 ft (4.6 m) between columns and building walls can be a further disincentive if it demands more walkway space than required.

Once the requirements for unobstructed pedestrian space needed purely for the purposes of circulation are satisfied, optional features such as space for sitting and for landscaping can be provided with a range of bonus incentives. It might be desirable to differentiate the bonus scale for three different types of plaza areas: (1) *active plaza space,* which should allow light commercial activities such as outdoor cafes, terraces for office cafeterias, vending kiosks and other outdoor sales activities, and display cases for stores; (2) *passive sitting*

space, which should not have any commercial intrusions but might have fountains and the like; and (3) *space for landscaping.*

Some minimum sitting space should be provided in every plaza. As for meaningful landscaping, it is suitable only for large sites. To allow for the growth of large trees, planting areas should be concentrated in groves of at least 1,000 sq ft (93 m²), good for about four respectable-size trees. The planting areas should provide 4- to 5-ft (say, 1.5 m) minimum depth of earth and preferably have no construction underneath; they should be protected from the intrusion of winter salt by at least a 1-ft (0.3 m) rim or curb and be equipped with automatic watering devices. Since planting areas require gardening expenses and offer no possibility of commercial return, the floor space bonus for them could be higher than for the active and passive plaza space.

Of course, *to the extent that bonuses for optional plaza features result in higher building densities, additional mandatory circulation space has to be provided.* Tables 4.16 and 4.17 indicate that these necessary increments, in the case of office buildings, are quite small—in the range of 1 to 2 units of walkway area for each 100 units of added floor area. Therefore, there is no need to fear moderate increases in office building density if they provide desirable amenities near the ground.

One last aspect of the mandatory walkway standards should be noted. An important constitutional reason for zoning is public safety, which includes provision for emergencies, for example, a case in which all building occupants find themselves on the sidewalk at once, as happened in New York during the blackout of 1965. From the figures presented earlier one can conclude that the peak occupancy of Manhattan's office buildings averages about 3 people per 1,000 sq ft (93 m²) of floor space. Should they all find themselves in the walkway at once, the standards of Table 4.17 would provide 5 sq ft (0.46 m²) per person or more, up to an FAR of 25. This would allow walking under JAMMED conditions but would avoid a crush seriously endangering life and limb. The peak average occupancy of all nonresidential floor space is about 3.4 persons per 1,000 sq ft (93 m²), which could justify appropriately higher allocations of walkway space in retail areas.

Zoning for Space Below Ground
The provision of off-sidewalk entrance space to below-ground walkway areas, notably to subway station mezzanines, is often achieved simply by public condemnation of the properties required; this has been the practice in Montreal and Washington as well as in many European cities. However, in very high-density areas with an active real estate market, attaining what has been often called "joint development"[40] at stations may be preferable through zoning. In Manhattan, two distinct possibilities exist. One is new stations on the Second Avenue subway, which are mostly in residential areas. The other is those stations on existing lines which are surround-

ed by sites with a potential for office redevelopment. The two situations differ primarily in the applicability of incentive bonuses. In the Second Avenue corridor, permitted residential densities are already very high, with an FAR up to 12. There is legitimate community resistance to raising them any further. By contrast, raising office building densities in limited areas around subway stations, following the "access tree" principle, can be quite appropriate. This principle is also applicable to residential areas outside Manhattan—in other cities as well—where present densities are too low to adequately support a transit line. Toronto presents an excellent example of clustering high-rise housing around subway stations.

On Second Avenue, to deal with that situation in greater detail, the 15-ft (4.6 m) wide sidewalk is just about adequate for UN-IMPEDED pedestrian flow at present, without the added pedestrian traffic to the subway stations. The avenue itself is a major artery whose importance for surface traffic could increase if other avenues were pedestrianized. So, there is no room for subway entrances in the sidewalk, and to gain it from the traveled way would be difficult. The only room is on private property. The most direct way to acquire this room for the public in new construction is through a mandatory setback at the ground level and below ground, applicable to buildings that abut stations.

The principle of setbacks above ground is widely established in

zoning law; there is nothing to prevent extending this principle below ground to apply to basement space. The public purposes are maintaining smooth pedestrian movement on the public sidewalk, encouraging the use of public transit, and providing an opening to the underground large enough to satisfy at least some of the ten purposes of sunken courts listed earlier, which have to do with the safety, health, orientation, and convenience of transit users.

The minimum size of the *transit access setback* is determined by the comfortable stair dimensions developed earlier and by the depth of the space, such as the subway mezzanine, to which access is to be provided. With a 7.5-ft (2.3 m) minimum stairway width (allowing three people to pass each other), a 6-ft (1.8 m) allowance for possible installation of an escalator, and room for walls on each side, the minimum width of the setback becomes 15 ft (4.6 m). This should be increased to 30 ft (9.2 m) at heavily used stations. With an average 22-ft (6.7 m) mezzanine depth, characteristic of all but a few deeper-level stations on the Second Avenue line, and a comfortable 50 percent stair incline, the horizontal stair dimension is 44 ft (13.4 m), or 50 ft (15.2 m) with two intermediate landings. The escalator requirement at this depth is similar. With standard 8 × 14 in. (20.3 × 35.6 cm) steps, the escalator will descend to the required depth in 33 steps, a horizontal distance of 38.5 ft (11.7 m); adding 6 ft (1.8 m) each for balustrade extensions at the top and at the bottom, its total length becomes 50.5 ft

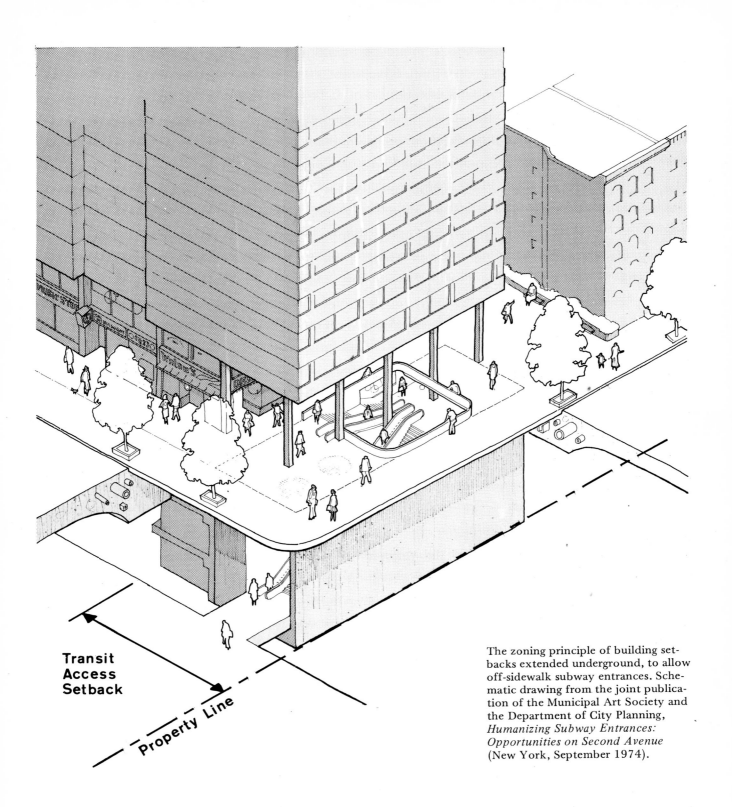

**Transit
Access
Setback**

Property Line

The zoning principle of building setbacks extended underground, to allow
off-sidewalk subway entrances. Schematic drawing from the joint publication of the Municipal Art Society and
the Department of City Planning,
*Humanizing Subway Entrances:
Opportunities on Second Avenue*
(New York, September 1974).

(15.4 m). Adding room for landings serving both the stairway and the possible escalator, the required minimum length becomes 80 ft (24 m). This 15 × 80 ft space should be unobstructed below ground to the depth of the mezzanine to which it connects and above ground up to a height of about 15 ft (4.6 m). Building over part of the setback above the height is desirable, to provide protection from rain and snow for people as well as for the escalator machinery.

The impact on the developer from what amounts to a public use of some 44,000 cubic feet (1,250 m³) of grade-level and basement space is modest and can be ameliorated in a number of ways. First, the transit access setback should be counted as plaza, arcade, or other open space for the purposes of calculating any applicable bonuses. Second, the permitted above-ground coverage of the building can be increased, allowing a lower but thicker building mass that will provide the needed cover for the transit access setback and that can be valuable for the developer of a smaller building. Third, the applicable off-street parking requirements can be waived; the typical use of basement space in the affected cases is for parking garages. Fourth, the substitution of commercial uses for garage use of basement space should be encouraged in areas fronting on the transit access setback. This can provide some direct compensation: annual rent for garage space may be on the order of $3 per square foot in 1975 prices, compared with $5 to $8 for mezzanine-type retail or office space.

To be attractive to potential customers, people-oriented commercial uses fronting the transit access setback must be open and inviting. The full horizontal dimension of the setback should be open to view from the sidewalk, unobstructed by any slabs. It can, in this way, act as somewhat of a lightwell. At stations where immediate requirements for stair capacity are satisfied, transit access setbacks should be provided anyway, to act as sunken courts providing light and air below ground and to allow possible later addition of stairs or escalators. Likewise, the space reserved for an escalator can act as a lightwell in the absence of an escalator.

Requirements generally similar to the ones described above were incorporated by the New York City Planning Commission into the 1974 Second Avenue Special Transit Land Use District legislation. As a minimum, the legislation attains the possibility of off-sidewalk station entrances on sites where new buildings will be erected next to transit stations. It does not, however, solve the problem of gaining off-sidewalk entrances in existing buildings, nor does it make provision for truly generous openings to the below-ground space. To attain these, the device of a benefit assessment district, often used to finance pedestrian improvements such as malls or overhead walkways, could be employed.

Among the benefits of a new transit line, such as the Second Avenue subway, is the reduction of walking distances to transit in the area. On the basis of data developed earlier in this book, the monetary value of that bene-

fit to a particular building can be calculated in an illustrative way.

Let us make the following assumptions: (1) The site in question was located an average distance from the nearest transit station, as defined by average walking distances in Chapter 2. The walking distance from the subway to the site now shrinks to near zero because a new station will be right under it. (2) People value the ability not to walk to a transit station at 1 cent for every 100 ft (30.5 m); at the end of Chapter 2 we pointed out that this figure is quite conservative. (3) The building on the site generates trips by subway at the average rates defined at the beginning of this chapter. (4) There are 296 equivalent average weekdays in a year, taking into account reduced subway travel on weekends and holidays to which the trip-generation rates apply. On this basis, the calculation is as follows:

Annual benefit to average non-residential building: 6.4 (two-way subway trips per day) × 12.4 (hundreds of feet average walk) × $0.01 ($ per 100 ft of walking) × 296 days = *$234/per year/1,000 sq feet of floor space.*

Annual benefit to residential building (Manhattan East Side location): 2 (two-way trips per day) × 14.5 (hundreds of feet average walk) × $0.01 ($ per 100 ft of walking) × 296 days = *$86/year/1,000 sq ft of floor space.*

The calculation shows that a building immediately adjacent to a newly built station will realize from that proximity an annual benefit of at least 23 cents per square foot if it has nonresidential use and 8 cents per square foot if it is an apartment house. The benefit from reduced walking distances will obviously be smaller for buildings farther from new stations, but any building that is closer to a new station than to any of the existing stations will realize some benefit.

That criterion can be used to define an area within which a special tax, or *benefit assessment,* can be levied to finance further pedestrian improvements. The reader will note that we are not dealing here with the broader benefits of increased accessibility. We are dealing strictly with recouping the private gain from public investment pertaining to pedestrian movement.

The proceeds from the benefit assessment can be used in two ways. First, the money can help to build sunken public squares off subway mezzanines and other more elaborate facilities not fundable from private resources or from regular public funds—a sort of pedestrian trust fund. Second, and perhaps more importantly in this context, access can be gained into existing buildings, by requiring, where necessary, a *transit entry easement in lieu of benefit assessment.* Thus, using the equivalencies calculated above, at $10 per square foot annual rental, a 100,000 sq ft existing nonresidential building ought to be able to "rent" to the transit agency, free of charge, 2,340 sq ft (217 m²) of space. This is not large enough for a plaza, but is certainly a commodious station entrance. Conversely, at $4 per square foot

annual rental, a 100,000 sq ft existing residential building with an East Side Manhattan location ought to be able to "rent," free of charge, a 2,150 sq ft (200 m²) station entrance. In both of the described cases, the transit agency would build the actual stairways in the privately provided easement.

In the situation in which floor space bonuses can be employed, a far-reaching change of the below-ground environment can be accomplished with private funds. Only limited efforts in that direction have been undertaken by the City of New York so far. They fall into three categories.

First, in return for certain zoning variances, monetary contributions to a special station reconstruction fund were sometimes obtained from developers. Because there was no clear plan, such monies are in the danger of being whittled away on minor tiling and transit furniture improvements, which should have been carried out with the general transit funds anyway and which are in the nature of renovation rather than a basic change in the spatial relationship between underground and above ground. If it is deemed desirable to supplement city and state transit funds with added levies from real estate, these can be collected from all buildings that profit by the subway's presence, not just those few that can make a direct contribution by being physically adjacent to a subway station. The main purpose of enlisting private builders in the reconstruction of stations is not to collect money; it is that station rehabilitation can have a full impact only when physically

integrated with new development on adjacent sites.

Second, underground connections from new buildings to adjacent stations were sometimes required by the City. These can be helpful to provide extra entrance width, but unless built to very generous standards, they do not necessarily represent a pleasing environment. Most of those built lack an essential prerequisite—openings to light and air. Some are so narrow and indirect that they had best not been built at all.

Third, and perhaps most promising, is the 1973 amendment to the zoning resolution, which allowed plazas to be depressed more than 10 ft below grade if they connect to a subway station, mezzanine, or concourse. One-half of the allowable plaza space can be at the lower pedestrian level. A subsequent 1975 amendment made more detailed provisions for what it called "open air concourses" and specified the size of the openings from the sunken plaza to the subway station spaces. This is important, because a wall between the subway station and the plaza can negate the entire purpose of a sunken plaza. However, the incentive for a sunken plaza connecting to a subway station is no different from the incentives for a surface plaza— 10 units of floor space for 1 unit of plaza space. While the developer may recoup the loss of below-grade floor space with higher rentals from the remaining space that is open to light and air by the plaza, this hardly encourages him to go deeper than one level. Meanwhile, the subway world is several levels deep, and all could profit from openness and visibility.

If the ten public purposes of sunken plazas enumerated earlier are to be fully satisfied, five design criteria are in order.

1.
Every new building in a fairly high intensity commercial zoning district *which abuts a transit station* or an underground corridor *should be required to have a sunken plaza connecting to the below-ground pedestrian space.*

2.
On-sidewalk stairways should be replaced by off-sidewalk stairways of adequate width in the sunken plaza or near it.

3.
The sunken plaza should have required minimum dimensions, perhaps a 40 × 80 ft (12 × 24 m) space, which constitute a meaningful opening to the street level. Its *maximum dimensions should be limited only to the extent that it cannot encroach on mandatory walkway space at the surface.* All other surface amenities can be waived in favor of station access because station entrances are few, while sites for the other amenities are many.

4.
The opening from the plaza to the abutting underground spaces should extend the full width of the surface that they have in common. This is perhaps the most important requirement, without which sunken plazas have little meaning. If considerations of noise and climate controls so dictate, *the opening can be glassed in* for the most part, but *it must provide maximum sunlight and visibility.*

5.
The developer must be encouraged, through adequate floor space bonuses, *to break down the wall between the subway space and the plaza* and rebuild the adjoining below-ground space to high architectural standards.

The magnitude of the bonus requires some elaboration. First, there is the need for compensation for the loss of basement space, which, in the case of a commercial building, can be higher-rent space than just garage space; computer operations or back-up space for retail are typically housed in basements. To make sunken plazas commercially attractive to the developer, it would seem reasonable to recompense him at least on a one to one basis for the basement space lost. Thus, a sunken plaza would get a floor space bonus not of 10 but of 11, if it is one level deep, and 12, if it is in two levels deep, and so on, provided it conforms to the other requirements listed.

Second, and large in magnitude, is the need for compensation for the underground construction needed to effect a real connection with the subway station environment. That construction can be costly and complex, involving not only demolition of existing station walls but also utility relocation. Estimates based on Transit Authority contract documents suggest that the average cost per cubic foot (0.0283 m^3) of finished construction, in 1970 prices, ranged from a high of $50 for platform extensions on eight BMT stations, to $35 for added stairways at the 77th Street IRT station, to a low of $20 for the Bryant Park pedestrian underpass.

The value of an added square foot of floor space can be as-sumed to equal the land value divided by the FAR: thus, if land is worth $450 a square foot, an added square foot of floor space is worth $25 in an FAR 18 district. Taking the higher of the construction cost figures, we can estimate, merely to gain a sense of scale, that each cubic foot of underground construction undertaken by the developer on public property should be recompensed with at least 2 sq ft of extra building floor space. In areas of lower land value, the compensation has to be higher, perhaps 1:7, based on figures developed for the Greenwich Street Special Development District. We can assume a 1:5 ratio for purposes of illustration.

Going back to our hypothetical 200 × 300 ft (61 × 91 m) site and assuming that we start with a basic FAR of 18, that we want the developer to provide a large sunken court (60 × 150 ft, or 18 × 46 m, or 15 percent of the site), and that we want him to undertake as much underground construction beyond his property line as could be reasonably expected on one Manhattan block face (a space 150 ft long, 20 ft wide, and 20 ft high [46 × 6 × 6 m] opening into the sunken court), then the arithmetic of bonuses would work out as follows:

Permissible with existing bonuses (60,000 sq ft site), FAR 18
                    1,080,000 sq ft
Extra bonus for 9,000 sq ft sunken court, 1:1   9,000 sq ft
Bonus for 60,000 cubic feet of off-site construction, 1:5
               +300,000 sq ft

Total allowable ————————
floor space   1,389,000 sq ft
Divided by site area FAR 23.2.

We see that the hypothetical bonus is not out of scale with the needs and that the bonus results in densities that are admittedly high but not beyond the bounds of what we have found reasonable for pedestrian space.

One factor not considered in this arithmetic is that of delays while the developer is negotiating agreements with public agencies. Available records on several privately built entrances into New York subway facilities suggest that the elapsed time between commencement of negotiations and the agreement to proceed on an approved plan is much more variable than construction costs and ranges from about three months (a new station entrance for a department store) to more than two years (the corridor between two subway stations on 50th Street). But, since the design and construction on most of the rest of the building can proceed while negotiations are in progress, it is hard to pinpoint exactly how much net delay the developer incurs. If the expansion of underground pedestrian spaces around transit stations by private developers becomes an accepted public policy— the Transit Authority has traditionally viewed such projects as if private gain were their main objective—appropriate safeguards must be established, similar to the 60-day limit for approval by the transit agency included in the Special Second Avenue District legislation.

On the positive side of the ledger, however, a benefit of reduced walking distances will accrue if more office floor space is clustered on top of transit stations

at high densities. Because stations in Midtown Manhattan are spaced closely and a large choice of lines exists, this benefit is not as pronounced as one that accrues to a formerly isolated building on Second Avenue which suddenly finds a transit station in its basement. Nevertheless, it is tangible and can be estimated at roughly 12 cents per year per square foot of floor space that exceeds average density, in 1969-71 prices.

It should be stressed that the total transit delivery capacity for future office floor space remains the same, regardless of whether floor space is clustered around stations or located haphazardly. Location closer to stations might lead to slightly higher peaking but will also encourage off-peak use in lieu of taxis and such.

In summary, the benefits of clustering are not limited to somewhat shorter walking distances and improved off-peak subway use. They include, first and foremost, the opportunity to change dramatically the below-ground pedestrian environment and, second, the opportunity to preserve more of the existing urban fabric away from stations. Figure 4.13 shows a schematic diagram of the special transit zoning districts, defined as areas abutting below-ground pedestrian passageways, where the principles described could be applicable.

Pedestrian Space as a Limit to Density
With our endorsement of selective increases in commercial building density to gain improvements in the public environment at and below the ground level, we come back to the issue raised

early in the book: Isn't there a point at which higher downtown densities become self-defeating? The issue has also been put another way: "The flaw of any plot ratio method of control of building bulk lies in its apparent arbitrariness. Developers cannot see why one figure rather than another should be enforced by a planning authority, and they feel confirmed in their doubts when they are promised disproportionate bonus floor areas . . . for features which the planning authority deems desirable".[41]

Responding to the second point first, we have demonstrated a rigorous method for relating open space for pedestrian circulation to building bulk and use and, in so doing, dispensed with much of the apparent arbitrariness. But what about the rest, pertaining to the optional open space features and the issue of inherent limits to building density?

While extrapolations from existing experience into nonexistent ranges of very high density are, as we said, somewhat shaky, the overall thrust of the calculations presented is that *the provision of pedestrian circulation space as such does not pose limits to urban density which are tangible at present, except for buildings serving retail use.*

In theory, the fairly conservative ratio of 1 square unit of walkway space supporting about 60 square units of incremental building floor space suggests that an FAR of 60 is a rough limit of general nonresidential building density from the viewpoint of pedestrian circulation, if one assumes that

A spacious sunken plaza at Market and Powell Streets in San Francisco (top view), carved out of formerly vehicular pavement. It provides pedestrian circulation space where it is needed most—at the junction of two pedestrian levels, and offers room for amenities, such as sitting and trees. It provides light and air to the subway station mezzanine (lower view). It also enhances security and visibility, provides orientation, and offers identity to the neighborhood and the subway station.

A similar sunken plaza on off-street property at Lake Merritt Station in Oakland sheds sunlight directly onto the subway platform—the most desirable condition.

New York's first attempt to break the street membrane and to open the underground to light and air. The concept, as advocated by Regional Plan Association, called for demolishing the subway walls and roof to create a huge "lantern" that would flood the Columbus Circle subway station with sunlight and provide orientation in its confused, cavernous spaces. After innumerable compromises, the builder of an adjacent office building provided a small, round, sunken court, and the Transit Authority, a new door to it. The tiny window seen on the right is false. No daylight penetrates the subway station. Photograph by Paul Cardell.

A somewhat more generous sunken court providing a new entrance to the subway station at Broadway and 51st Street. Unfortunately, the path offered to transit users is indirect—they have to walk around the wall on the right to enter the turnstile area. Again, though the possibility is tantalizingly close, daylight cannot be seen from the subway platform, which remains hidden just behind the stairway on which people are walking down. In future construction, openings from sunken plazas to the abutting underground spaces must be made mandatory, and extend the full width of the surface which the two spaces have in common.

Transit station mezzanine connected to adjacent buildings and a bus station through off-street sunken courts open to light and air. Early Regional Plan Association proposal for Jamaica, Queens designed by Donald H. Cromley. Final design for the Jamaica Center station prepared by the Transit Authority followed the principle of off-sidewalk open entrances and direct linkages to major adjacent generators of pedestrian traffic. However, in view of rather sparse projected off-peak use, the mezzanine area was divided in two and substantially reduced, among other things to improve policing and maintenance.

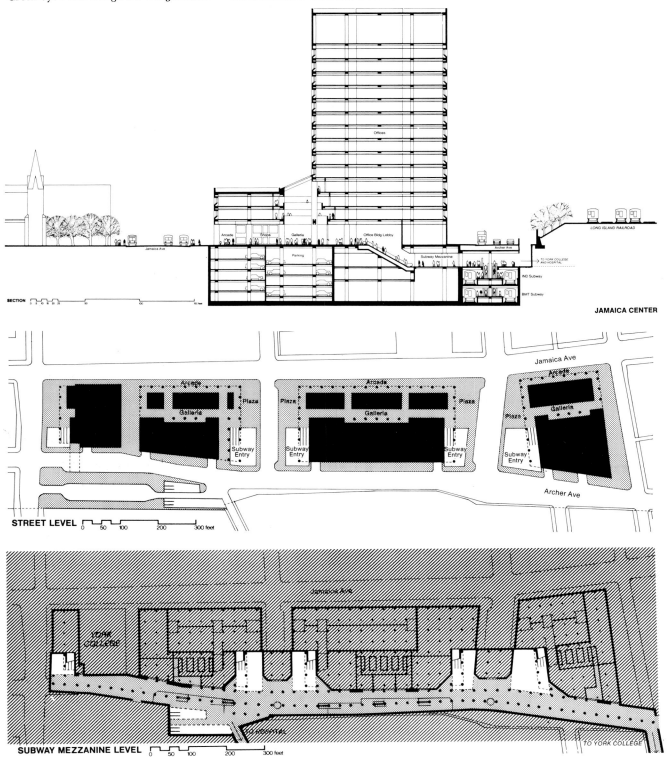

SECTION 0 5 10 15 20 25   50   100   150 feet

JAMAICA CENTER

STREET LEVEL 0 50 100 200 300 feet

SUBWAY MEZZANINE LEVEL 0 50 100 200 300 feet

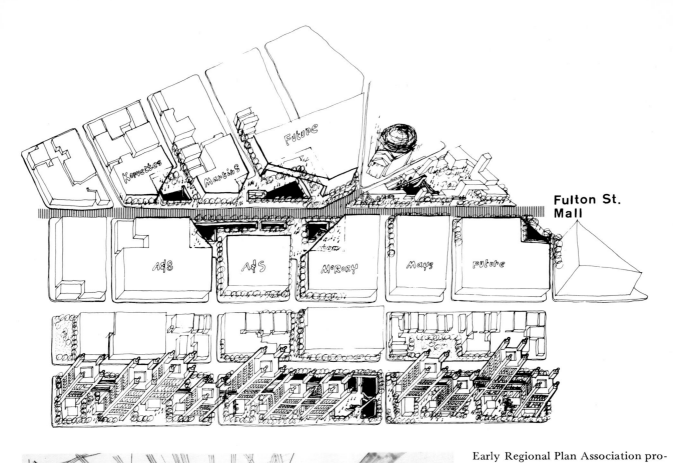

Early Regional Plan Association proposal for opening underground pedestrian passageways to light and air in Downtown Brooklyn. Enabling legislation was passed in 1972 in the form of the Special Brooklyn Center Development District, and further design and implementation has been carried forward by the Office of Downtown Brooklyn Planning and Development.

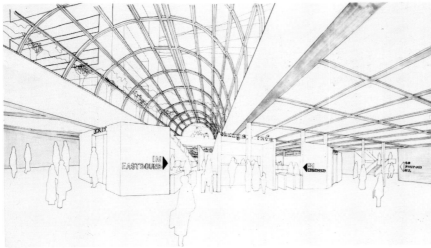

Early Regional Plan Association proposal for opening the extensive mezzanine area of the Hoyt-Schermerhorn subway station in Brooklyn to daylight. Extensive redesign of the station, incorporating new shopping areas, was approved by the City in 1973, as a cooperative venture of the Transit Authority and the New York State Urban Development Corporation. Both drawings are by Felix Martorano.

Pedestrian space on the grand scale. Huge pylons raise the forty-six floors of the new Citicorp building in Midtown Manhattan ten stories above the street level. A 10,000 sq ft (920 m²) sunken plaza is carved out of the open space thus created. Most of the common wall between the sunken plaza and the adjacent subway mezzanine under 53rd Street is removed (the space in the shadow to the right in the upper right view). Pedestrians passing through turnstiles emerge in the sunlight of the plaza and see trees. The mezzanine is also architecturally unified with the plaza through the use of common surface materials. The space to the left of the open subway entry serves as an outdoor cafe. The open-air concourse design is by Sasaki, Dawson, Demay Associates. Location was proposed in Regional Plan Association's *Urban Design Manhattan* (1969). Photo credit: Citicorp Center.

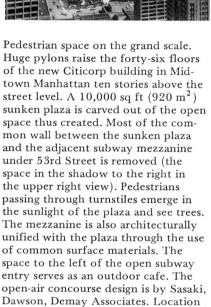

Daylight seen from the underground shopping concourse in Place Ville Marie in Montreal.

Pedestrian space at a subway station in a residential area. Proposal for a redevelopment site in Harlem, developed by the New York City Planning Commission and Municipal Art Society. The mezzanine level and connected sunken concourses create a neighborhood focus, with shopping and community facilities. Though intended for the new Second Avenue subway line, this kind of treatment could be the prototype for the reconstruction of New York's existing 265 underground subway stations, most of which are in predominantly residential areas.

the equivalent of the entire site is devoted to walkways. This compares with a floor-area ratio of 33 for the world's tallest building, the Sears Tower in Chicago. Of course, smaller buildings in New York, such as the Empire State, the Chrysler, and the Chanin, also have floor space densities around 30. The pedestrian space they provide is grossly inadequate, but this does not have to be so. One can visualize a 180-story tower covering one-third of its site, with extensive multilevel walkways taking care of mandatory pedestrian circulation needs, providing enough room for emergency evacuation, and having space left over for fountains and trees.

Four such 180-story towers would exhaust the delivery capacity of a two-track rapid transit line, feeding passengers from both directions. We might note here that this delivery capacity is limited less by technological considerations, such as electronic control of train headways, than it is by human needs for adequate space while on the train and by pedestrian movement while disembarking from the train. Even proposed high-performance systems, such as Gravity-Vacuum Transit,[42] while achieving very high speeds, do not differ markedly from conventional systems in terms of the number of people delivered in an hour at comfortable space standards. So, the theoretical limits to urban density imposed by comfortable pedestrian circulation and comfortable transit delivery capacity are rather similar.

A more stringent limitation emerges in an area that has been

the traditional concern of zoning limitations on building bulk, the provision of light and air. A 180-story megastructure containing 15 million sq ft (1.4 million m^2) may some day be erected in some city if enough tenants can be found who do not mind their ears popping in the elevators or if it is deemed acceptable to pressurize the higher floors. But four such structures clustered around a transit station would mean, assuming 100-ft (30 m) wide streets at an FAR of 60, that the window-to-window distance between them would be only about 300 ft (90 m). That is an acceptable spacing for 20-story buildings but probably not for 180-story buildings, particularly if there are more than four. Furthermore, in each building only about 25 percent of the interior space would be within 20 ft (6 m) of windows.

Without belaboring the hypothetical 180-story situation, we can observe 40-story buildings at an FAR of 18 which are, despite ample plaza space, uncomfortably close together. It is probably the identical close spacing—about 130 ft (40 m) window to window—that contributes most to the undesirable image of "slab city" sometimes created by present Midtown Manhattan zoning.

Generalizing, we can single out three spatial factors that define the degree of openness in a high-density area and that are quite independent of pedestrian space. These are (1) the distance of the view from windows, (2) the proportion of interior space accessible to windows, and (3) the exposure of the ground level to sunlight.

The trade offs among these factors are rather complex. For example, with the same density, the thinner the building, the more exposure of interior space to windows and the longer the immediate view, but also, the more obstruction to view by others. The thinner the building, the more room for sun in the streets, but also, the longer the shadow from the sun. Short, stubby buildings have little exposure of interior space to windows, and their own views are short, but they enable tall buildings to have a long view and lots of light. These complex relationships have never been modeled mathematically in a comprehensive way to answer the question: Given a certain average floor space density, what zoning envelope, or arrangement of building mass, would provide, in the aggregate, the longest sum of all views, the most interior exposure, and the greatest openness to sunlight? If such calculations were performed under realistic constrains (that is, short of putting everybody into one very thin building, which would maximize all three factors), the result would be a highly uneven zoning envelope, with sharp contrasts between highs and lows. This is precisely the result that higher floor areas near stations would produce.

However, the notion that, to maximize the common good, what is proper for some sites cannot be the rule for all sites implies a probabilistic, rather than an egalitarian, view of the universe, which runs somewhat counter to constitutional provisions of equal treatment to which zoning must conform. The

The three-dimensional city, perceived in movement. Top view shows glass-enclosed exterior elevators on the St. Francis Hotel in San Francisco, where at long last the claustrophobic box that typifies vertical transportation was broken to open an exhilarating view of the city.

Lower view, likewise in San Francisco, shows a pedestrianized section of Powell Street, where cable cars are the only vehicles allowed. A mode of transportation that offers civilized pleasure, the cable car could be a prototype for technologically new downtown systems, in scale with the pedestrian.

most direct way to resolve this contradiction is to make equality a function of accessibility—in simplest terms, of distance from transit stations. This way, truly high-rise clusters would be encouraged near transit stations, while in the surrounding areas densities would be lowered. This, in essence, is the architectonic message of the predecessor to this book, *Urban Design Manhattan.*

With an FAR on the order of 25 in the station clusters, or "access trees," distances between towers do not have to be uncomfortably close if proper precautions are taken. One device is to stagger the towers in a checkerboard pattern so that one faces the other's plaza. Given Manhattan's street dimensions, this can result in distances of 360 to 540 ft (110 to 165 m) from building face to building face, ample in a cluster of six 75-story towers at an FAR of 25. Alternatively, the Office of Midtown Planning and Development has proposed the device of turning large towers at a 45 degree angle to the street, which insures a perpendicular distance between buildings of about 300 ft (90 m). This is probably the closest that large buildings ought to be allowed to come near each other. Given Manhattan's orientation, the 45-degree placement also improves the exposure to sunlight; it has been implemented in one building on Park Avenue South.

A full exploration of the environmental consequences of and designs for high density must also consider the effects on microclimate, including wind. Plazas in front of isolated tall buildings have been found to experience exceptionally strong winds;[43] it is easier to ameliorate some of these effects in a building cluster. The issue is raised here merely to stress that high-density urban design includes a multitude of factors beyond the sheer provision of space for pedestrians, to which this book is addressed.

Within that chosen discipline we find that, contrary to public prejudice, higher densities can mean more, rather than less, amenity for pedestrians—more room for people and trees at the expense of buildings and vehicles. In the long run, one can visualize the area devoted to buildings shrinking from the present 53 percent to less than 40 percent of the total land area of Midtown Manhattan. Vehicular space could be reduced from the present 26 percent to less than 20 percent. And the pedestrian area could then be more than doubled to almost half the land in Midtown Manhattan. With this amount of walkway space, proportionately allocated, it would be feasible to support, if necessary, twice the present amount of building floor space and yet offer far superior levels of pedestrian comfort and amenity.

The underground would no longer be underground but rather open to the sun. About one-fifth of the private land would be devoted to outdoor amenities such as sitting areas, cafes, and groves of trees. These seeming miracles would be achieved primarily by rearranging the rules of the game, providing powerful, not marginal, incentives and constraints, so that both the public and the private sectors could reap the benefits of urban concentration.

In terms of design, this book starts from the functional objective of making walkway space proportionate to the pedestrian flow in it. It ends with a new esthetic, in which unused monuments get no steps leading to them at all, whereas subway entrances become the new palaces, with 100 ft (30 m) wide staircases on which people can arrive to celebrate the city.

To return to the allocations of urban space with which we started and to maintain some perspective, we should remember that cities designed for pedestrians were never in history distinguished by low densities. The urban land per resident in ancient Athens was roughly the same as that in present-day Manhattan, and in the larger medieval cities was comparable to that of New York City as a whole. In time, the tendencies of spread—a twentieth-century overreaction to the inhumanly high urban densities that followed the industrial revolution—are likely to run out and settle toward an equilibrium in which urban space will be in scale with humans. It is as a step in this long search that this book was written.

Notes for Chapter 4

1. Regional Plan Association, "CBD Cordon Crossings Analysis 1965." Tri-State Regional Planning Commission, *Hub-Bound Travel; Trips Crossing the Manhattan Central Business District Cordon in 1971* (New York, 1973).

Regional Plan Association, *Hub-Bound Travel in the Tri-State New York Metropolitan Region; Persons and Vehicles Entering Manhattan South of 61st Street 1924-1960,* Bulletin no. 99 (New York, 1961).
2. *Highway Capacity Manual,* Highway Research Board Special Report 87, (Washington, D. C., 1965), pp. 111-159.
3. *Ibid,* pp. 62-66.
4. Tri-State Regional Planning Commission, *Auto-free Zones in CBDs and an Example for Lower Manhattan,* Interim Technical Report 4447-3306 (New York, June 1974).
5. Kai Lemberg, *Pedestrian Streets and Other Motor Vehicle Traffic Restraints in Central Copenhagen,* City of Copenhagen, General Planning Department (1973), p. 19.
6. Tri-State Regional Planning Commission, *Subway Riders and Manhattan Autos* (New York, October 1971).
7. "The Metropolis Speaks; a Report to the New York Region on Its Mass Media Town Meetings, Choices for '76." *Regional Plan News,* 95 August 1974. P. 16.
8. Kenneth C. Orski, "Car-Free Zones and Traffic Restraints: Tools of Environmental Management," Paper prepared for presentation to the Highway Research Board (1972).

William Lieberman, "Environmental Implications of Auto-Free Zones," Paper prepared for presentation to the Highway Research Board (1973).
9. Kai Lemberg, *Pedestrian Streets in Central Copenhagen,* p. 16.
10. *Downtown Malls: Feasibility and Development* (New York: Downtown Research and Development Center, 1974). See also:

Arrowstreet, Inc., *Streets for People: The Design of the Pedestrian Environment in the Downtown Retail Core of Washington, D. C.* (Washington, D. C.: District of Columbia Redevelopment Agency, 1973).

Frederick T. Aschman, "Nicollet Mall: Civic Cooperation to Preserve Downtown Vitality," *Planners Notebook* 1, no. 6, American Institute of Planners, (Washington D. C., September 1971).

David Carlson and Mary R. S. Carlson, "The Pedestrian Mall; Its Role in Revitalization of Downtown Areas," *Urban Land,* May 1974.

R. W. Cottle, "The Experience of Cities in the Improvement of the Pedestrian Environment" *Greater London Council Intelligence Unit Quarterly Bulletin,* no. 21 (December 1972).

Institute of Traffic Engineers, *Traffic Planning and Other Considerations for Pedestrian Malls* (Washington, D.C., 1966).

"We Could Have America's First Pedestrian City," *The Providence Sunday Journal Magazine,* May 27, 1973.

Jaquelin Robertson. "Rediscovering the Street." *The Architectural Forum,* November 1973. pp. 24-32.
11. Franklin D. Becker, "A Class-Conscious Evaluation: Going Back to Sacramento's Pedestrian Mall," *Landscape Architecture,* October 1973, pp. 448-457.
12. Jorg Kuehnemann and Robert Witherspoon, *Traffic Free Zones in German Cities,* Organization for Economic Co-operation and Development, Economic Directorate (Paris, 1972), p. 19.
13. American Society of Planning Officials, *Sidewalks in the Suburbs,* Planning Advisory Service Information Report no. 95 (Chicago, February 1957). Also: Joseph DeChiara and Lee Koppelman, *Planning Design Criteria* (New York: Van Nostrand Reinhold, 1969). pp. 107-111, 277.
14. H. Levinson (First Deputy Highway Commissioner), City of New York Intra-departmental Memorandum (January 27, 1964).
15. Simon Breines, "Planning for Pedestrians," in Whitney North Seymour, ed., *Small Urban Spaces* (New York, New York University Press, 1969), pp. 59-71.
16. Berry Benepe, "Pedestrian in the City," *Traffic Quarterly,* January 1965, pp. 28-42.
17. Office of Downtown Brooklyn Development, *Fulton Arcade* (New York, December 1973).
18. Marvin Marcus and John Petit West, "Urban Design through Zoning: the Special Greenwich Street Development District," *Planners Notebook* 2, no. 5, American Institute of Planners (Washington, D. C., October 1972).
19. William H. Whyte, "Please, Just a Place to Sit," in *Citizen's Policy Guide to Environmental Priorities for New York City,* part 2, *Townscape* (New York: Council on the Environment, April 1974), pp. 28-36.
20. Rai Y. Okamoto and Frank E. Williams, *Urban Design Manhattan; A Report of the Second Regional Plan* (New York: Viking Press, 1969). See

also Rai Y. Okamoto, "Urban Design Determinants in Seattle and New York," *Journal of Franklin Institute* 286, no. 5 (Philadelphia, November 1968), p. 401-422.

21. Marguerite Villecco, "Urban Renewal Goes Underground," *Architecture Plus* 1, no. 5, (New York, June 1973), p. 20 ff.

22. Hartmut Steinbach, *Zweite Fussgaengerebene* [The Second Pedestrian Level] (Wiesbaden: Lenz Planen und Beraten, 1969).

23. Los Angeles Department of City Planning, *Central City Elevated Pedway System* (Los Angeles, 1971).

24. Minneapolis Planning and Development, *Minneapolis Skyway System* (Minneapolis, 1970).

25. Vincent Ponte, "Montreal's Multi-Level City Center," *Traffic Engineering* 41, no. 12 (Washington, D. C., September 1971), p. 20 ff.

26. Dallas Central Business District Association, *Prologue to the 70's* (Dallas, 1969), pp. 10, 12.

27. The City of New York, "Special Brooklyn Center Development District," *Calendar of the City Planning Commission* (May 17, 1972), pp. 20-38.

28. Downtown Brooklyn Development Committee, *Downtown Brooklyn Development Progress,* Annual Report (New York, January 1971).

29. The Port Authority of New York and New Jersey, *Pennsylvania Station Pedestrian Systems Analysis* (New York, 1972).

30. Institute for Rapid Transit, *Guidelines and Principles for Design of Rapid Transit Facilities* (Washington, May 1973), see esp. pp. 5-6.

31. Cambridge Seven Associates, *Manual of Guidelines and Standards,* 1-4 (Boston: Massachusetts Bay Transportation Authority, 1966).

32. Arcop Associates, *Rehab Path; Station Modification and Rehabilitation Technical Study* (New York: Port Authority Trans-Hudson Corporation, 1971).

33. Felix J. Martorano, "Psychological Analysis of Subways" (Paper for Columbia University).

34. San Francisco Planning and Urban Renewal Association, *Market Street Subway Stations* (San Francisco, December 1964).

35. F. Carlisle Towery, *Mezzanine Shopping Avenue of the Americas; A Sketch Proposal* (New York: Regional Plan Association, August 1965).

36. Boris Pushkarev, "The Future of Subways," *New York Affairs* 1, no. 2 (1973), pp. 72-91.

37. The Fifth Avenue Association, et al., *petitioners,* v. John V. Lindsay, et al., *respondents,* Supreme Court New York County 694/73, Abraham J. Gellinoff, J. S. C. (March 5, 1973).

38. Simon Breines, "Pedestrian Engineering Should be a City Agency," *The New York Times,* April 12, 1970.

39. City of San Francisco, Department of City Planning, *Downtown Zoning Study Working Paper no. 2.* (San Francisco, 1966).

40. National League of Cities, *Transit Station Joint Development,* Prepared for the Department of Transportation and the Department of Housing and Urban Development (Washington: National Technical Information Service, June 1973).

41. Gerhard Rosenberg, "A Standard for the Control of Building Bulk in Business Areas," *Journal of the Town Planning Institute* 55, no. 8 (London, Sept./Oct. 1969), p. 345.

42. L. K. Edwards, "Urban Gravity-Vacuum Transit System," *Transportation Engineering Journal, ASCE* 95, no. TE 1 (February 1969), pp. 173-202.

43. James MacGregor, "Why the Wind Howls Around Those Plazas Close to Skyscrapers; It's the Marilyn Monroe Effect . . . and it's Not Funny Either," *Wall Street Journal,* February 18, 1971.

A Note on Bibliography and Future Research

Most of the references consulted in the preparation of this book are listed among the over 180 items referred to in the notes at the end of each chapter and at the foot of tables. Many of them deal with pedestrians only indirectly, and repeating them here in the form of a bibliography would be redundant. Furthermore, there are bibliographies available, to be referred to shortly, and it may be more helpful as a guide to further reading to give the reader an overview of the major topics in the field and to relate this book to them.

Pedestrian Safety
In the nineteen seventies, about 400,000 pedestrians each year are hit by motor vehicles in the United States; about 10,000 die as a result, representing about 20 percent of all traffic fatalities. The figures are down from about 15,000 pedestrian deaths a year in the nineteen thirties, when they represented about 40 percent of all traffic fatalities; the proportion is still around 30 percent in Europe. Thus, there is small wonder that the largest part of any bibliography on pedestrians has traditionally been taken up with items dealing with pedestrian safety, and the engineering, enforcement, and education measures to enhance this safety. The subject is an integral part of standard traffic engineering literature and is outside the scope of this book.

Engineering of Pedestrian Facilities
A large number of minor items in the engineering, and to some extent in the architectural,

journals deal with the physical design of pedestrian facilities, including such things as the relative merits of zebra versus panda crossings, the use of sheet metal for pedestrian underpasses under freeways, or wire fencing to control pedestrians. Some thirty illustrations of the broader planning principles can be found in H. Blachnicki and E. Browne, "Over-Under; A survey of Problems of Pedestrian-vehicle Segregation," *Architectural Review,* May 1961.

Generally speaking, most of this kind of literature lacks an analysis of behavioral responses to these various facilities and thus also remains outside our purview.

Architectural Qualities of Pedestrian Space
This is a very broad and amorphous topic that ranges from architectural history to picture books of textures encountered in pedestrian spaces, from descriptions of buildings and landscaped spaces in architectural and landscape magazines to didactic journalism on the subject of "streets for people." Design studies of street furniture and "outdoor information systems" can also be included under this heading. Important as it is in many ways, this kind of material, too, had to remain outside the much narrower discipline of our book. A synthesis of the various conceptions from the planning viewpoint can be found in Caniglia Rispoli, *Spatio publico per la città - Problemi de la mobilita pedonale* [Public space in the city - problems of pedestrian mobility] (Naples, 1970).

For a good synthesis of pedestrian-related urban design accomplishments in New York, see: Jonathan Barnett, *Urban Design as Public Policy,* (New York: Architectural Record Books, 1974).

Perception of Space by Pedestrians

This is a rapidly emerging interdisciplinary subject that involves anthropologists, biologists, psychologists, and designers, in which interesting empirical work is being done, reported in such journals as *Environment and Behavior,* in the references listed at the beginning of Chapter 1, and in Edward Hall's popular summary quoted in Chapter 3. Of course, the fact that the people whose interaction with their physical environment is being studied may be moving on foot at any particular instance is quite incidental to this kind of basic research, and thus it is only rather narrowly reflected in this book. For an important recent contribution, see: Jonathan L. Freedman, *Crowding and Behavior,* (New York: Viking Press, 1975).

Physiology of Pedestrians

Material relevant to this topic is generally dispersed among journals on applied physiology, including the physiology of work, and medical journals, including such topics as rehabilitation medicine. A brief bibliography is included in John Fruin's *Pedestrian Planning and Design* (Chapter 3, note 2). With respect to design implications, there are useful manuals, such as Wesley E. Woodson and Donald W. Conover, *Human Engineering Guide for Equipment Designers* (Berkeley: University of California Press, 1964).

Pedestrian Travel Inventories

As we pointed out in Chapter 2, pedestrian travel inventories are deficient; the only extant region-wide survey is that done in Chicago in 1960 (note 2), which, despite its small sample, focuses rigorously on trip generation, trip length, trip purpose, and geographic location. Downtown traffic counts are fairly numerous but very spotty and frequently of little use for mathematical analysis; several are listed in other references in Chapter 2; notes 8, 11, and 27 focus on cyclical variation.

Mathematical Modeling of Pedestrian Travel

The dominant approach to the problem of pedestrian trip distribution, mostly focused on downtown areas, has been through various adaptations of the gravity model (see Donald Hill, et al., source note to Table 2.15). For an alternate approach, see Dietrich Garbrecht, "The Binomial Model of Pedestrian Flows, Implications and Experiments," *Traffic Quarterly,* October 1969, pp. 587-595, as well as other articles by this author.

The direct pedestrian estimation approach employed by us has two antecedents: first, helicopter aerial photography of pedestrians, developed by the Port Authority of New York and New Jersey and first reported in *Cameras Aloft—Project Sky Count,* The Port Authority Operations Services Department, Operations Standards Division (New York, 1968); second, Morton Schneider's basic theory of trip distribution, Einstein-esque in its elegance, and its

follow-up, developed at the Tri-State Regional Planning Commission and referred to in 33 and 34 in Chapter 1. A similar approach was adopted for forecasting pedestrian travel in the city of Helsinki: Kari Lautso and Pentti Murola, "A Study of Pedestrian Traffic in Helsinki," *Traffic Engineering and Control,* January 1974, pp. 446-449.

Pedestrian Flow Characteristics

In terms of data collection, flow characteristics have generally fared somewhat better than trip generation characteristics, and a number of studies are available, focusing mostly on issues of interest to traffic engineers, such as behavior at signalized interactions; several are theses for the Bureau of Highway Traffic at Pennsylvania State University. Others are referred to in Chapters 2 and 3.

Mathematical Modeling of Pedestrian Flow

An indispensable work on the subject is Oeding's 1963 study referred to in note 4 of Chapter 3. An important contribution, in some ways more detailed, is Fruin's work (Chapter 3, note 2). There are perhaps half a dozen more limited studies in speed-flow area, listed in notes 4 and 5 of Chapter 3. Unfortunately, few of them venture beyond extremely dense flow conditions; to our knowledge, the only look at fairly relaxed movement was taken by Hirsch (note 10).

Behavioral Studies in the Non-walking Mode

A somewhat separate topic is the behavior of pedestrians other than in sheer locomotion—in their modes of relaxation in malls and plazas. Particularly notable is the work of William

H. Whyte (Chapter 2, note 30 and Chapter 4, note 19) and the studies in Copenhagen (Chapter 2, note 27) and Sacramento (Chapter 4, note 11).

Pedestrian Malls
Beginning in the late sixties, there has been a tremendous awakening of interest in the subject of vehicle-free zones, pedestrian precincts, and pedestrian malls, which now has a respectable body of literature. A selection of items is cited in Chapter 1 in notes 27 and 28 and in Chapter 4 in notes 8 through 12. The views of a long-time advocate are expressed in: Simon Breines and William J. Dean, *The Pedestrian Revolution: Streets Without Cars.* (New York: Vintage Books, 1975) 151 pp.

Grade Separation
That subject is treated in notes 22 through 28 in Chapter 4. An important subdivision of it, the rehabilitation and design of underground transit stations, is illustrated by notes 31 through 36.

Mechanical Assistance Devices
In this study, we touch on two types of mechanical assistance devices, escalators and moving walks, because the modes of behavior on them are related to walking; selected references appear under notes 21 through 24 in Chapter 3. We do not deal with elevator operation, which has traditionally been a subject unto itself, nor with various "peoplemover" systems, to the extent that their characteristics are closer to those of mechanical transport modes.

Bibliographies
A great number of the studies cited, particularly those by Oeding and Fruin, include extensive bibliographies. Among the special bibliographies we can single out:
Katherine Sigda Bartholomaus, *Pedestrian Movement: Selected References 1965-June 1972* (Evanston, Ill.: Transportation Center Library, Northwestern University, 1972), 19 pp.
Dietrich Garbrecht, *Pedestrian Movement; a Bibliography* (Monticello, Ill.: Council of Planning Librarians, 1971), 27 pp.

Numerous bibliographic references are included in: *Proceedings of the Pedestrian/Bicycle Planning and Design Seminar San Francisco 1972.* (Berkeley, Calif.: The Institute of Transportation and Traffic Engineering, University of California, 1973) 241 pp.

A good list of German literature, with an emphasis on the pedestrian movement at mass transit facilities, is included in Joachim Westphal, *Untersuchungen von Fussgaengerbewegungen auf Bahnhoefen mit starkem Nahverkerhr* [Studies of pedestrian movement in railroad stations with heavy commuter traffic] (Hannover: Technishe Universitaet, 1971).

Future Research Needs
As usual, some gain in knowledge creates awareness of greater areas of ignorance. The gaps that had to be bridged in this study suggest the following spectrum of directions for future research:
1. Refinement of the direct pedestrian estimation approach by introducing measures of accessibility and coverage of smaller urban centers;
2. A much larger sample of trip-generation rates for particular building uses;
3. Measures of nighttime, weekly, and seasonal variation in pedestrian flow;
4. More data on walking distances in different urban environments and on the effect of environmental factors on encouraging or discouraging walking;
5. Flow analysis in the comfortable, rather than congested, range, including a more rigorous definition of platooning and of the ability to walk in voluntary groups;
6. The effect of obstacles on pedestrian flow;
7. The dynamics and the physiology of the movement of the individual pedestrian on stairways and around corners, accelerating and decelerating;
8. Psychological reactions at different degrees of spaciousness;
9. Value structures as reflected in trading off money, time, walking distance, congestion under different conditions of physical environment, amenity, and weather; and
10. Microdata on travel by mechanical modes in a central business district, both in absolute quantities and in relation to the different tradeoffs listed; in fact, a reasonable evaluation of various mechanical pedestrian assistance devices is not possible without more knowledge in the latter two fields.

Index